Dictionary of the Tarot

Dictionary of the Tarot

Bill Butler

SCHOCKEN BOOKS · NEW YORK

First published by SCHOCKEN BOOKS 1975
First SCHOCKEN PAPERBACK EDITION 1977
10 9 8 7 6 5   80 81 82

Library of Congress Cataloging in Publication Data

Butler, Bill.
  Dictionary of the tarot.

  Bibliography: p. 253
  1. Tarot. I. Title.

BF1879.T2B87   133.3′2424   74-9230

Manufactured in the United States of America

Contents

5 Systems Design

The facility which the cards afford a receptive mind to use them in divination to evoke an already formed answer in the Querent's mind. Description of variant decks and a suggested future for the Tarot itself.

6 Glossary

Containing the chief terms and symbols used in the design of the cards themselves and in the commentaries on the cards. The purpose of the glossary being to enable the reader to gain further insight into the meaning of individual elements within designs and interpretations.

Bibliography

Primary works used

Short Cartography of Tarot Decks Consulted in this Book

GRINGONNEUR
Jacquemin Gringonneur, 1392
Originals Bibliothèque Nationale, Paris
Reproduced in *History of Playing Cards,* Dover Pub.

VISCONTI
Bembo early fifteenth Century
Originals mostly in the Pierpont Morgan Library
Reproduced in *The Tarot Cards Painted by Bembo,* New York Public Library

MARSEILLE
B.P. Grimaud, 1748

SWISS, INSIGHT, ITALIAN, and WIRTH are all later variants on the MARSEILLE

WAITE
A.E. Waite, designs; Pamela Coleman Smith,
Rider & Co., 1910 and 1971.

CROWLEY
Aleister Crowley; design; Frieda Harris, executor. Llewellyn, 1972.

B.O.T.A.
Paul Foster Case, design; Jessie Burns Parke, executor, n.d. (c 1927?)
B.O.T.A., n.d.

AQUARIAN
David Palladini, 1970

NEW
John Starr Cooke, design; Rosalind Sharpe, executor, 1969

Most of these decks or any others mentioned in this book are available in England through the following bookshops:

Atlantis, 49A Museum Street, London W.C.1.
Compendium, 240 Camden High Street, London N.W.1.
Watkins Bookshop, 19-21 Cecil Court, Charing Cross Road, London W.C.2.

In the United States the best source for books on the Tarot and for cards is:
Samuel Weiser, 734 Broadway, New York, N.Y. 10003

Dictionary
of the Tarot

Introduction

It is incredible the amount of nonsense that has been written over the past 170 years regarding the Tarot Cards and the 'science' of fortune telling with their assistance. From the eighteenth century Parisian barber, Alliette, down to present day 'experts' book after book has been produced to prove that the Tarot derives from the Ancient Egyptians, from Mahatmas in Tibet, from the Gypsies, from the Kabbala, from Chinese Sages or from Arcane sources too esoteric to be named.

This book attempts to look at the symbolism of the cards themselves and at the commentaries on the Tarot of a number of writers. Based upon these two sources a theory of the Tarot is formulated which works for this writer and may work as a way-station for someone else.

The cards are not magic. They do not tell the future, they cannot evaluate the past. In the hands of a skilled practitioner they can be used in two different ways for the study of the unconscious mind. The first is for a reader to relate the symbology of the cards as they 'fall' in a reading. This method is passive, the reader of the cards adding as little personal interpretation as possible. The evaluation is performed by the Querent, to whom the question is real and known and the answer is made manifest through the reading within the Querent's mind. The obvious advantage of this procedure is that it can be performed by a relatively unskilled reader.

In the second method the reader, a skilled clairvoyant, uses the Tarot as a vehicle for concentration, a sort of patterned mirror reflecting to an inner eye the features of a landscape in someone else's mind. Both methods rely on the Querent to provide the answer, on the theory that some shadow of events to come is thrown across the unconscious days and perhaps years before the eruption of physical event. As shadows by their nature are not 'fixed' it seems likely that shadows of the future are no more fixed. What is reflected is possibility. With the knowledge of possibility the Querent may choose his future.

Another theory of the mechanism of the Tarot would be possible if one considered Time as 'simultaneous' rather than linear. In linear Time Past and Present are said to be 'fixed', the Future is changeable, and Time is considered as a line which runs from Past through Present and on to Future. Utilizing the concept of 'Simultaneous Time' the Tarot can be conceived of as a window overlooking any point in all of Time, and in all possibilities of Time. From a

1

standpoint of consciousness expansion Simultaneous Time may be more useful as a consideration than Linear Time. Perhaps neither of these theories is true. Perhaps one or the other or both is relevant. They are given to show that the Tarot, like the I Ching, can be used as a map. To show the individual where he has been, where he is, where he has to go.

1 History

The Tarot Cards date with certainty from 1392, when an entry was made in the Court accounts of Charles VI of France referring to the payment of a sum of money to Jaquemin Gringonneur for the purchase of three sets of the Major Arcana. These 22 cards of the Tarot deck *triumph* over all the other 56 cards in the game of tarocchi. Thus, in Italian, the Major Arcana are referred to as *trionfi*. In English games the equivalent terms are triumph and, of course, *trump*.

The earliest reference to cards of any kind is in 1332, when Alfonse XI, King of Leon and Castile, banned them. In 1377 there is a more detailed account concerning them in the Latin manuscript of a German monk, Johannes. He writes of the introduction of the game of cards into the monastery where he lived and of its possible uses as a guide to morality. While his descriptions are similar to a description of present day playing cards there are significant differences: a deck could have up to six kings, up to eight marschalli or knaves, up to four queens, etc. So at the time that he wrote there was no established convention for playing card design. Nor was there any for some years. In the fifteenth century an Italian game, Tarrocchino, was devised which had over one hundred cards. Included were all the Signs of the Zodiac, the Virtues, in short all that was necessary for the proper instruction of the young. Which, as Johannes suggests, was probably an early use for the Tarot and for playing cards. Though the earliest remaining cards are those from the Tarot decks of Charles VI which have been preserved in the Bibliothèque Nationale in Paris it seems likely that playing cards evolved independently at about the same time and developed on their own to become the standard 52 card deck used throughout most of Europe and America. The Tarot, on the other hand, began with an unknown number of Major Arcana and subsequently added 56 cards of the Minor Arcana to become what is today the standard deck of 78 cards.

The deck is divided as follows:

MINOR ARCANA:

Pentacles/Coins/Diamonds	1-10, Page, Knight, Queen, King
Wands/Batons/Clubs	1-10, Page, Knight, Queen, King
Cups/Chalices/Hearts	1-10, Page, Knight, Queen, King
Swords/Epees/Spades	1-10, Page, Knight, Queen, King

MAJOR ARCANA:

0	The Fool	11	Justice
1	The Magician	12	The Hanged Man
2	The High Priestess or Papess	13	Death
3	The Empress	14	Temperance
4	The Emperor	15	The Devil
5	The Hierophant or Pope	16	The Tower
6	The Lovers	17	The Star
7	The Chariot	18	The Moon
8	Strength	19	The Sun
9	The Hermit	20	Judgement
10	The Wheel of Fortune	21	The World

The earliest purposes of these cards were probably for gambling (which could explain why they were banned by Alphonse XI) and as mnemonic devices for impressing upon the young the concepts of virtue. Comparison of the earliest Tarot designs with, for example, the designs for the Triumph of Maximilian by Hans Burgkmair will readily show correspondences. Burgkmair was endeavouring by Royal Commission, to portray in a procession, the glories of Maximilian. Though the triumph seems never to have taken place it remains as a series of designs originating in the same legends and customs of medieval times as does the Tarot.

The resemblance between the genesis of the cards and Burgkmair's inspiration is particularly strong in the seventh card. *The Chariot*. More than any other card this one adapts the medieval concept of the Triumph, the subject of all Burgkmair's designs. In Roman and Greek times the Triumph had been a celebratory procession. By the thirteenth century a custom tailored to honour returning army generals had come to be incorporated into Lenten festivals, where th e figure of a fool, a king or a general was frequently drawn through the streets in a Triumphal Car. In the present day the same symbolism is still with us in the circus parade or in parades for any great public holiday: Remembrance Day, Independence Day, or Trooping the Colour, for example.

It is uncertain just when the divinatory aspects of the Tarot first came to be regarded. No literature survives which is contemporary with the invention of the cards and which could pin down their use in fortune-telling. But by the end of the eighteenth century Tarot cards were employed almost entirely for divination with the earlier purposes of gambling and instruction largely forgotten.

During that interval the cards were extensively redesigned from the rather ornate originals of Charles VI and the slightly later Visconti deck. By 1748 they had become simplified and standardized in what is now referred to as the Marseille Tarot, which is the closest thing to a 'traditional' Tarot that exists.

Then, in the early twentieth century, A.E. Waite and Pamela Colman Smith produced what has come to be known as the Waite Tarot, based upon the Marseille pack together with additional symbols derived from Waite's involvement with the Rosicrucians and with the Golden Dawn. A few years after the Waite deck Aleister Crowley reinterpreted the cards yet again. Drawing partially on Rosicrucian teaching and partially on teachings of the Order of the Golden Dawn he designed a new Tarot deck which is heavily influenced by his own morbid sense of the ridiculous.

Within the past few years the Crowley deck, as painted by Frieda Harris, has been issued. And a new deck, the Aquarian Tarot, designed by David Palladini and published in the United States is also available. The Aquarian Tarot reinterprets the Waite designs as does the Brotherhood of the Adytum pack, designed by Jessie Burns Parke. And each new interpretation changes a few of the cards or emphasizes a different aspect of their meaning. Waite, for example, transposes Major Arcana numbers 8 and 11; Crowley retitles some cards and omits others; Oswald Wirth interprets them in the light of a 19th-century France which was undergoing a revival of interest in witchcraft and black magic. (See J.K. Huysmans, *La Bas*.)

Not only the designs of the Tarot deck have changed, the interpretations have also evolved, particularly during the past 100 years. MacGregor Mathers first published his book, *The Tarot*, in Covent Garden in 1888. It is a slender treatise from which stems practically all of the lengthy studies of the Tarot that have been published in English since. A.E. Waite, in *his* book on the Tarot, relies on Mathers for many of his interpretations. Waite expands the meanings, gives them added dimensions, and the result is a book vastly longer than that of Mathers. Eden Gray, Paul Huson and Alfred Douglas have all obviously studied Waite; but each of them interprets Waite, and through him Mathers, in the light of his own occult experience. Even the great iconoclast. Aleister Crowley, does not hesitate to quote from Waite and Mathers when it suits his purpose.

Which adds up, if you have been following this, to a vast divergence of opinion on what the Tarot is and what it means. All of which contributes to the sum of possibility which defines this area of experience. Yet none of the people who have worked with the Tarot believes that he has necessarily found 'The Way'. For as the Tao Te Ching says, "The Way that can be known is not The Way." Perhaps the Way changes, perhaps each man has to find it for himself. So the numbering, the naming, the designs and the interpretation of the Tarot cards may be largely a matter of individual choice.

This book compares the various Tarot decks which are currently available and the readings given by most of the standard authorities, suggests further interpretations and outlines a number of systems for reading the cards. A full bibliography of books and decks appears at the end. The philosophy and the bias of each source described, of each authority consulted will be apparent to the reader. MacGregor Mathers regarded the Tarot as of comparatively small importance, and his interpretations reflect this. Waite and Gray both regard the Tarot as primarily a mechanism for spiritual development as does Paul Foster Case. Their interpretations define this spiritual interest. And for Aleister Crowley the Tarot was, as everything, a joke and at the same time, an intellectual and magickal discipline. His attributions fit his philosophy. From the contradiction each reader will select his own meanings or reject them all and make his own. Thus using the Tarot as it may have been originally intended, by an unknown Maker, to be used: as an intellectual and intuitive system, for making systems, for destroying them, and for creating.

2 The Book of Thoth

Aleister Crowley titled his work on the Tarot, *The Book of Thoth*. And, according to some western occult traditions, it is exactly that; the remnants of an Egyptian initiatory rite. And the 22 Major Arcana are the steps through which the neophyte passes in his progress towards enlightenment. Court de Gebelin first postulated the legend at the end of the eighteenth century and it has grown steadily ever since. According to the story the 22 Atout are representations of 22 stone tablets which are in a small temple between the paws of the Sphinx. The temple itself has been lost beneath the sands of Egypt.

Unfortunately for legend de Gebelin's theories date from 25 years before the translation of the Rosetta Stone and seem to be based entirely upon wishful thinking. No sign of either temple or tablets has been found.

Nevertheless, even if no direct connection between Thoth and the Tarot can be shown it may be useful to consider Thoth and the corresponding gods of European mythology (Odin, Lugh, Llew, Hermes, Ogma, *et al.*) The attributes of Thoth include: the counter of the stars, measurer and enumerator of the earth, twice great or thrice great lord of books, the mouse, the ibis, and the dog-headed ape. He is a sun god, a recorder of sins, a punisher of evil, a healer, a moon god, the deputy of Ra when the sun god is resting (at night), a navigator, a rain god, a thunder god, a teacher of grammar, speech, the alphabet and hieroglyphics. Thoth is the personification of divine speech and the teacher of words of power and their correct pronunciation. In the Theban Recension it was necessary for the candidate to address each god and each doorway by the correct name. Those names were each comprised of a number of syllables which together formed a spell. And that spell, properly said, gave the candidate power over the doorway or the God.

In Egyptian mythology Thoth assists Isis to escape from the tower where she is imprisoned by Set, who hopes to marry her by force when he has killed her husband, Osiris. According to the story Isis is either pregnant by her dead husband or is already the mother of the child, Horus. And her husband is either Osiris or Horus, who is either dead or alive. It's a little difficult to tell as Egyptian mythology is contradictory; there are two Horus gods, for example, one a child and one an adult. Though different gods they are frequently interchanged or considered as father and son.

Anyway, accompanied by seven Scorpion goddesses, Isis sets out for the reed swamps where she is going to hide from Set. On the way she stops at a house to ask for shelter. But the woman of the house slams the door in her face. In revenge one of the Scorpion goddesses forces her way inside and stings the woman's child to death for her inhospitality. At which the mother breaks down, implores forgiveness, and Isis, with a spell, restores the child to life.

So far in the story there has been no mention of the child, Horus; but suddenly he is stung by another Scorpion and dies. Isis is inconsolate and is advised to appeal to Ra by her sister, Nephthys, and one of the Scorpion goddesses, Serqit. When she does so the boat of Millions of Years, the Solar Bark of Ra, stops in midheaven and Thoth, the author of spells and words of power, descends with The Word which all Heaven and Earth and Hell must obey. He talks with Isis, then utters The Word, thus transferring some of the fluid of life from Ra to the body of the child, Horus, who lives again.

Thoth promises that he will protect Horus, that he will defend him in the Hall of Judgement in Anu, that he will give him power to repel any attack which may be made upon him, and that he will ensure his succession to the throne of Egypt, thus acing-out Set who is offstage throughout the entire legend. The story closes with Thoth proclaiming that it was through the spells of Isis (presumably taught to her by Thoth) that the Solar Boat had been made to stand still. (The parallel between this legend and that of Joshua in the Book of Joshua, 10: 12, 13, is obvious. But, as the Book of Joshua occurs historically after the Captivity it is likely that the Old Testament borrows from Egyptian sources.) The contradictions in the Isis legend—if Isis was able to raise one newly Scorpion-dead, why couldn't she raise her own child?—are glossed over. The possibility that the two children are the same is never resolved.

In another legend Thoth teaches Isis the spell by which she can revive Osiris (Horus) who has been slain by Set and have a child by him. And in the final showdown between that child, the other Horus, and Set, just as Horus is about to utterly wipe out Set, Isis intervenes. Horus cuts off her head in a fit of pique and Thoth replaces it with that of a cow, thus restoring her to life and, at the same time, commenting upon her personality. Set is also preserved from death which makes for cosmic equilibrium between Good and Evil, Law and Chaos.

The concept of Thoth as a God of Equilibrium does not imply in any way that he is a God of Happy Endings, but rather that he is a god of everything in its season. In a sense he is a God of Change, tension within the concept: 'The more it changes, the more it is the same.' Which can be considered an aphoristic view of the I Ching. And when this consideration of Turn and Re-Turn is applied to the cards, Justice and the Wheel of Fortune, then quite different attributes than those normally clutched by Judaeo-Christian mythology will be apparent.

Thoth, as the inventor of the alphabet, of spells, of the Naming of Things, is closely related to Odin, Hermes, Lugh, Ogma and Llew, all of whom were likewise supposed to have invented alphabets and to have been Magicians of Great Power. For to be able to paint an animal or a man (as at Lascaux or Tassili) or to name it (as in Odin's Rune Song) is to have power over it. Which power ranges from the corn of nineteenth century melodrama to Zanoni and

Mejnour, the lofty magicians of Bulwer-Lytton's novel, *Zanoni,* who appear to seek power (knowledge) solely for its own glory and not as the means to any other end. And from a similar point of view the spells of Odin, the runes from the Lay of the High One, are of less interest as tools than they are as weapons made to hang on the walls of the High One's mind.

The words of Thoth from the Papyrus of Ani translated for the Rosicrucian Society suggest yet another use of his spells: they are ritual:

'I have done battle on account of thee. I am one of those divine judges making true of voice OSIRIS to his opposers on the day of the weighing of words.

I am of thy kindred, oh! OSIRIS, I am of those gods who are children of the Heavenly abyss, who work vengeance on the opposers of OSIRIS, imprisoning the executors of Fate on his account.

I am Thoth, making true of voice OSIRIS to his opposers, on the day of the weighing of words in the Great Temple of the ancient one who dwelleth in the City of the Sun.

I am the two pillars, and the Son of the two pillars, I am brought forth between the pillars.

I am with the mourners and the wailing women of OSIRIS, in the two earths of initiation making true of voice OSIRIS to his opposers.'

The resemblance to other ritual, for example to the words of the Sioux medicine man, Black Elk, is striking. Particularly in that much of the meaning of what is being said is not conveyed by the words but rather by their repetition. And the power which is here evident is power which comes into being by stating its own existence. Again, with correspondences to the Lay of the High One.

Like Thoth, Hermes is a magician. Like Thoth he is the inventor of an alphabet. He is also a conductor of souls who leads the newly dead to Tartarus and brings back to life those who are allowed to return (Persephone/Kore). He was also the governor of the second degree of the Mithraic Initiation, the sphere of occult powers, of magic and of resurrection. To Thoth is attributed the *Egyptian Book of the Dead* or *Book of Coming Forth by Day* and an additional 42 books on forms of worship, history, geography, the law, astronomy and astrology, religion and medicine. To Hermes is attributed the Corpus Hermeticum which contains the following passage in the translation by Scott:

'If you do not make yourself equal to God, you cannot apprehend God; for like is known by like. Leap clear of all that is corporeal, and make yourself grow to a like expanse with that greatness which is beyond all measure; rise above all time and become eternal; then you will apprehend God. Think that for you, too, nothing is impossible; deem that you too are immortal, and that you are able to grasp all things in your thought, to know every craft and every science; find your home in the haunts of every living creature; make yourself higher than all heights, and lower than all depths; bring together in yourself all opposites of quality, heat and cold, dryness and fluidity; think that you are everywhere at once, on land, at sea, in heaven; think that you are not yet begotten, that you are in the womb, that you are young, that you are old, that you have died, that you are in the world beyond the grave; grasp in your thought all this at once, all times and places, all substances and qualities and magnitudes together; then you can apprehend God. But if you shut up your soul in your body, and abase yourself, and say, "I know nothing, I can do nothing; I am afraid of earth and sea, I cannot mount to heaven; I know not what I was, nor what I shall be"; then, what have you to do with God? Your thought can grasp nothing beautiful and good, if you cleave to the body, and are evil.

For it is the height of evil not to know God; but to be capable of knowing God, and to wish and hope to know him, is the road which leads straight to the Good; and it is an easy road to travel. Everywhere God will come to meet you, everywhere he will appear to you, at places and times at which you look not for it, in your waking hours and in your sleep, when you are journeying by water and by land, in the nighttime and in the daytime, when you are speaking and when you are silent; for there is nothing which is not God. And do you say 'God is indivisible?' Speak not so. Who is more manifest than God? For this very purpose he made all things. Nothing is invisible, not even an incorporeal thing; mind is seen in its liking and God in his working.

'So far, thrice-greatest one, I have shown you the truth. Think out all else in like manner for yourself and you will not be misled.'

The Hermes speaking in this passage is a philosopher; but He is also a God of mystic learning and rebirth. In the *Discourses of Arrian,* the Slave, Epictetus, says:

'Great is God: this is the rod of Hermes: *touch what you will with it,* they say, *and it becomes gold.* Nay, but bring what you will and I will transmute it into Good. Bring sickness, bring death, bring poverty and reproach, bring trial for life — all these things through the rod of Hermes shall be turned into profit.' This text, from the fourth century B.C. manages to combine a number of different attributes of Hermes . . . his inclination toward change (that is, his *Mercurial* quality), his mysticism (which could easily be taken from the words of an Alchemical tract) and his mercantile values ('. . . shall be turned into profit.')

Robert Graves, writing in *The White Goddess* and *The Greek Myths,* identifies Hermes with Thoth. And Graves specifies Hermes' role as 'Psychopomp' or 'Leader of Souls' in which capacity he was sent to the Underworld to fetch back Persephone (Kore). This is of some importance in another legend where Hermes is credited with fathering Ceryx, traditionally the first Herald of the Eleusinian Mysteries. Although nothing is known of the content of the Mysteries (it being a verbal tradition passed on from Hierophant to Hierophant) it is likely that they were concerned with the 'Death' of Persephone and her subsequent 'Resurrection'. This connection of Hermes and the Eleusinian Mysteries is one of the few provable links between Egyptian mythology and the Tarot. For Hermes was an Egyptian god as well as being a Greek one. His worship was established in Graeco-Egyptian times at Hermopolis. A further link exists between Hermes and the Tarot in the fifth card of the Major Arcana, The Hierophant. (Or, more frequently, the Pope.) The Hierophant was the High Priest of the Mysteries at Eleusis; and, in function, he is the spiritual predecessor of the Pope, having many of the same attributes.

Other accounts of Hermes specify his invention of Astronomy (and therefore Astrology) and his origination of flesh sacrifice when he slaughtered two of the cattle which he had stolen from his half-brother Apollo. Flesh sacrifice is interesting not only for its possible connection with the Eleusinian Mysteries but also in considering Odin, the Hanged God, who is also a God of Sacrifice. But in the story of Odin the Sacrifice is self-sacrifice; and its purpose is the

XIX

The Sun, *Aquarian Tarot*

acquisition of knowledge. During this period (nine days) that Odin hung from the tree (Yggdrasil, the World Tree) he is said to have discovered Runes, the Norse form of writing, thus linking him again with Hermes/Mercury and with Thoth.

Another link (tenuous, but there) between Hermes and Odin lies in the snake. Odin, the name, corresponds directly with Wodin or Wotan (Germanic forms of the name). The Mayan god, Votan, has for his symbol the snake. As does Hermes, who bears the Caduceus, a rod on which two snakes are coupling or fighting. The symbol for trickery and wisdom is the snake, who is thus a suitable persona for both Odin and Hermes. On one occasion Odin transformed himself into a snake. And the snake is closely associated with Hermes from Classical times down as far as the early centuries after Christ. Initially it is Hermes, thief/trickster/psychopomp who bears a serpent rod. Later he becomes Hermes Trismegistus, Egyptian Thoth combined with Egyptian Hermes; and the snake becomes a Gnostic symbol for spiritual wisdom.

Still later, at about the same time as the Tarot was developed, Hermes Trismegistus was honoured in alchemical tradition as the Lord of the Highest Wisdom, patron of the desire to transform that which is human and ignorant into that which is divine and wise. With which aim no Gnosticist could disagree. In later times that motivation degenerates from the pursuit of wisdom to a search for methods to turn base metals into gold. And Hermes Trismegistus degenerates from being a patron of spiritual wisdom to an identity as a carnival magician and mountebank. The Magician, second card of the Major Arcana.

Alchemy also incorporated into its philosophical structure the Hermaphroditic attributes of Hermes (literally a reference to the son of Hermes and Aphrodite who was born half male and half female). The snakes of Hermes' staff became the dragon of Sulphur or the Sun and that of Mercury or the Moon. The Egyptians painted these as a circle, biting each other's tail, thus illustrating that they came from the same thing, that they were Hermaphroditic. And the Lion, central to other alchemical tracts, is also Hermaphroditic.

Hermetic tradition (literally, tradition of Hermes, but with an added modern connotation of closed or secret) whether Greek, Egyptian or medieval can be seen in such cards of the Major Arcana as The Fool (Postulant or Novice in the Mysteries), The Magician (Hermes/Thoth), The High Priestess (Secrecy, Hidden Wisdom), the Hierophant (High Priest of the Mysteries of the Triple Goddess, also a symbol of Hidden or Revealed Wisdom), the Lovers (Choice), the Chariot (Balancing of Power), Strength (The Taming of the Alchemical Lion), Justice (Equilibrium again), The Hanged Man (The Quest for Wisdom, also represented by the Fool), Death (Change), Temperance (Equilibrium of Forces, in a sense the combination of Strength and Justice), The Devil (an admonition against folly, or misuse of power), the Tower (the Divine Irrational), The Star (that which is hidden), The Moon (The Female principle or metallic Mercury), the Sun (The Male Principle or Sulphur), Judgement (over what has been done, *not* the Last Judgement), the World (represented in some decks as androgynous, the highest metamorphosis). So a connection between Hermetic tradition of the Middle Ages (Alchemy) and the Major Arcana, at least, doesn't seem too far-fetched.

The Magician God, of Wisdom or Trickery, is not confined to the Mediterranean basin. In Europe there were Lugh (a Celtic sun god) and Llew (a British god who could be killed neither in a house, nor in the open nor on horseback, nor afoot) and Odin (a Norse god, equivalent to Hermes and to Zeus). What seems significant about all of them are their shared attributes: a link between sorcery and the invention of writing or Runes, shape-changing or trickery, and patronage of poetry or singing. They are not identical gods; but the resemblances are great and they can be said to be the inspiration of, if not the authors of, the Tarot.

Court de Gebelin's theories about the Tarot have not been borne out by the translation of the Rosetta Stone in 1822. The 'hidden' temple between the paws of the Sphinx has not been found. The 22 Tablets of the Major Arcana are lost as well. But if the theory of Egyptian initiation cannot be proven literally the connection of the Tarot with traditions of Hermes, Mercury, Odin and the rest seems likely. Those traditions became, over many years, part of the heritage of all Europe, moving with every migration and every invasion. By the end of the first millennium A.D. the names had changed many times and the legends had become common property. For example: the story of Isis, the Scorpion woman, and the child Horus: this story parallels the stories of Demeter and Kore, Ishtar and Tammuz, and the Virgin Mary with the Crucified Jesus. Unessential details have been changed, the vital belief, that of life beyond death and death beyond life, cyclic, eternal is common to them all.

So, when Aleister Crowley named his book, *The Book of Thoth,* in a sense it was literally that. The Tarot cards, invented by some unknown in the late twelfth or early thirteenth century, would seem to be the sum of a system of belief in death and resurrection up to that time. And one of the largest figures in that deck is that of the Magician/Fool/Devil/Hierophant/Hermit/Hanged Man. Call him by what name you will . . . he is Hermes, he is Thoth.

3(a) *The Minor Arcana*

The Minor Arcana are seldom illustrated in traditional decks. Up until Waite and the Rider (or Waite) deck it was customary to emphasize the Major Arcana with pictures. The Minor Arcana from one through ten were illustrated sketchily, for example, by nine wands or three chalices. The 'face cards' or court cards were much the same as occurs in an ordinary deck of playing cards. With the Waite deck the Minor Arcana came into their own; and most of the twentieth century decks—the Crowley Tarot, the Brotherhood of the Adytum Tarot, the Aquarian Tarot—follow Waite's lead and illustrate the Minor Arcana fully. The New Tarot deck returns to the older tradition of the Marseille pack except that the arrangements of the geometric forms of the New Tarot are numerologically significant, using geometric form to emphasize numerical value, in a manner similar to the nineteenth century Grand Tarot de Belline. Thus, seven of a suit is reinforced by a square and a triangle: $3 + 4 = 7$.

Brief descriptions of the Minor Arcana as represented in the Marseille deck and in several modern decks together with various interpretations of the cards follow. If, in some cases, meanings appear contradictory according to the same authority then the reader should allow for 'reversed' positions of the cards, when they are dealt in an upside-down position. In interpretation it is this writer's opinion that a reversed position merely implies one of the poles of interpretation of a card, the upright position providing the other. And the meaning is a fluctuation between those poles with reference to the surrounding cards.

In card design the term 'Traditional' refers to the Gringonneur, Bembo and Marseille Tarots. In interpretation it refers to Mathers and Waite.

Pentacles

Money, coins, stars, pentagrams. The lowest suit of the entire deck. It corresponds to the Primal or Solar Fire, to pure sensation. Most commentators equate it with Earth, which, as wands seem more likely to be of Earth, I think unlikely

Case:	Business, money, possessions. Unfriendly to Swords, friendly to Wands
Crowley:	The powers of Earth
Douglas:	Material and financial interests
Gray:	Traditional implications of finance + the direction east, one who is ill-tempered. The Apocalypse Creature (Cherub) is the Bull
Huson:	Traditional
Kaplan:	Traditional
Mathers:	Those not so dark, money
Papus:	Man, winter, new moon, night, old age. Money and interest. Court cards represent fair people
Waite:	Court cards generally indicate dark people. The sign of the pentagram indicates the correspondence of the four elements in human nature, the suit pentacles indicates change (and, in old packs, money)

Design

Ace of Pentacles

Marseille:	A flower, quatrefoil, centred in the sun in glory
Waite:	A hand from the heavens holding a yellow coin in which is inscribed a pentagram. Below it is a garden, hedged with red roses, filled with white lilies
Aquarian:	A single pentacle, with a flower on either side

16

Crowley:	Ace of Discs. The sign of the Great Beast. According to Crowley's book, *The Book of Thoth*, this card has been inadvertantly printed upside down in the version recently issued in St. Paul, Minnesota. Two concentric circles. In the space between the circles is the text TO MEGA THERION. (English translation from the Greek: The Great Beast.) Within the smaller circle are inscribed two concentric seven pointed stars. Within the smaller of these are three circles, each containing a '6'. Thus forming 666, the Sign of the Great Beast of the Apocalypse. It should also be noted that the three circles are so arranged as to be symbolic of the male sexual apparatus seen head-on. Crowley was presumably aware of this reference. The sexual symbolism, in the form of wing and ball shapes, is consistent throughout the card
New:	One of Stones. A green, crystalline stone

Interpretations

Case:	Material gain, wealth, contentment
Crowley:	The Root of the Powers of Earth. In his commentary on this card Crowley refers to Alliette as 'the grotesque barber', Wirth as 'obscurely perverse', and Ouspensky as an 'Autolycus quack' of 'verbose ignorance'. He then points out that his Ace of Discs incorporates his personal sigil. As noted elsewhere this includes the phallus seen head-on + the sun and the moon (or testicles)
Douglas:	As Waite; but with an element of stoicism under adversity, greed or avarice possible
Gray:	As Waite or the opposites implied by his interpretation
Grimaud:	Material success by invoking aid from on high. A card of chance. No meaning of itself
Huson:	Prosperity, abundance
Kahn:	Traditional
Kaplan:	Traditional
Mathers:	Perfect, contentment, felicity, prosperity, triumph. Purse of gold, money, etc.
Papus:	Commencement of fortune. Inheritance, gifts, economy
Thierens:	Creative energy, fulfilment of hope, wish and desire. Good luck, bright prospects etc. Profit

17

Lust, *Crowley Tarot*

| Waite: | Perfect contentment, felicity, ecstasy, speedy intelligence, gold. Comfortable material conditions. The most favourable of all cards. A share in the finding of treasure |
| Suggested: | The active principle of Solar Fire, sensation conscious of its existence. Vulcanism. The first card of the Tarot deck. Beginning. |

Two of Pentacles

Design

Marseille:	Two flowers, quatrefoil, each centred in a coin. The two coins are joined by what could be intended to be a lemniscate on which is printed the maker's name and two dates, 1748 and 1930.
Waite:	A young man dancing near the sea. In his hands he is juggling two pentacles which are surrounded by the lemniscate.
Aquarian:	As Waite
Crowley:	A lemniscate formed from a crowned snake. Within either end is a ball in the form of the T'ai Chi. Each ball includes two of the signs of the four elements. At top the sign for Jupiter. At bottom, that of Capricorn.
New:	Two of Stones. With the lemniscate

Interpretation

Case:	Harmony in the midst of change
Crowley:	The Lord of Harmonious Change. Jupiter in Capricorn. Change
Douglas:	Change in all forms, whether to do with money, travel, news, communications. He suggests possible instability implicit in the card, perhaps leading to drunkenness
G. Dawn:	Pleasant change, visit to friends
Gray:	The juggler and all that his character implies. Essentially traditional
Grimaud:	Man can elevate himself by thought, alliance in all spheres, spiritual and physical riches
Huson:	Monetary obstacles, need for financial dexterity
Kahn:	A dancer, thus leading to the same type of manipulation implicit in the image of the juggler. Traditional

19

Kaplan:	An expression of the difficulties of attempting to juggle. Also contains a suggestion of literary ability. Traditional
Mathers:	Embarrassment, worry, difficulties. Letter, missive, epistle, message.
Papus:	Opposition to the commencement of fortune. Difficulty in firmly establishing the first landmarks of good fortune
Thierens:	Good work, reasonable satisfaction, satisfactory results or occupations, a warning to use economy in the display of one's forces, means, money, health, difficulty of choice, trustworthy and good servants, good treatment of servants, joy, gaiety, recreation, feeling of physical well-being, machinery, techniques, abilities with machinery
Waite:	Gaiety, recreation etc. News and messages in writing, obstacles, agitation, trouble, embroilment (all written). Enforced gaiety, simulated enjoyment, handwriting, composition, letters of exchange. Troubles more imaginary than real, bad omen, ignorance, injustice.
Suggested:	The creative power of fire. Reflective qualities. The moon as an element of the first creation. The absolute primal female energy

Design

Three of Pentacles

Marseille:	Three coins, each with a four-petalled flower at its centre
Waite:	A monk and a hooded man observing a stonemason at his work
Aquarian:	A stonemason working
Crowley:	A three-sided pyramid, the angles of which intersect the centre of a wheel. Above the sign of Mars (male) and below that of Capricorn
New:	Three of Stones. With an equilateral triangle

Interpretation

Case:	Construction, material increase, growth, financial gain
Crowley:	Material works. Mars in Capricorn. Work (the title of the card according to Crowley, used in the sense of engineering or construction)

20

Douglas:	The businessman, merchant or craftsman. Cognate generally with Waite interpretations
G. Dawn:	Business, paid employment, commercial transactions
Gray:	As Waite, but with the added suggestion of Freemasonry
Grimaud:	Forces taken from the occult to obtain gains in the physical world. Relative equilibrium
Huson:	Status, earned esteem, honour
Kahn:	Craftsmanship, either good or poor
Kaplan:	Similar to Kahn
Mathers:	Nobility, elevation, dignity, rank, power. Children, sons, daughters, youths, commencement
Papus:	Realization of the commencement of fortune
Thierens:	Civilization, aristocracy, good workmanship, skill, civil treatment, noblesse, agreeable relation, métier, employment, profession, marriage, good done to others, bounty, profitable relations in business, restoration, reparation, beneficial arrangement, a marriage will do much good
Waite:	Métier, trade, skilled labor, a card of nobility, aristocracy, renown, glory. Mediocrity, puerility, pettiness, weakness. Celebrity for man's eldest son
Suggested:	The child of money or the child of fire. Adam in paradise

Design

Four of Pentacles

Marseille:	Four coins, each with a quatrefoiled flower at its centre. At the centre of the card is a double, concentric square which surrounds a flower, a lotus, perhaps
Waite:	A king sits brooding. On his crown rests one pentacle. He hugs another in his lap. The third and fourth are beneath his feet.
Aquarian:	One on his head, one on his breast, one on either hand
Crowley:	A castle with four turrets as seen from above. Each of the towers bears one of the elemental signs. Sol in Capricorn
New:	Four of Stones. A square

Case: Earthly power, physical forces and skill in directing them

Crowley: Earthly power, Sun in Capricorn. Power

Douglas: Traditional but with the additional contrary suggestion of inability or opposition to change or to delegate authority

G. Dawn: Gain of money and influence, a present

Gray: Gain or loss

Grimaud: The expansion of the psychic, equilibrium between the planes, halt, plan brought to a halt by contingencies which hold it fast, sometimes not an abrupt halt. Just a great reversal

Huson: Material benefits, acquisitiveness

Kahn: Security or insecurity

Kaplan: The miser, the polarity of the card being between the possibilities of future further gain or opposition to future gain

Mathers: Pleasure, gaiety, enjoyment, satisfaction. Obstacles, hinderances

Papus: Opposition of fortune. Loss of money

Thierens: Desire, delay, retreat, secret possession, legacy, debt, limitation, enclosure, some good which is not in reach of the querent

Waite: The surety of possessions, cleaving to that which one has, gift, legacy, inheritance. Suspense, delay, opposition. For a bachelor, pleasant news from a lady. Observation, hindrances

Suggested: False economy, financial institutions, established money. Undiscovered talents

Design

Five of Pentacles

Marseille: Five coins, each with a four-petalled flower at its centre

Waite: Two beggars pass a brightly lighted church window. They hurry through the snow. The pentacles are incorporated into the tree design of the stained-glass windows

The Devil, *Crowley Tarot*

Aquarian:	As Waite, except that the pentacles in the window are arranged in cruciform design
Crowley:	A pentagram, each of whose angles terminates in a circle. Each circle bears one of the following symbols: triangle, square, crescent, oval, circle. Mercury in Taurus
New:	Five of Stones. A pentragram, inverted

Interpretation

Case:	Concordance, affinity, adaptation. (Interior rather than exterior, see Waite.)
Crowley:	Material trouble, Mercury in Taurus. Retitled, 'Worry'. 'Intense strain coupled with long-continued inaction.'
Douglas:	As Waite but not as extreme
G. Dawn:	Loss of profession, loss of money, monetary anxiety
Gray:	Similar to Waite but with a suggestion that loss of fortune may lead to a renaissance of spiritual feeling
Grimaud:	Human reason should be able to come to terms with immaterial knowledge. Attack on physical life. A malleable card
Huson:	Head ruled by heart, business loss through emotions
Kahn:	Loss generally
Kaplan:	Loss or the reversal of loss
Mathers:	Lover or mistress, love, sweetness, affection, pure and chaste love. Disgraceful love, imprudence, licence, profligacy
Papus:	Opposition to the opposition of your fortune. A success coming which will balance the loss
Thierens:	Emanation, expansion, love-making, sure to indicate love outside the confines of legal marriage, brilliance but sometimes with a lack of responsibility. Travelling or emigration will do much good. (To remove oneself from importunate mistresses?)
Waite:	Material trouble, love and lovers, concordance, disorder, chaos, ruin, etc. Conquest of fortune by reason. Troubles in love
Suggested:	Money in its power or prime. Pay day

24

Six of Pentacles

Marseille:	Six coins, each with a quatrefoil flower at its centre
Waite:	A wealthy merchant giving alms to beggars. He holds a golden scales in his left hand
Aquarian:	A merchant with scales weighing money
Crowley:	Six milky globes. The Moon in Taurus. Each of the globes bears one of the following planetary symbols: Saturn, Jupiter, Venus, Moon, Mercury, Mars. In the central hexagon of the card is a Mandala
New:	Six of Stones. Arranged in two groups of three. A hexagram

Interpretation

Case:	Material prosperity, philanthropy, presents
Crowley:	Material success, the Moon in Taurus. Success. The condition is transient
Douglas:	Traditional with implications of either philanthropy or prodigality
G. Dawn:	Success in material things, prosperity in business
Gray:	The positive interpretations are those of Waite. Negative aspects include tendencies toward jealousy, threats to prosperity, bribery or irrecoverable debts
Grimaud:	Psychic force exerting its authority over the elements. Success, sure judgement, stabilization in the midst of uncertainty
Huson:	Traditional
Kahn:	Fortune telling, gift, charity. Small business dealings, a special favour which is likewise returned
Kaplan:	As Eden Gray
Mathers:	Presents, gifts, gratification. Ambition, desire, passion, aim, longing
Papus:	Realization to the opposition to money and trade. Ruin.
Thierens:	Charitable action, prosperity, fruitfulness, seizing of opportunity, desire, cupidity
Waite:	Presents, gifts, gratification, attention, vigilance, now is the

hour, present prosperity. Desire, cupidity, envy, jealousy, illusion. The present must not be relied upon. (Pun on *present*? Waite's card shows a man giving *alms*, i.e., presents.) A check to ambition

Suggested: The ambivalence of money, considered as a useful or as a destructive tool. The two-faced quality of power

Design # Seven of Pentacles

Marseille: Seven coins, each with a quatrefoiled flower at its centre

Waite: A farmworker contemplates gloomily six pentacles on a vine, apparently nearly ripe, and a seventh at his feet

Aquarian: Seven pentacles on a tree. The man in this card rests his left hand on the head of a goose

Crowley: Seven circles, each of which contains the symbol for Taurus or that of Saturn. The background design is suggestive of a Scarabaeus Beetle. Saturn in Taurus

New: Seven of Stones. In four and in three. An equilateral triangle mounted on a square

Interpretation

Case: Success unfulfilled, delay but with growth

Crowley: Success unfulfilled, Saturn in Taurus. Retitled, 'Failure'. The atmosphere of the card is that of Blight

Douglas: Substantially traditional

G. Dawn: Unprofitable speculations, employments, honorary work undertaken for the love of it and without hope of reward

Gray: Impotence in a financial situation after a promising beginning, an implication of monetary stagnation

Grimaud: Cosmic harmony, equilibrium between matter and the psychic, indecision, lack of precision, difficulty

Huson: Ardent pursuit of wealth, greed

Kahn: Some small financial gain, birth or a child. Inertia similar to that in Eden Gray

Kaplan: Polarized between success and ingenuity on the one hand, anxiety and imprudence on the other

26

Mathers:	Money, finance, treasure, gain, profit. Disturbance, worry, anxiety, melancholy
Papus:	Success assured. A large fortune
Thierens:	Friendship, concord, cooperation, natural outcome of what was sown previously
Waite:	A card of business, money, barter, altercation, innocence. Cause for anxiety concerning money that the Querent may lend. Improved position for a lady's future husband. Impatience, apprehension
Suggested:	Man in perfect control of power, whether solar power or money

Eight of Pentacles

Design

Marseille:	Eight coins, each containing a four-petalled flower
Waite:	A woodworker chiselling out a pentagram within a circle. Five of them hang beside him, a seventh rests against his bench and the eighth is on the ground beside him
Aquarian:	Basically as Waite; but the eight pentacles are mounted on the wall of his room
Crowley:	A tree of eight five-petalled flowers. The Sun in Virgo
New:	Eight of Stones. An octagon

Interpretation

Case:	Skill in material affairs
Crowley:	Prudence, the Sun in Virgo. Intelligence lovingly applied to material matters
Douglas:	Traditional with the added negative implications of concentration on short-term rather than long-term goals
G. Dawn:	Skill, prudence, artfulness, cunning
Gray:	Compares with Waite
Grimaud:	Equilibrium of extremes in every realm, harmony of the worlds. Violent stopping of something or success or stability according to the cards around it
Huson:	Prudence, economy

27

The Devil, *Aquarian Tarot*

Kahn:	A virtuous brunette woman. His contrasting meaning is a vain woman, working to get what she wants or a shameless hussy. 'Minor illicit arts'
Kaplan:	Corresponding to Waite
Mathers:	A dark girl, beauty, candour, chastity, innocence, modesty. Flattery, usury, hypocrisy, shifty
Papus:	Partial success, just as you appear to be securing your fortune you lose a lot of money
Thierens:	Devotion, possibly to charity, the mysteries of nature, religious work, medicine, prisons or the arts. A possibility of Bohemian love ending in degradation, deprivation, waste of money. The conversion of a good for nothing to labour. Dark girl
Waite:	Work, employment, commission, craftsmanship, skill in craft or business, perhaps in the preparatory stage. Voided ambition, vanity, cupidity, exaction, usury, the skill of the ingenious mind turned to cunning and intrigue. A young man in business who has relations with the Querent. A dark girl. The Querent will be compromised in a matter of money-lending
Suggested:	Established power properly applied, the rejuvenation of fire

Nine of Pentacles

Design

Marseille:	Nine coins, each with a flower in its centre
Waite:	A woman seen in her vineyard of ripe grapes. On her upraised left hand she holds a bird. Her gown is patterned with flowers in the form of the planetary sign for Venus
Aquarian:	The same woman, no pattern on her gown. The bird she holds is a white cockatoo
Crowley:	Six smaller discs around three larger ones. The larger discs are reminiscent of the Ace of the suit. Venus in Virgo. Within the smaller discs are the planetary signs of Saturn, Jupiter, Venus, Moon, Mercury, and Mars incorporated into stylized faces
New:	Nine of Stones

29

Case: Prudence, material gain, completion

Crowley: Material gain, Venus in Virgo. Retitled, 'Gain'. Good luck attending material affairs. Favour and popularity

Douglas: As Waite

G. Dawn: Inheritance, much increase of money

Gray: Private concerns: pleasures of life, inheritance or one's own interests. Her reverse is assorted dangers: thieves, cancellations, loss of home or friend. A need for caution

Grimaud: Unattainable agreement between the spiritual and the material. Difference or agreement, concealed or latent plans

Huson: As Waite, prudence

Kahn: Future gain, endeavors accomplished for the benefits they will bring in the future, mystic arts, spiritual practices and gifts on a large scale. Dealing, money games, risky venture, chance, fate, gambling, cards, dice, roulette, big business

Kaplan: Traditional

Mathers: Discretion, circumspection, prudence, discernment. Deceit, bad faith, artifices, deception

Papus: Equilibrium of equilibrium. A durable fortune

Thierens: Honesty, positive action, it means to the Querent: 'Go ahead, you will succeed.' Strong affirmative answer on questions, the effect is certain

Waite: Prudence, safety, success, accomplishment, certitude, discernment. Roguery, deception, voided project, bad faith. Prompt fulfilment of what is presaged by neighboring cards, vain hopes

Suggested: Impotence, either through lack of power or money or the lack of the ability to use power or money. Can denote avarice

Design

Ten of Pentacles

Marseille: Ten coins arranged in two 'X' forms, one above the other. Each coin has a four-petalled flower in its centre

Waite:	A patriarch seated before his gate. Near him are his dogs, his children and his grandchild. Ripe grapes and crescent moons also figure in this card
Aquarian:	A man, woman and child entering the gate to a castle which stands on a high eminence. The pentacles are incorporated into the design of the gate
Crowley:	Ten coins with Cabbalistic designs upon them. The signs include the planetary sign for Mercury, a combination of the signs for Mercury and Saturn; The Caduceus formed from the three Hebrew 'Mother' letters . . . Aleph, Shin and Samekh, the zodiacal sign for Aries, an eight-pointed star, a hexagram inscribed within a hexagon, the Hebrew letter Beth, the planetary sign for Mercury combined with the sign for the setting sun. Of the two central coins which complete the ten, one is illegible, the other contains the Hebrew for Raphael, the Archangel of the East, the Sixth Sephiroth (Tiphareth) and Angel of the Planet Mercury. (This coin illustrates adequately Crowley's delight in mystification for its own sake.)
New:	Ten of Stones. Arranged in two five-pointed stars

Interpretation

Case:	Wealth, riches, material prosperity
Crowley:	Wealth, Mercury in Virgo. The great and final solidification of the force, completely expended and resulting in death. A hieroglyph of the cycle of regeneration
Douglas:	Traditional with emphasis upon inheritance and its effects, for benefit or for restriction. Wills or dowries
G. Dawn:	Riches and wealth
Gray:	Traditional
Grimaud:	Success, agreement, equilibrium, satisfaction, complete joy
Huson:	Stable home, family life, the house
Kahn:	Assignations and conferences. Money. Peace, amity, a mate
Kaplan:	Prosperity. Possible loss
Mathers:	House, dwelling, habitation, family. Gambling, dissipation, robbery, loss
Papus:	Uncertainty in the fortune, great successes and great reverses

31

Thierens:	Fortune, riches, favourable chance, economy, agriculture, music and painting, may give a beautiful voice, advantage in world affairs, possessions, domains, lands or property, banking, insurance, art dealing, laziness, dull luxury, full midsummer in human life, you cannot escape this good ripe fruit of Karma, nor the fullness of Nature at its height. The attitude of the wise must be to enjoy
Waite:	Gain, riches, family matters, archives, extraction, the abode of a family. Chance, fatality, loss, robbery, games of hazard, gift, dowry, pension. Represents house or dwelling, deriving its value from other cards, an occasion which may be fortunate or otherwise
Suggested:	The solar fire exhausted. Numbness, lack of sensation. Winter. The dark star

Design

Page of Pentacles

Waite:	A young man stands in a field of flowers holding a pentacle
Aquarian:	A young man, a dreamer, holding a pentacle
Crowley:	Princess of Discs. A Germanic princess wearing a ram's head crown. Her left hand rests on a pentacle formed by combining a lotus and the symbol, T'ai Chi. Her left hand holds a spear with a diamond point, downward. The spear sheds light on the earth near it.
New:	Reminiscent of some Amerindian art. The zodiacal sign for Virgo at the bottom

Interpretation

Case:	A diligent, careful, deliberate youth
Crowley:	The Princess of the Echoing Hills. The Lotus of the Palace of the Earth. Rules a quadrant around Kether. The earthy part of Earth. Womanhood in its ultimate projection, bewildering inconsistency
Douglas:	Virtues: thrift, diligence, honour, administrative sense, business acumen. Vices: Idleness, stupidity, humourlessness, over-cautious or hypercritical, tendency toward pride and pride in power
G. Dawn:	Princess of the Echoing Hills, Rose of the Palace of Earth. Generous, kind, diligent, benevolent, careful, courageous,

preserving, pitiful. If ill-dignified she is wasteful and prodigal. Rules one quadrant of the heavens around the North Pole of the Ecliptic (Kether). Earth of Earth, Princess and Empress of the Gnomes. Throne of the Ace of Pentacles

Gray: Boy or girl with black hair and eyes, swarthy complexion. Otherwise traditional

Grimaud: Material work to ensure existence, disinterested work bringing riches as a reward. Tentative advance, mediocre results

Huson: Crass young materialist, dull person, avarice

Kahn: Traditional

Kaplan: Traditional

Mathers: A dark youth, economy, order, rule, management. Prodigality, profusion, waste, dissipation

Papus: A fair child, a messenger, a letter

Thierens: Disciple, student, messenger, newsagent, liberal treatment of the Querent, a director, book-keeper, assistant, editor, honorable mention, application. A meeting, committee or board of directors

Waite: Application, study, scholarship, reflection, news, messages, the bringer of messages, rule, management. Prodigality, dissipation, liberality, luxury, unfavourable news. A dark youth, a young officer or soldier, a child. Sometimes degradation and sometimes pillage

Suggested: The bringer of fire or power or money, either a human agency or a force. Prometheus. Loki. See also Five of Swords to which this relates

Design # Knight of Pentacles

Marseille: A knight, wearing loose clothing, mounted. He holds a baton over his right shoulder. In the upper right hand corner of the card is a coin with a four-petalled flower at its centre

Waite: A knight on a black horse bears a pentacle before him. His helmet is crowned with oak

33

Aquarian:	A partially visored knight, his armour has pentacles upon it
Crowley:	A dark knight on a dark horse in a field of ripe wheat. His helmet is topped by a stag's head
New:	A desert canyon. In it are a Tau cross, a war bonnet, the lemniscate within the yoni figure, a volcano and the sun above

Interpretation

Case:	Laborious, patient, dull young man
Crowley:	The Lord of the Wide and Fertile Land. The King of the Spirits of Earth. 20 degrees Leo to 20 degrees Virgo. The fiery part of Earth, tends to be dull, heavy, preoccupied with material things, laborious, patient, little intellectual grasp even of matters which concern him closely. Strong instincts. Ill-dignified he is hopelessly stupid, slavish, incapable of foresight, churlish, surly, instinctively jealous of the superior state of others, meddling in petty matters, interfering
Douglas:	A crusader or an upholder of established tradition. Practicality. Smugness or the defense of what should be allowed to fall
G. Dawn:	Lord of the Wild and Fertile Land, King of the Spirits of Earth. Attributions the same as Crowley. Fire of Earth, King of the Gnomes
Gray:	Black-haired young man with black eyes, swarthy skin. Laborious, patient, responsible man. Otherwise cognate with Waite
Grimaud:	Fortune or attainment cannot come from laziness, success due to force, perseverance and will. Discouragement, abandonment of the struggle
Huson:	Traditional
Kahn:	Money/poverty axis, otherwise traditional
Kaplan:	As Waite
Mathers:	A useful man. Trustworthy. Wisdom, economy, order, regulation. A brave man unemployed, idle, negligent
Papus:	A young fair man, a stranger, an arrival
Thierens:	Discreet aid in financial difficulties, advantage, interest, a

messenger bringing these, loan, inheritance, happy memories, savings. Indolence, secret enjoyment, idleness

Waite: Utility, serviceableness, interest, responsibility, rectitude. Inertia, idleness, stagnation, placidity, discouragement, carelessness. A useful man, useful discoveries. A brave man out of employment

Suggested: Protector or defender of the Sun, of money, of fire or power. Earth of Fire

Queen of Pentacles

Design

Marseille: A queen, seated, holding aloft in her right hand a pentacle, the flower at its centre being eight petalled. In her left hand she holds a sceptre which rests upon her left shoulder

Waite: A queen, seated upon a ram's head throne. She sits in a flowery field beneath roses. Near the throne is a rabbit

Aquarian: A queen in an ermine robe. Her helmet is winged

Crowley: A queen wearing a helmet which incorporates gigantic ram's horns. Before her stands a ram. She holds a globe with an interlocking disc design in her left hand. In her right she holds a diamond tipped spear upright.

New: A crown, a bear, a Phoenician or Egyptian ship and, at the bottom of the card, the sign for Capricorn.

Interpretation

Case: Generous, intelligent, charming, moody married woman

Crowley: The Queen of the Thrones of Earth. 20 degrees Sagittarius to 20 degrees Capricorn. The watery part of Earth, the function of water as Mother. Passivity, usually in its highest aspect. Possesses the finest of the quieter qualities. Ambitious in useful directions, immense funds of affection, kindness, greatness of heart, strong in intuition and instinct, weaker in intelligence, quiet, hard working, practical, sensible, domesticated, and often (in a reticent and unassuming fashion) lustful and even debauched. Inclined to the abuse of alcohol and drugs. Ill-dignified they are dull, servile, foolish, drudges rather than workers

Douglas: Traditional

G. Dawn: Impetuous, kind, timid, charming, great-hearted, in-

35

telligent, melancholy, truthful. Ill-dignified she is undecided, foolish, capricious, changeable. Water of Earth, Queen of Gnomes

Gray: As Waite

Grimaud: Disappointment in a given situation due to lack of wisdom, struggle to acquire and keep that which is acquired. Sale of possessions

Huson: Parallel to the traditional

Kahn: Traditional

Kaplan: Prosperity/false prosperity. Similar to the traditional interpretations

Mathers: A dark woman, a generous woman, liberality, greatness of soul, generosity. Certain evil, suspicious woman, woman justly regarded with suspicion and doubt

Papus: A fair woman, indifferent or inimical

Thierens: Good intelligent woman who will render service to the querent. Help, assistance, woman of good standing, sometimes timidity, material benefit, earnings, wealth, rent, products, security, insurance, diploma, patronage of science and technical and industrial works

Waite: Greatness of soul, a dark woman, serious cast of intelligence, opulence, generosity, magnificence, security, liberty. Evil, suspicion, fear, mistrust. Dark woman, presents from a rich relative, rich and happy marriage for a young man. An illness

Suggested: The Queen of Pentacles, fire, power or suns. The mother of the Ace of Wands or of the Fool. Those things and people working through established institutions to further the attributes of fire. Water of Fire

Design

King of Pentacles

Marseille: A seated king, holding in his right hand a pentacle which contains a six-petalled flower

Waite: A king on a bull's head throne. In his right hand he holds the sceptre with orb at its end. His left rests upon a pentacle. In the background is a stone castle. His robe is decorated with a pattern of grape vines and ripe grapes

Aquarian: A king. In the background a bull with a halter around its neck

Crowley: A naked king in a chariot drawn by a bull. His left hand rests on a globe. In his right he holds a sceptre surmounted by an orb. The orb is itself surmounted with a Maltese Cross. His helmet is crowned with the head of a bull, apparently winged. Throughout the card the motifs of pomegranates and flowers are repeated

New: King of Stones. A white stag bearing a bow. In his antlers the crystal sign which has represented all the cards within this suit. Below the stag is a swastika, reversed. (Reversed, that is, from the more familiar Nazi swastika.) A field which consists of a fringed blanket above which is an Indian head-dress for crown and below which is the zodiacal sign for Taurus

Interpretation

Case: Friendly, steady reliable married man

Crowley: The Prince of the Chariot of Earth. 20 degrees Aries to 20 degrees Taurus. The airy part of Earth, great energy brought to bear on practical matters, energetic and enduring, a capable manager, steadfast and persevering worker, competent, ingenious, thoughtful, cautious, trustworthy, imperturbable, constantly seeks new uses of common things adapting circumstances to his purposes in a slow steady well thought out plan. Lacking in emotion, somewhat insensitive, may appear dull but only because he makes no effort to understand ideas beyond his scope, may appear stupid, inclined to be resentful of more spiritual types, slow to anger but can be an implacable enemy

Douglas: Practicality/implacability ranging to dullness/stupidity/materialistic qualities, weakness, servility

G. Dawn: Increase of matter, increase of good and evil, solidifies, practically applies things, steady, reliable. If ill-dignified, animal, material, stupid. Slow to anger but furious if aroused. Air of Earth, Prince and Emperor of Gnomes

Gray: Black-haired, black-eyed man with swarthy skin. A chief in industry, banking, real estate, dependable married man, possibly a mathematician with considerable financial

37

ability. Negative aspects include stupidity, waste or perversion of abilities, thriftlessness, bribability etc. A weak person

Grimaud: The occult and fatal action of cosmic forces, possessions in a precarious state

Huson: Traditional

Kahn: Traditional, except for the negative aspects of the card, possibly morbidity, illness. Possible danger to others because of his state of mind

Kaplan: Traditional with additional qualities of loyalty and with additional negative aspects of avarice and unfaithfulness

Mathers: Dark man, victory, bravery, courage, success. An old and vicious man, a dangerous man, doubt, fear, peril, danger

Papus: A fair man, inimical or indifferent

Thierens: Noble, good and honest man, influential, whom you must go to see, banker, speculator, gambler, benefic influence, wealth, luxury, in weak cases vanity, pride. Success in mechanics and machinery

Waite: Valour, realizing intelligence, business and normal intellectual aptitude, sometimes mathematical gifts and attainments, success in mathematics or business. Vice, weakness, ugliness, perversity, corruption, peril. Rather dark man, merchant, master, professor. An old and vicious man

Suggested: The King of Power, Pentacles, Money, Solar Fire, Sensation. People or agencies acting to establish or to destroy the institutions related to the suit. The judge of matters having to do with the suit. Father of the Fool and Father of the Ace of Wands. Air of Fire

Wands

The second of the suits of the Minor Arcana, corresponding to Feeling, to Earth, to Emotions. In many of the Tarot decks some or all of the Wands are shown as either in leaf or as having been cut from living wood. For this reason the attribution to Earth and Feeling, seems to me to be more logical than that to Fire

Case:	Energy, opposition, quarrel. Inimical to cups, friendly with swords and pentacles
Crowley:	The powers of fire
Douglas:	Inspiration, ideas and intellect, exercise of will
Gray:	Animation and enterprise, energy and growth. Associated with the salamander. Apocalyptic beast, the lion. South. Of courageous, hopeful, or amorous disposition. The suit of the labourer
Huson:	Things to do with work and creativity
Kaplan:	Enterprise and glory. Air
Mathers:	Very fair people. Feasting
Papus:	Eagle, spring, first quarter, dawn and childhood. Enterprise and glory. Court cards represent dark people
Waite:	Court cards indicate dark people

Design   ## Ace of Wands

Marseille:	A hand brandishing a stout branch cut from a tree. The card is completed by 29 Solar 'Yods', eighteen to the left of the branch and eleven to its right
Waite:	A hand holding forth a wand in leaf from the clouds. Other leaves, in the shape of 'Yods', are also seen
Aquarian:	A rod in flower

39

Crowley:	Design based on the Tree of Life, suggesting lightning
New:	The Ace of Snakes. A two-headed snake

Case:	Energy, strength, enterprise, principle, beginning
Crowley:	Root of the powers of fire. Blind, solar, phallic fire
Douglas:	Creativity, inspiration or intuition. Barrenness, sterility, most major vices
Gray:	Beginnings of enterprises/journeys/inventions/families. Cancellation of any of these
Grimaud:	The power of man over matter. Success due to force, force overcome, results of force annulled by some other force
Huson:	Activity, beginning, wisdom, initiative, male libido
Kahn:	A letter, a book, an important piece of writing
Kaplan:	Traditional
Mathers:	Birth, commencement, beginning, origin, source. Persecution, pursuit, violence, vexation, cruelty, tyranny
Papus:	Commencement of an enterprise
Thierens:	Birth, beginning, innovation, creation, initiative, impulse, origin, principle, source, cause, reason, parentage, handing over a message, news, revelation, initiation. Fall, decline, descent, depreciation, profanation, that which will happen once only and which cannot be taken back
Waite:	Creation, invention, enterprise, powers which result in these, principle, beginning, source, birth, family, origin, the virility behind the family, starting point of enterprises, money, fortune, inheritance. Fall, decadence, ruin, perdition, to perish, a certain clouded joy. Calamities of all kinds. A sign of birth
Suggested:	The active principle of Earth, the first emotions. Phallic

Two of Wands

Marseille:	Two rods, crossed
Waite:	A man standing on a battlement looking out over the sea. In his right hand he holds a globe, in his left, a wand. To his

Death, *Aquarian Tarot*

right, resting against the wall, is another wand. To his left and upon the wall is a St. Andrew's Cross, one transverse arm of which is white lilies, the other being formed from red roses

Aquarian: A man holding a pink, pearly globe in his right hand. A flowering staff in his left. Before him is another flowering staff. On his left shoulder is a design of a crossed white lily and red rose

Crowley: St. Andrew's Cross formed from two Jester's sceptres superimposed on the zodiacal sign, Pisces. Mars in Aries

New: Two of Snakes, a lemniscate

Interpretation

Case: Dominion

Crowley: Mars in Aries. Dominion. The will in its most exalted form

Douglas: Crowley interpretation expanded with additional negative implication of loss of will or the achievement of worthless goals

G. Dawn: Influence over another. Dominion

Gray: Similar to the interpretation of Douglas, which appears to be based on that of Aleister Crowley rather than Waite or Mathers

Grimaud: Occult knowledge, in physical matters this card holds an evil power, destroying the kindly influences of cards around it

Huson: Novelty, turmoil, restlessness

Kahn: Waiting, a dry spell, a hotel room, patience required, firm position from which to contemplate the world. A long wait

Kaplan: Maturity, ruler, fulfilment of purpose. Sadness, restraint, loss of faith.

Mathers: Riches, fortune, opulence, magnificence, grandeur. Surprise, astonishment, event, extraordinary occurrence

Papus: Opposition to the commencement of the enterprise. An unexpected obstacle suddenly prevents its execution

Thierens: Music, art, artistic ability in general, capital riches, heavy responsibility, pressure, obsession, melancholy, fear, weakness, impossibility, material power, gloom, dullness,

42

spleen, impotence, subjection to material circumstances, attitude of wait and see, the future is for those who can afford to wait, country life

Waite: Riches, fortune, magnificence, physical suffering, disease, chagrin, sadness, mortification, the sadness of Alexander amid the world's wealth. Surprise, wonder, enchantment, emotion, trouble, fear. A young lady may expect trivial disappointments

Suggested: The creative power of Earth or emotions

Three of Wands

Design

Marseille: Three wands

Waite: A man looking out over what could be the sea or a desert. (The background colour in this card is sometimes yellow, yielding a yellow sea.) His right hand holds one wand, to his left stands another. Slightly behind him and to his right stands a third

Aquarian: The grouping is roughly the same, two on the right, one on the left

Crowley: Wands tipped with lotus flowers. Superimposed on a design of a ten-pointed star repeated twice. The Sun in Aries

New: Three of Snakes. An equilateral triangle

Interpretation

Case: Established strength

Crowley: Established strength, the Sun in Aries. Virtue (as retitled in *The Book of Thoth)*

Douglas: Contrasts sharply with most other authorities in that he emphasizes the successful beginning of a great project or the inspiration and fire of the artist or the inventor. His negative meanings are those derived from failure of nerve or paralysis of will

G. Dawn: Pride and arrogance, sometimes power

Gray: Traditional

Grimaud: A card of departure, beginning, groping or advancing, research. Success depending upon surrounding cards

43

Huson:	Derived through Waite
Kahn:	A business from which material goods will be shipped to distant markets, business at hand, creative perspective, analysis of matters underway
Kaplan:	Essentially traditional
Mathers:	Enterprise, undertaking, commerce, trade, negotiation. Hope, desire, attempt, wish
Papus:	Realization of the commencement of the enterprise. The basis of the work is now firmly established and the undertaking can be fearlessly continued
Thierens:	Communication, instruction, reflection, message, writing, postage and letters, passing impressions, commerce, theft and loss. The end of troubles
Waite:	Established strength, enterprise, effort, trade, commerce, discovery, cooperation in business. The end of troubles, suspension or cessation of adversity, toil and disappointment. Collaboration will favour enterprise
Suggested:	The child of feeling. Resolution after struggle

Four of Wands

Design

Marseille:	Crossed wands with the old style numeral IIII on either side
Waite:	Wands in leaf garlanded with flowers. Behind are people apparently celebrating
Aquarian:	Wands garlanded with flowers
Crowley:	Eight rods arranged in the form of an eight pointed wheel. Possibly a variant on the Gnostic Sun monogram. Venus in Aries. Each rod is tipped with either the head of a white ram or a white dove pointing towards the centre of the circle which is fire
New:	Four of Snakes. A square

Interpretation

Case:	Perfected work
Crowley:	Perfected work, Venus in Aries. Completion
Douglas:	The traditional meaning of the card, perfected work,

probably derives from Crowley or the O.T.O. Douglas refines this to make the card represent a particular kind of achievement: that of civilization, the aesthetic arts, or culture generally. Its negative aspects are therefore decadence or snobbishness, the qualities of effete civilization

G. Dawn: Settlement, arrangement completed

Gray: As Waite

Grimaud: Tendency towards psychic equilibrium. Agreement in a durable enterprise yielding a fruitful result. A master card

Huson: Standstill, family bond, demands of society, refuge

Kahn: A fortunate partnership, a satisfying project, friends, work that is enjoyed

Kaplan: Traditional but with the added implication of recently perfected work or recently achieved satisfaction in love or partnership

Mathers: Society, union, association, concord, harmony. Prosperity, success, happiness, advantage

Papus: Obstacles to the enterprise

Thierens: Family-spirit, clan, home, ideas which rule us, that which is familiar (i.e., home) memory, imagination, fantasy, augmentations, decrease, unstable conditions, popularity, vacillation, profanation, a gathering of people, cosiness

Waite: Harvest-home, repose, domestic tranquillity, prosperity, peace. Increase, felicity, beauty. Unexpected good fortune, a married woman will have beautiful children

Suggested: The tyranny of feeling

Five of Wands

Design

Marseille: The wands, crossed. The roman numeral, V, on either side

Waite: Five youths playing with wands as staves

Aquarian: Two youths, two men carrying wands. One extra wand

Crowley: Five wands, one larger than the others. Two of the smaller rods are tipped with phoenix heads at the top and inverted bull's horns at the bottom. The other two small rods are tipped at the top with lotuses. The large rod has at the top a winged solar disc and two snakes, at the bottom Crowley's variant on the winged phallos. Within the disc is inscribed a seven-pointed star, and within the star is a variant on Crowley's three-ring monogram. Saturn in Leo. In the background is a ten-pointed cross of fire

New: Five of Snakes. A pentacle

Interpretation

Case: Strife, competition

Crowley: Strife. Saturn in Leo. Leo shows the element of fire at its strongest and most balanced, Saturn weighs it down and embitters it

Douglas: Traditional meaning of strife or competition with the suggestion of mental agility as a successful weapon

G. Dawn: Quarrelling, fighting

Gray: Corresponds to Waite

Grimaud: A wish to understand and penetrate mysteries without impeding material life. Plan whose outcome cannot be determined

Huson: Wealth and success

Kahn: Making arrangements necessary for a venture, discussion, plans, strategy, acquiring specific information, struggle, hassle, indisposition, effort

Kaplan: An elaboration of the traditional meanings

Mathers: Gold, opulence, gain, heritage, riches, fortune, money. Legal proceedings, judgement, law, lawyer, tribunal

Papus: Opposition to the obstacles to an enterprise. Victory after surmounting them

Thierens: Egotism, positive speech, speaking in a self-centred way and taking no notice of others, possibly leading to trickery, little or no evil, good for health and wealth in a general way, promoting both, but it is not riches in itself

Waite: Imitation fight, competition, the battle of life, gold gain, opulence. Litigation, disputes, trickery, contradiction. Success in financial speculation. Quarrels may be turned to advantage

The mystical power of Earth. The 'force that through the green fuse drives the flower . . . '

Six of Wands

Design

Marseille: A bundle of crossed wands. To either side the roman numeral, VI

Waite: A young man on horseback, riding in triumph. His wand has a victor's wreath. He is accompanied by other men on foot who bear wands

Aquarian: Central figure as Waite. The other figures are not visible

Crowley: Six wands crossed, three over three. Two of the rods are tipped with the winged solar disc, two are tipped with Phoenix heads, two with lotus flowers. From each intersection burns a small flame. (Nine points altogether.) Jupiter in Leo

New: Six of Snakes. Arranged three and three. A six-pointed star

Interpretation

Case: Victory after strife, gain

Crowley: Victory, Jupiter in Leo. Crowley implies a stable victory as the meaning for this card in *The Book of Thoth*

Douglas: Traditional

G. Dawn: Gain and success

Gray: Traditional

Grimaud: Halt in the evolution of things to allow something to be brought to perfection. Victory but only on a practical plane. A firm, stable card

Huson: Domesticity

Kahn: Carrying out of a project, execution of desire, staying above apprehension. Cunning people, dispute

Kaplan: Traditional

Mathers: Attempt, hope, desire, wish, expectation. Infidelity, disloyalty, treachery, perfidy

Papus: Realization of the opposition. At last the obstacles succeed. Failure of the enterprise in the midst of its execution

Thierens: Knowledge, decorative art, efficiency, practical solutions

47

Ace of Pentacles, *Crowley Tarot*

with perhaps some discrepancy, persons in subordinate positions waiting for orders or for the results of experiments, for the answer to questions

Waite: A victor in triumph, great news, expectations crowned, the crown of hope. Apprehension, fear, treachery, disloyalty, indefinite delay. Servants may lose the confidence of their masters, a young lady may be betrayed by a friend. Fulfilment of deferred hope

Suggested: The dual nature of, the measure of Earth

Design

Seven of Wands

Marseille: Wands crossed. At either side is the roman numeral, VII

Waite: An embattled man using his wand as a staff to fight off six attacking staves

Aquarian: As Waite but with the added implication: 'You shall not pass'

Crowley: Similar to his design for the Six of Wands; but with the addition of a wooden rod, superimposed upon the others. Mars in Leo

New: Seven of Snakes. Three above, four below. A triangle on top of a square

Interpretation

Case: Valour, courage in the face of difficulties

Crowley: Valour, Mars in Leo

Douglas: Cognate with the traditional

G. Dawn: Opposition, sometimes courage therewith

Gray: As Waite

Grimaud: Violence, conflict

Huson: Skilful exchange of ideas, good communication

Kahn: Discourse for the present, present plans, music, live theatre. Means a great deal of whatever card is next to it. (Kahn humour)

Kaplan: As Waite

49

Mathers:	Success, gain, advantage, profit, victory. Indecision, doubt, hesitation, embarrassment, anxiety
Papus:	Certain success of the enterprise
Thierens:	Discussion, negotiation, contract, measure, rules for conduct
Waite:	Valour, discussion, wordy strife, negotiations, war of trade, barter, competition, success. Perplexity, embarrassment, anxiety, caution against indecision. A dark child
Suggested:	Earth in its most developed aspect. Can also indicate stubbornness. Valour, perhaps in an attempt to conquer overstrong emotions

Design
Eight of Wands

Marseille:	Wands crossed. On either side the roman numeral, VIII
Waite:	Eight wands flying through the air parallel to each other. Their flight is apparently terminating
Aquarian:	As Waite
Crowley:	Four lightning bolts crossed to form a double (or solar) cross. Above, a rainbow. Mercury in Sagittarius
New:	Eight of Snakes. Arranged in a wheel

Interpretation

Case:	Activity, swiftness, approach to goal
Crowley:	Swiftness, Mercury in Sagittarius. The energy of high velocity
Douglas:	An inventive synthesis of the Crowley and Waite attributions. He suggests that a time for initiative is indicated when hopeful change or movement will take place. Additional meanings are more/less traditional and include journeys or communications on the one hand, rashness and brilliance dissipated on the other
G. Dawn:	A hasty communication, letter or message, swiftness
Gray:	Substantially the same as Waite
Grimaud:	Transition between life and death, new beginning
Huson:	Stability, understanding, a rural matter
Kahn:	The country, gain, gold. Travel, rumination, sorrow

Kaplan:	Traditional
Mathers:	Understanding, observation, direction. Quarrels, intestine disputes, discord. (Intestine disputes?)
Papus:	Opposition to its success, the enterprise will only partially succeed
Thierens:	Examination, interrogation, misgivings, sometimes misunderstandings, quick response, pleasure and pain, life at or on the sea, students of occultism, poetry, music and sculpture, secret message, hidden meaning, sex question, private interview or rendezvous, bad weather. (This list is typical Thierens, including everything)
Waite:	Activity in undertakings, swiftness, that which is on the move, the arrows of love. Arrows of jealousy, internal dispute, conscience, domestic disputes
Suggested:	Emotions in their most fruitful aspect, perhaps maternal

Nine of Wands

Design

Marseille:	Crossed wands. On either side is the roman numeral, VIIII
Waite:	A man leaning upon a staff. His head is bandaged. Behind him stand eight other stave
Aquarian:	Nine rods, flowering
Crowley:	Eight small wands, one large one. The smaller ones are arrows pointing downward, the feathers formed from stylized crescent moons. The tips are also crescents. The arrows are crossed. The ninth wand has the solar disc at its top and the crescent at the bottom. Moon in Sagittarius
New:	Nine of Snakes

Interpretation

Case:	Preparedness, strength in reserve, victory after opposition
Crowley:	Great strength, the Moon in Sagittarius. Retitled, 'Strength'. Change in stability, the best that can be obtained from the energy of the suit of Wands
Douglas:	As Crowley
G. Dawn:	Strength, power, health, energy
Gray:	Similar to Waite but with added implications of eventual

51

victory after the application of considerable force. The negative aspects include suggestions of physical debility or sickness

Grimaud: Desire to attain the realms of the psychic which goes beyond the bounds of physical safety. Abstract or physical sciences

Huson: Delays

Kahn: Gain, separation and advantage, knowledge of special value, a stalwart position. Threat, mishap

Kaplan: Traditional but with the negative possibilities ranging from obstacles to calamity and disaster, presumably touching all the bases along the way

Mathers: Order, discipline, good arrangement, disposition. Obstacles, crosses, delay, displeasure

Papus: Realisation of success, success is continued

Thierens: Teaching, planning, travel, editors and journalists, prophecy, unruliness, controversy, contradiction wherever this card appears, preaching, excitement of the people, revolution

Waite: Strength in opposition, delay, suspension, adjournment. Obstacles, adversity, calamity. Generally speaking a bad card

Suggested: The emotions debilitated. An aged person. Possible insanity

Design
Ten of Wands

Marseille: Crossed wands, at either side the roman numeral, X

Waite: A man carrying a bundle of ten heavy wands

Aquarian: As Waite

Crowley: Four small rods crossed with four others. They are tipped with flame. Two larger rods, vertical, superimposed, and having at the top fools' heads, at the bottom, spear points. Saturn in Sagittarius

New: Ten of Snakes. Five and five

Interpretation

Case: Oppression, burden of ill-regulated power

Crowley:	Oppression, Saturn in Sagittarius. The most violent form of the energy of wands
Douglas:	Traditional; but elaborates the negative position to include malicious deceit, guile or lies . . . mischief with the object of watching the ants run about in circles
G. Dawn:	Cruelty and malice towards others, overbearing strength, revenge, injustice
Gray:	Traditional
Grimaud:	Temporary power in the realm of the psychic, difficulties, plans which do not succeed or only with difficulty, with other cards can indicate halt, sterility
Huson:	The traditional aspect of oppression is changed to treachery
Kahn:	Change of style, place, occupation, activity, location. Gold and the sea
Kaplan:	Similar to the traditional; but with the change of oppression as the prime meaning for excessive pressure or the quality of being overburdened. Implication of a situation which has within itself at least some of the seeds of its own solution
Mathers:	Confidence, security, honour, good faith. Treachery, subterfuge, duplicity, bar
Papus:	Uncertainty in the management of the enterprise
Thierens:	Karma, obedience, executive ability, duplicity, falsehood, oppression, overestimation of the importance of things
Waite:	Oppression, fortune, gain, any success as well as its oppression, a card of false-seeming, disguise, perfidy, success is stopped if the nine of swords follows, and if it is a lawsuit there will be certain loss. Contrarieties, difficulties, intrigues. Difficulties and contradictions if near a good card
Suggested:	The exhaustion of emotion. Perhaps the end of a love affair. Sterility, the desert, catatonia, despair

Page of Wands

Design

Marseille:	A young man, standing with a club which has been cut from a tree branch

Waite:	A young man, his clothing decorated with salamanders, standing in a desert with a wand
Aquarian:	A young man, his hat decorated with a flower in bud, standing with a flowering rod before a swamp of cat tails (bulrushes)
Crowley:	A princess drawn upward with a leopard past an altar with burning sacrifice. She carries in her left hand a sun-tipped wand. Her hair forms the sign of Leo
New:	Serpent page. A drum, a snake, a spilled cauldron, a zebra. The sign of Sagittarius

Interpretation

Case:	Dark, young man, messenger, brilliance, courage
Crowley:	The Princess of the Shining Flame. The Rose of the Palace of Fire. Rules one Quadrant of the Heavens about the North Pole. The Earthy part of Fire. The dance of the virgin priestess of the Lords of Fire, for she attends upon an altar ornamented with rams' heads symbolizing the fires of Spring. Brilliance, daring, vigour, energy, the impression of beauty, sudden, violent, implacable, ambitious, aspiring, patient only when it is a matter of revenge. Can be superficial, theatrical, shallow, cruel, faithless, domineering
Douglas:	Employs the traditional meaning of a messenger which is elaborated in its negative aspect to include betrayal of trust, bearer of scandal, slander, misleading information. Additional suggestions: Ambition, resource, enthusiasm
G. Dawn:	Same titles as Crowley. Brilliance, courage, beauty, force, sudden in anger, in love. Desire of power, enthusiasm, revenge. Ill-dignified as Crowley. Earth of Fire, Princess and Empress of the Salamanders. Throne of the Ace of Wands
Gray:	As the suit of Wands, for her, always indicates blonds with blue or hazel eyes, this card represents a fair-complexioned boy or girl. (Compare with Case and Waite). Traditional meanings plus courage, beauty, volatile in love and anger. Negatively, he may break your heart
Grimaud:	Man faced by d fficulty becoming aware of his forces and who can prevail or stagnate according to his abilities, hard work with chances of success. Powerlessness yielding in the face of effort

Huson:	Traditional
Kahn:	Traditional
Kaplan:	Traditional
Mathers:	A good stranger, good news, pleasure, satisfaction. News, displeasure, chagrin, worry
Papus:	A dark child, a friend, a message from a near relation
Thierens:	A brother, schoolmate, messenger, younger man sometimes on an errand, news, friend, telegraph, telephone, radio, telepathy. Invention. Helpful influences in general, helpful people, dustmen
Waite:	He is unknown but faithful and his tidings are strange. Dark young man, faithful, a lover, an envoy, a postman, beside a man he will bear favourable testimony concerning him. A dangerous rival if followed by the Page of Cups. The chief qualities of Wands. May signify family intelligence. Anecdotes, announcements, evil news, indecision, instability which accompanies it
Suggested:	Messages or the bearers of messages concerning love or hate. The coming of love. Fire of Earth

Knight of Wands

Design

Marseille:	A mounted knight carrying a club cut from a tree branch
Waite:	A knight riding through a desert. His clothing is decorated with salamanders. A fiery plume streams from his helmet
Aquarian:	A knight carrying a flowering rod over his left shoulder
Crowley:	A fiery knight. The sign of Leo also appears. His horse is black and fiery as well
New:	Serpent knight. A scorpion, holly, a volcano, a lemniscate. The solar disc and T'ai Chi

Interpretation

Case:	Dark, friendly young man, departure, change of residence
Crowley:	The Lord of the Flame and the Lightning. The King of the Spirits of Fire. 20 degrees Scorpio to 20 degrees Sagittarius. Fiery part of fire, activity, generosity, fierceness, impetuosity, pride, impulsiveness, swiftness in unpredictable

actions. Ill-dignified he is evil-minded, cruel, bigoted and brutal

Douglas:	Traditional Waite interpretation with implications of Crowley readings
G. Dawn:	As Crowley but: Fire of Fire, King of the Salamanders
Gray:	Traditional with the addition of possible change of residence or emigration
Grimaud:	Providential aid, support given in everything, protection, support and strength brought by the unknown. Protection delayed if inverted
Huson:	Change of residence, departure, emigration
Kahn:	Traveller. Abandonment and flight
Kaplan:	Traditional with the suggested implication of travel or movement augmented to imply possible journey into the unknown
Mathers:	Departure, separation, disunion. Rupture, discord, quarrel
Papus:	A dark young man, a friend
Thierens:	A representative of the father or family, someone who brings new, perhaps disturbing influences into the home, the disturbance of domestic happiness, changes in the home, an investigator, an occultist, a stranger, a tramp, possibly an enemy, translation, transmutation, disturbing influences, unrest
Waite:	A precipitate mood, departure, absence, flight, emigration, a friendly dark young man, change of residence. Rupture, division, interruption, discord. A bad card, alienation. For a woman, marriage; but probably frustrated
Suggested:	The defender of or the defence of feelings/emotions/love. Perhaps love in trouble? Earth of Earth

Design   # Queen of Wands

Marseille:	A queen, with a roughly carved club over her right shoulder
Waite:	A queen on a lion throne. She holds a sunflower in her left hand, a wand in her right. A black cat is before the throne. The designs of lions and sunflowers appear behind her on the canopy

Morgan Tarot

Aquarian:	A sunflower in her left hand, a flowering rod in her right
Crowley:	A queen, crowned with the winged solar disc. Her wand is tipped with a pine cone. Her throne is of flame. A leopard sits near her
New:	Serpent queen. An alligator, a daffodil, a snake, a ship, another daffodil. Above is a crown with the lunar crescent

Interpretation

Case:	Dark woman, magnetic, friendly, business success
Crowley:	The Queen of the Thrones of Flame. 20 degrees Pisces to 20 degrees Aries. The watery part of fire, adaptability, persistent energy, calm authority, kindly and generous, impatient of opposition, immense capacity for friendship and love on her own initiative. Pride which lacks spontaneous nobility, self-complacent vanity, snobbery, tendency to brood which results in a wrong decision executed with great savagery, may be easily deceived, can be stupid, obstinate, tyrannical, may be quick to take offence, can harbour revenge without good cause
Douglas:	General aspect of fertility, kindness, sympathy, a lover of the country and of the home. Generally matriarchal interpretation with both positive and negative poles of that quality represented
G. Dawn:	Adaptability, steady force, steady rule, great attractive power, power of command, well liked, kind and generous when not opposed. Obstinate, revengeful, domineering, tyrannical. Water of Fire, Queen of the Salamanders or Salamandrines
Gray:	A blond, blue or hazel eyes. Powers of attraction, mentally and physically fruitful, lover of both country and home. Negatively: domineering, obstinate, revengeful, possibly treacherous without warning. (And, incidentally, without cause.) Possibly unfaithful if married
Grimaud:	Fatality, defence by means of brutality, passionate anger, stubbornness, efforts to avoid the blows of fate
Huson:	Astute woman, honesty, business transaction
Kahn:	Similar to the interpretations of Eden Gray and Douglas, with added aspects of a social woman, a gossip or flirt. Possibly a meddler or a dangerous woman

58

Kaplan:	As Eden Gray with the negative additions of jealousy, deceit, instability in emotional matters, fickleness
Mathers:	Woman living in the country, lady of the manor, love of money, avarice, usury. A good and virtuous woman, strict, economical, obstacles, resistance, opposition
Papus:	A dark woman, a friend, serious, good counsellor, often the mother of a family
Thierens:	A practical woman, wealthy or desiring wealth, more/less artistic, perhaps honest, passive and cool, not easily roused to passion. Money matters, i.e. banking, stocks and shares etc., not actually money
Waite:	A dark woman, countrywoman, friendly, chaste, loving, honourable, well-disposed towards adjacent card if it signifies a man, interested in the Querent if the adjacent card signifies a woman, love of money or certain success in business. Good, economical, obliging, serviceable, opposition, jealousy, deceit, infidelity. A good harvest in all senses. Goodwill towards the querent but unable to exercise it
Suggested:	The Queen of Earth/Feelings/Emotions. Those people or forces which work through established institutions to rule them. The Mother of the Ace of Cups and of the Fool. Can also imply Diana the Huntress and her attributes, Aradia. Water of Earth

King of Wands

Marseille:	A seated king holding, in his right hand, a carved staff or club
Waite:	A king on a salamander and lion throne in the desert. His robe is decorated with salamanders. He holds a wand in his right hand. There is a salamander beside him
Aquarian:	A king in a winged helmet. A flowering rod
Crowley:	Prince of Wands. He rides in a fiery chariot drawn by a lion. On his breast is the seven-pointed star inscribed within a circle. Inscribed within the star is the crescent and three-ring device. In his right hand he carries a Phoenix Wand
New:	Serpent king. A shield crowned with a fez. A black lion rampant and a snake. A smaller shield with a flaming torch and arrow. Below is the sign of Leo

59

Interpretation

Case: Dark man, friendly, ardent, honesty, possible inheritance

Crowley: Prince of the Chariot of Fire, Rules 20 degrees Cancer to 20 degrees Leo. The airy part of fire, swiftness and strength, impulsive, sometimes easily led, sometimes indecisive, particularly over trifles. Sometimes violent, states a proposition for the sake of stating it, slow to make up his mind, always sees both sides of a question, essentially just but feels that justice is not necessarily to be obtained in the intellectual world, intensely noble and generous, romantic, may be practical joker, proud, holds meanness and pettiness in scorn, fanatical courage, strong endurance, enormous capacity for work. Great cruelty, sadism, callousness, indifference, laziness, intolerance, prejudice, a boaster, a coward

Douglas: A man possessing the following characteristics: nobility, courage, strength, fortitude, virility, passion, loyalty, generosity, a love of the traditional ways and family life, swift thinker, ability to mediate well, good at moral support. Negatively his characteristics are: an autocrat, an ascetic, an unfeeling person, a prejudiced person, one who is ruthless, virtuous in an individual fashion, ethical in an intolerant manner

G. Dawn: Swift, strong, hasty, violent, just, generous, noble and scorning meanness. Ill-dignified he is cruel, intolerant, prejudiced, and ill-natured. Air of Fire, Prince and Emperor of Salamanders.

Gray: Blonde man, blue or hazel eyes. His qualities include rashness, handsomeness, agility of mind or body, loyalty, nobility, of good family, perhaps hastiness, honesty, friendliness. Can also indicate passion, unforeseen legacies, advantageous marriage. Negatively he shows a lack of tolerance, prejudice, ill-temper, severity, ruthlessness, and high principles. (High principles negative?)

Grimaud: Spiritual force brings mediation in discussions, moral support. Discussion able to come to agreement on their own

Huson: Clever man, honesty, good advice

Kahn: A fair man with firm desires, possibly a manager, possibly pursuing some worthwhile objective. A shrewd person

Kaplan: Similar to the interpretation of Eden Gray

Mathers:	Man living in the country, country gentleman, knowledge, education. A naturally good but severe man, counsel, advice, deliberation
Papus:	A dark man, a friend, generally represents a married man, the father of a family
Thierens:	Governor, director of business, austerity, security, initiative and honesty, in weak cases.there may be doubt as to his absolute integrity, notary, clergyman, High Priest, Grand Master
Waite:	Dark man, friendly, countryman, generally married, honest and conscientious, honesty, an unexpected heritage. Good but severe, austere yet tolerant. Generally favourable, may signify a good marriage. Advice that should be followed
Suggested:	Associations with the King of the May (the Green Man). The King of Earth, Feeling, Emotion. Father of the Ace of Cups and of the Fool. Those persons or forces which work to establish or to destroy institutions having to do with the suit. In this sense that card may relate to the 'King of the Mountain' or 'King of the Grove', the Sun King, sacrificed every year by his successor. Judgement. Air of Earth

Cups

Traditionally the suit associated with love; but, as indicated earlier, Wands might seem a more likely suit for the emotions, including love. Other traditional associations with cups, i.e., the Grail, chalices, and the Cauldron of Dagda (which fed all who came to it), that of Brân (which brought the dead back to life), that of Ogyrvran the Giant (from which the Muses ascended) or that of Ceridwen (the Cauldron of Inspiration) would seem to suggest an attribution of Intuition to the suit of Cups. The other association, Water, which is common, has been retained. Therefore: Cups . . . Water, Intuition

Case:	Pleasure, merriment. Inimical to Wands, friendly to Swords. Fair people
Crowley:	The powers of water
Douglas:	Creation, love, feeling and all emotional matters
Gray:	Water: knowledge and preservation relating to love, pleasure and enjoyment. Subconscious or instinctual behaviour. If an individual, someone who is cool or self-possessed. People with light brown hair, hazel eyes. If a direction is indicated, west. Governed by the Apocalypse figure, Aquarius. (In most decks this figure occurs as a Cherub in card XXI, The World.) The suit of the priest
Huson:	Traditional
Kaplan:	Traditional
Mathers:	Rather fair people. Lovemaking
Papus:	Lion, summer, full moon, noon, youth, love and happiness. Court cards represent fair people
Waite:	The court cards generally indicate fair people

Ace of Cups

Marseille: An ornately carved cup, surmounted by a castle with seven towers

Waite: A hand from the heavens, holding a golden chalice which is also a fountain. From the fountain five streams of water and 'Yods' fall into a lotus pool. On the cup is inscribed the letter 'M' reversed. A white dove flies downward into the cup bearing a white circle with a cross (perhaps the Host) in its beak

Aquarian: A chalice from which the sun rises. It stands on a lotus pool

Crowley: A chalice of light which stands in another chalice of lotuses. On the upper chalice is a stylized key design

New: The One of Pears

Interpretation

Case: Fertility, productiveness, beauty, pleasure

Crowley: The root of the powers of water. Admirable or hidden intelligence. God. Union with God. Water in its most secret and original form. The feminine counterpart of the Ace of Wands, derived from the Yoni and the Moon

Douglas: Traditional and as Crowley

Gray: The coming of transcendent love, joy, contentment. The mind filled with the spirit or with love. Negatively, the opposites of these

Grimaud: Great psychic protection, knowledge which will be realized. Plans, latent thoughts. Benefits to be scorned

Huson: As traditional; but in very general terms: Passion, inspiration, pleasure etc.

Kahn: A house, creative things generally. Forced joy

Kaplan: Abundance, perfection or joy. Change, alteration or sterility. Unrequited love

Mathers: Feasting, banquet, good cheer. Change, novelty, metamorphosis, inconstancy

Papus: Commencement of a love affair

Thierens:	Sanction, permission, inspiration, idealism, enthusiasm, blessing. May denote a leader, teacher, guide or any influence of this nature. Legislation, direction, instruction, hospitality, sympathetic reception, driving, hunting, travelling, planning for the future, invitation, convocation, appeal, mutation and transmutation. Translation and interpretation
Waite:	House of the true joy, content, abode, nourishment, abundance, fertility, holy table, felicity thereof, house of the false heart, mutation, instability, revolution. Inflexible will, unalterable law, unexpected change of position
Suggested:	A card of potential. Water or intuition hidden, perhaps under the Earth of the preceding suit

Two of Cups

Design

Marseille:	Two carven chalices, two dolphins
Waite:	Two lovers holding cups. Above them hovers the winged head of a lion with caduceus
Aquarian:	Two lovers with cups
Crowley:	Two cups resting upon a sea. From a fountain, composed of two fish and two lotuses the cups are filled and overflow. In the sky are visible the symbols to show Venus in Cancer
New:	Two of Pears. With lemniscate

Interpretation

Case:	Reciprocity, reflection
Crowley:	Venus in Cancer. Love, love under will. The harmony of the male and the female interpreted in the largest sense. Perfect and placid harmony, radiating an intensity of joy and ecstasy
Douglas:	As Waite and Crowley; but with the addition of negative aspects to all the possibilities of the attributions: Love, affinity, understanding, sympathy
G. Dawn:	Marriage, love, pleasure. Warm friendship
Gray:	As Douglas. Similar to traditional
Grimaud:	Possession in the realm of occult power. Separation,

64

	disagreement, parting, divorce, shared fortune. Temporary separation
Huson:	Traditional
Kahn:	Traditional with the additional meaning of something peculiar concerning a meeting, perhaps conditional upon something else
Kaplan:	Traditional with negative implications
Mathers:	Love, attachment, friendship, sincerity, affection. Crossed desires, obstacles, opposition, hindrance
Papus:	Unimportant obstacles raised to the commencement of a love affair
Thierens:	Lovemaking, passion, friendship, attraction, concord, good action, hospitable meeting or reception, interrelation of sexes, desire. Lust, cupidity, 'cupboard love'
Waite:	Love, passion, friendship, affinity, union, concord, sympathy, interrelation of sexes, favourable in pleasure, business and love, wealth and honour, passion
Suggested:	The most creative form of water/intuition. Resurrection. Springtime. Artistic creation, perhaps after a sterile spell

Three of Cups

Design

Marseille:	Three carven chalices
Waite:	Three women in an abundant field holding aloft cups
Aquarian:	Three women holding cups before a giant lotus. One is crowned with roses, one with circles and one is uncrowned
Crowley:	Three cups in designs reminiscent of ripe pomegranates or grapes. There are also eight Lotus flowers. Mercury in Cancer
New:	Three of Pears. Joined by a triangle

Interpretation

Case:	Pleasure, liberality, fulfilment, happy issue
Crowley:	Abundance. Mercury in Cancer. Fulfilment of the Will of Love in abounding joy. The spiritual basis of fertility
Douglas:	The traditional meaning of abundance generally; but

Morgan Tarot

Douglas additionally interprets this to include maternity, comfort, healing. Negative aspects include unbridled passion, self-indulgence, sex without love, etc

G. Dawn: Plenty, hospitality, eating, drinking, pleasure, dancing, new clothes, merriment

Gray: Traditional with the added negative of pleasure surfeited, turning to pain

Grimaud: Spiritual riches brought about by a balance between the physical and the mental. Plenty . . . irregular and intermittent. Fruitful contribution by the union of two beings

Huson: Fulfilment

Kahn: Good beginning of a new venture, eve of journey. Extravagance, business close by

Kaplan: As Eden Gray

Mathers: Success, triumph, victory, favourable issue. Expedition of business, quickness, celerity, vigilance

Papus: Realization of the commencement of love. The love is mutual

Thierens: Above meanings plus good health, recuperation, healing

Waite: Conclusion of a matter in plenty, happy issue, etc. Excess of physical enjoyment and sensuality. Unexpected advancement for a military man. Consolation, cure, or the end of the business

Suggested: The child of intuition. That which is created (as opposed to the act of creation, Two of Cups) or that which is felt strongly without rational support

Four of Cups

Design

Marseille: Four carven chalices

Waite: A dreamer sitting before a tree. On the ground near him are three cups. From heaven a hand offers a fourth cup

Aquarian: As Waite

Crowley: Four cups filled by a lotus fountain. The Moon in Cancer

New: Four of Pears. The symbol of a square

67

Case:	Contemplation. Dissatisfaction with material success
Crowley:	Pleasure, the Moon in Cancer. Retitled, 'Luxury'
Douglas:	Satiety, either of emotions or happiness generally, becoming dissatisfaction with achievement or with the things of this world. Possibly excesses
G. Dawn:	Blended pleasure. Receiving pleasures or kindnesses from others. Waking from a period of contentment or contemplation, new relationships now possible, new goals, new ambition
Gray:	Traditional
Grimaud:	Plenty as a result of agreement and equilibrium. Difficult agreement
Huson:	Traditional
Kahn:	Persons or environments known to Querent but not as yet utilized. Far away. Near by
Kaplan:	Traditional
Mathers:	Ennui, displeasure, discontent, dissatisfaction. New acquaintance, conjecture, sign, presentiment
Papus:	Serious obstacles to love arising from other than the lovers
Thierens:	Discontent with present conditions, estrangement, unrest, aversion, troubles, disgust, discord, failing to understand others or to make oneself understood, new discoveries, researches in unknown countries or territories, meeting with strangers, instability, changes generally for the worse but with some distant aim, at war with current opinion, better to be silent than to talk
Waite:	Weariness, disgust, aversions, imaginary vexations, blended pleasure. Novelty, presage, new instruction, new relations, contrarieties. Presentiment
Suggested:	Intuition retarded by sensation, by emotions or by intellect. Intuition betrayed

Five of Cups

Design

Marseille:	Five carven cups

68

Waite:	A man in black standing disconsolate beside a river. On the ground are three cups before him, overturned, and two behind him upright
Aquarian:	Roughly the same as Waite
Crowley:	Five cups and lotuses which together form an inverted pentagram design. Above is the sign of Mars (male) and below is that of Scorpio
New:	Five of Pears. A pentagram

Interpretation

Case:	Loss in pleasure, partial loss, vain regret
Crowley:	Loss in pleasure. Mars in Scorpio. Retitled Disappointment. Crowley associates the card with the geomantic sign, Rubeus, which he describes as being of such evil omen that some schools of geomancy destroy a map on which appears this sign and wait for several hours until Rubeus appears in the ascendant. One of the societies practising this was apparently the Golden Dawn, as Regardie includes the note that if Rubeus appears in the First House the figure is to be destroyed as 'not fit for judgement'
Douglas:	Traditional
G. Dawn:	Disappointment in love, marriage broken off, unkindness from friends (whether deserved or not is shown by surrounding cards), loss of friendship
Gray:	Parallels Waite
Grimaud:	Lack of harmony. Indefinite plan which comes to nothing, temporary material prosperity, a plan which misfires
Huson:	Having to do with inheritance or gift
Kahn:	A soulmate, broken engagement, short but lingering love affair, letting go of a person or life style or job, meeting up with your ex. New beginning for old affair, vain regret for that same affair, unusual frustration or separation
Kaplan:	Traditional
Mathers:	Union, junction, marriage, inheritance. Arrival, return, news, surprise, false projects
Papus:	Opposition to the obstacles to love. Victory over the obstacles after a struggle
Thierens:	Family matters, care to be taken of them, sorrow or

69

pleasure, emotion, material difficulties, some advantage or loss at the same time, certain news, apt to react too quickly to surrounding influences

Waite: A card of loss but with something remaining, inheritances which fail to measure up to expectations, marriage accompanied by bitterness or frustration. News, alliances, affinity, consanguinity, ancestry, return, false projects. Generally favourable, happy marriage, patrimony, legacies, gifts, success in enterprise. Return of a relative who has been away for a long time

Suggested: The element of uncertainty in intuition. Do you see what you think you see? Limitation but with an element of hope, particularly if followed by the Seven of Cups

Six of Cups

Design

Marseille: Six carven cups

Waite: Six cups filled with white, five-pointed flowers. A small boy offers a girl one of them

Aquarian: Six cups filled with assorted flowers

Crowley: Six cups. Incorporated into each is the lotus. The Sun in Scorpio

New: Six of Pears. At the centre a six-pointed star

Interpretation

Case: Beginning of steady gain, new relations, new environment

Crowley: Pleasure, the Sun in Scorpio. Well being, harmony of natural forces without effort or strain. Fulfilment of sexual will

Douglas: Traditional expressed partially as 'The past, working through the present, will create the future'

Gray: Basically traditional with the possibility of clinging too much to the past

Grimaud: Equilibrium, assured and durable success

Huson: Traditional

Kahn: Elements of the traditional: happy couple, satisfying partnership, old friends and acquaintances, return home. But also other meanings: new projects, sexual fulfilment

Kaplan: Traditional

Mathers: The past, passed by, faded, vanished, disappeared. The future, that which is to come, shortly, soon

Papus: The obstacles to love triumph. Love destroyed, in the midst of happiness. Widowhood

Thierens: Happiness, feeling of interior riches, good health, lots of good things all over the place, impressions of the past and future

Waite: Memories, nostalgia. The future, new knowledge, new environment, etc. Pleasant memories, inheritance to fall in quickly

Suggested: The measure of intuition. Tests or testing. The double-edged nature of intuition

Design

Seven of Cups

Marseille: Seven carven cups

Waite: Seven cups seen in the heavens by a silhouetted figure. From one cup arises the head of an angel. From another arises a serpent. From another, a castle. In a fourth, jewels. In the fifth, a monster. In the sixth is a shrouded figure with a halo. And in the seventh is a wreath. The seventh cup is doubly interesting in that the skull design on its side comments upon the contents. It is the only one of the cups to do so

Aquarian: Seven cups containing: A hand brandishing a flower in bud, a deep-sea diver's helmet, a head, a flower, fruit with a butterfly, a cobra, and a rainbow

Crowley: Seven lily cups from which drips a poisonous green liquid. Venus in Scorpio

New: The Seven of Pears. A group of four and a group of three. A triangle surmounting a square

Interpretation

Case: Illusionary success, ideas, designs, resolutions

Crowley: Illusionary success. Venus in Scorpio. Retitled, 'Debauch'. External splendour and internal corruption

71

Douglas:	Exceptional promise or mystical experience. Self-delusion in the card's negative aspect, being false mystical experience
G. Dawn:	Lying, deceit, promises unfulfilled, illusion, error, slight and transient success
Gray:	Traditional
Grimaud:	Difficulty in the realization of a happiness of mind and in raising oneself above matter, pleasure, transient joys, unexpected transience, disappointment
Huson:	Traditional
Kahn:	Traditional
Kaplan:	Traditional
Mathers:	Idea, sentiment, reflection, project. Plan, design, resolution, decision
Papus:	Success assured to the lovers
Thierens:	Thoughts, ideas, imagination, fantasy, reflections, short travels, impressions, unstable conditions, promise and surprise but more promise than fulfilment, illusion
Waite:	Imagination and vision, some attainment but nothing permanent or substantial suggested. Desire, will, determination or project. Fair child, idea, design, resolve, movement. Success, if accompanied by the Three of Cups
Suggested:	Intuition at its most developed level. Possible enlightenment. A very good, if solemn, card

Eight of Cups

Design

Marseille:	Eight carven chalices
Waite:	A desolate night scene. A man turns his back on eight cups and walks away under a waning crescent moon
Aquarian:	As Waite
Crowley:	Eight Lotus cups. Saturn in Pisces
New:	Eight of Pears

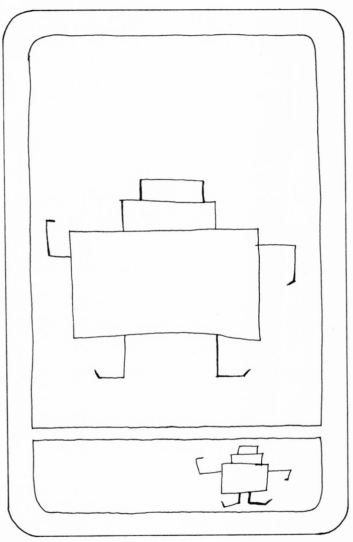

Morgan Tarot

Case:	Abandoned success, instability, leaving material success for something higher
Crowley:	Abandoned success, Saturn in Pisces. Retitled, 'Indolence'. The soul poisoned
Douglas:	Traditional
G. Dawn:	Success abandoned, decline of interest in a thing, ennui
Gray:	As Waite substantially
Grimaud:	Abandon of the psychic, return to matter, mental imbalance. Agreement and success. Disappointment without success, reversal of fortune
Huson:	Gentle attachment, casual association
Kahn:	A blonde woman, nourishment, room and board, partial love, preparation. Pleasures for the moment, parties, sexual enjoyment, dancing, theatre, fun
Kaplan:	Compares with Waite
Mathers:	A fair girl, friendship, attachment, tenderness. Gaiety, feasting, joy, pleasure
Papus:	Partial failure of love, love only partially succeeds
Thierens:	Leaving the house or home, changes in the family, shyness, little chance to see ambitions realized, disorder and waywardness, despondency, dissatisfaction, fair-haired girl
Waite:	Deserting the cups of felicity or enterprise, joy, mildness, timidity, honour, modesty, the decline of a matter or the revealing of a previously thought to be important matter as unimportant or trivial. Great joy, happiness, feasting. Marriage with a fair woman. Perfect satisfaction
Suggested:	The fruits of intuition. A card of peace or terror

Design
Nine of Cups

Marseille:	Nine carven chalices
Waite:	A merchant sitting in satisfaction before a row of cups
Aquarian:	As Waite
Crowley:	Nine Lotus cups. Jupiter in Pisces

New: Nine of Pears. Eight pears surrounding a ninth

Interpretation

Case: Material success, physical well being

Crowley: Material happiness, Jupiter in Pisces. Retitled, 'Happiness'. The most complete and most beneficial aspect of the force of water

Douglas: Stability, security or well being. Contrasting meaning of the above without justification and attendant troubles

G. Dawn: Complete success, pleasure and happiness, wishes fulfilled

Gray: Similar to the traditional and Golden Dawn interpretations; with the added meaning of wish fulfilled/wish unfulfilled

Grimaud: Success in the realm of intellect, success in everything, especially matters of the heart

Huson: Traditional

Kahn: As Waite

Kaplan: Traditional, emphasizing the material aspect, either for good or ill

Mathers: Victory, advantage, success, triumph, difficulties surmounted. Faults, errors, mistakes, imperfections

Papus: Motherhood. (He does not say if this means the Love succeeded or if it failed)

Thierens: Happiness, contentment. etc

Waite: Concord, contentment, etc. Truth, loyalty, liberty, mistakes, imperfections. Of good augury for military men, good augury for business

Suggested: The senility of intuition. Blind faith. This card may describe some miracles. It also describes the beneficiaries of blind faith, fat churches

Ten of Cups

Design

Marseille: Nine carven chalices vertical surmounted by one larger chalice horizontal. The last has a quatrefoil flower design within it, possibly a reference to the Host

Waite: A man and woman beholding a rainbow of cups in the heavens. Near them two children are dancing

Aquarian:	A pair of lovers. She wears a rose in her hair. Above are nine small cups and a tenth larger one into which a rainbow is pouring
Crowley:	Ten Cups, their design implying Aries. The planetary sign for Mars. The sign for Pisces should also be on this card, as Crowley's attribution is Mars in Pisces; but either it was not included in the original design or it was omitted for some reason in this printing of the Thoth Tarot
New:	Ten of Pears. Arranged in two groups of five

Interpretation

Case:	Lasting success, happiness to come
Crowley:	Perfected success, Mars in Pisces. Retitled, 'Satiety'. The work proper to water is complete: and disturbance is due
Douglas:	Traditional with the additional meanings implied by the negative aspects of peace and security
G. Dawn:	Perpetual success. Matters definitely arranged and settled in accordance with ones wishes, complete good fortune
Gray:	Contentment, friendship, trust and their opposites
Grimaud:	Separation of matter and mind, burning need for evolution, spiritual progress. Transition, passage from life to death, halt
Huson:	Home life or homeland, adjacent cards indicate final outcome
Kahn:	The city, envious people, material well being. A strange turn of fortune, miraculous event, meeting of a friend from the distant past, the unusual, the unexpected, the remarkable and unbelievable
Kaplan:	Traditional with severe negative possibilities
Mathers:	The town wherein one resides, honour, consideration. esteem, virtue, glory, reputation. Combat, strife, opposition, dispute
Papus:	Uncertainty in the management of the love affair
Thierens:	Well-earned security, the city, birthplace, physical constitution, organic life in the body and in the community, irritability and agitation, a weak nervous system must avoid the full sway of emotions

Contentment, repose of the entire heart, perfection of human love and friendship. If with several picture cards a person who is taking charge of the Querent's interests, the town, village or country inhabited by the Querent. Repose of the false heart, indignation, violence. For a male Querent a good marriage and one beyond his expectations, sorrow, a serious quarrel

Suggested: Intuition destroyed. Dead. Midwinter with all its potential

Design

Page of Cups

Marseille: A young man carrying an ornate chalice in his right hand, from his left hand droops his hat

Waite: A page standing beside the sea. He holds a cup from which a fish is jumping

Aquarian: As Waite except that the page is standing beside tulips, not beside the sea

Crowley: Princess of Cups. She holds a giant cup in the form of a shell in which seems to be a tortoise. Behind her is a swan. Next to her, a fish. Her gown is decorated with diamond figures

New: Page of Pears. A wreath of white roses on a circle. Above is an inverted cup from which comes light. In the centre are a pear, a mandolin, a cup of blood, and an inverted stalk of a green plant. Below is the sign of the waxing and waning moon (or perhaps Pisces)

Interpretation

Case: Fair, studious youth, reflection, news

Crowley: The Princess of the Waters, the Lotus of the Palace of the Floods. Rules one of the four quadrants of the heavens about Kether. Earth of Water. Represents the faculty of crystallization, the power of water to give substance to idea, to support life and to form the basis of a chemical combination. She is infinitely gracious, all sweetness, all voluptuousness, gentleness, kindness, tenderness are in her character. She lives in the world of romance, in the perpetual dream of rapture. A dependent person but unsurpassed as a helpmeet

Douglas: As Waite, generally

77

G. Dawn:	Princess of the Waters and Lotus of the Palace of the Floods. Sweetness, poetry, gentleness, kindness, imagination, dreamy, at times indolent, can be roused to courage, ill-dignified she is selfish and luxurious. Princess and Empress of Nymphs and Undines. Throne of the Ace of Cups
Gray:	Traditional
Grimaud:	Spiritual and moral riches obtained as a reward and giving full satisfaction, work rewarded and giving wealth. Happiness in wealth and affections is elusive
Huson:	A sensitive youngster
Kahn:	A bachelor dreaming of his pleasure
Kaplan:	Traditional
Mathers:	A fair youth, confidence, probity, discretion, integrity. A flatterer, deception, artifice
Papus:	A fair child, a messenger, birth
Thierens:	Friendly message, good news, proposal of marriage or love affair, solicitation, change of relations and sympathies, possibility that someone will try to seduce the Querent. Praise and persuasion. A man very much open to sex influences
Waite:	A fair young man, one impelled to render service and with whom the Querent will be connected, a studious youth, news, messages, application, reflection, meditation, the same conditions directed towards business. Taste, inclination, attachment, seduction, deception, artifice. Good augury, a young man who is unfortunate in love. Obstacles of all kinds
Suggested:	The coming of or messages of intuition. Fire of Water

Design

Knight of Cups

Marseille:	A mounted knight, carrying a carved chalice in his right hand
Waite:	A knight, wearing a winged helmet, rides over a desert toward a river and the mountains. He carries a cup. His clothing is decorated with red fish

Aquarian:	A knight with a winged helmet seen near flowers in bud, perhaps tulips
Crowley:	A winged knight riding a white horse from the sea. His upraised right hand holds a cup, above which is a crab. His wings are in stylized extension of the tail of a peacock in the lower right
New:	Knight of Pears. A pear, on the side of which is a figure eight design, suggesting eight-ball as in pool. Below it is a white rose. Another white rose decorates a helmet from under which a black cat stares. The helmet is horned (or perhaps decorated with a crescent moon). In the sky is a crescent moon. Water pours from the sky

Interpretation

Case:	Fair man, Venusian, indolent, arrival, approach
Crowley:	The Lord of the Waves and the Waters. The King of the Hosts of the Sea. Rules from 20 degrees Aquarius to 20 degrees Pisces. The fiery part of water, its power of solution, passive, graceful, dilettante, Venusian, amiable, quick to respond but not enduring, sensitive but with little material depth. Ill-dignified he is sensual, idle and untruthful. Essence of his nature is innocence and purity
Douglas:	As Mathers and Waite
G. Dawn:	Same as Crowley except: Fire of Water. King of Undines and of Nymphs
Gray:	As Mathers and Waite
Grimaud:	Frail destiny, passing destiny which must be seized. Shattered, broken destiny
Huson:	Lover, rival, seducer, a proposition or a message
Kahn:	A lover, an offering. An offer of love or work unappreciated
Kaplan:	Traditional
Mathers:	Arrival, approach, advance. Duplicity, abuse of confidence, fraud, cunning
Papus:	A young fair man, a friend, the young man loved, a lover
Thierens:	A stranger, sailor, man coming from far away. Intoxicants, drugs, merchants of the same, imagination, vision, dreams, occultism, strong sexual tendencies, falsehood, venomous reports, slander, blackmail, possibly a change of life caused

79

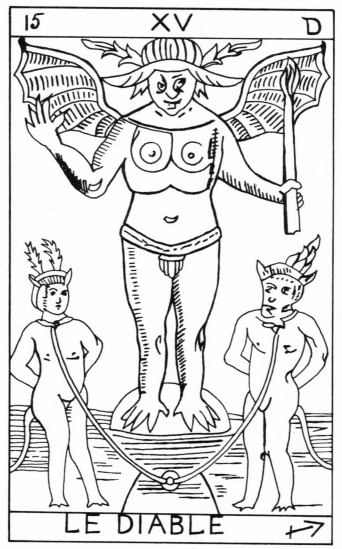

The Devil, *Nineteenth Century French Tarot*

by the above, an unknown or anonymous messenger to the soul

Waite: A dreamer haunted in his vision, arrival, approach, a messenger, a proposition, incitement. Trickery, artifice, subtlety, swindling, duplicity, fraud. A visit from a friend bringing unexpected money to the Querent. Irregularity

Suggested: The defender of intuition. Perhaps one who, though not possessed of intuitive faculties yet promulgates their use. Possibly a teacher. Earth of Water

Queen of Cups

Design

Marseille: A seated queen, holding in her left hand a naked sword. In her right hand she holds an ornate, covered cup. So elaborate is this chalice that she must rest it upon her knee

Waite: A queen sitting on a throne by the sea. She holds an ornate cup decorated with angels. Her throne is decorated with cherub-mermen and incorporates a scallop motif in the heading

Aquarian: A queen with a cup. At the base of the cup is a flower

Crowley: A shadowy queen beside a lotus pool. Near her is a crane and a fish. The cosmic lemniscate motif is repeated throughout the card in variant forms

New: Queen of Pears. At the top a golden crown. At the botom is the sign of Cancer. In the central figure are white roses, a pear, a crab, and a viking ship

Interpretation

Case: Fair woman, imaginative, poetic, gift of vision

Crowley: The Queen of the Thrones of the Waters. 20 degrees Gemini to 20 degrees Cancer. The watery part of water, its power of reception and reflection. Dreaminess, illusion, tranquility, able to receive and transmit everything without herself being affected. Ill-dignified, everything that passes through her is distorted

Douglas: As Waite

G. Dawn: Kind, imaginative, poetic, not willing to take much trouble for others, coquettish, good natured underneath a dreamy

81

appearance, imagination stronger than feeling, affected by other influences. Water of Water, Queen of Nymphs and Undines

Gray: Traditional

Grimaud: Her wisdom prevails, prudence, good advice. Good advice which will be disregarded

Huson: Traditional

Kahn: Traditional with the addition of the meanings: best friend of the querent and barmaid

Kaplan: Resembles Waite

Mathers: A fair woman, success, happiness, advantage, pleasure. A woman in good position but intermeddling, not to be trusted. Success with attendant trouble

Papus: A fair woman, a friend, the woman loved, the mistress

Thierens: Good intelligent, active and practical woman whom the Querent will do well to obey and who deserves his full esteem, careful and attentive, loving intelligence, success, pleasure, happiness, virtue, natural growth, promotion in the world, fame

Waite: Good fair woman, honest and devoted, will do service to Querent, loving intelligence, gift of vision, success, happiness, pleasure, wisdom, virtue, perfect spouse and good mother. Good woman, distinguished woman but not to be trusted, perverse woman, vice, dishonour, depravity. Sometimes a woman of equivocal character, a rich marriage for a man, a distinguished one for a woman

Suggested: Queen of Cups and Mother of the Fool and Ace of Swords. Those things or people who work to rule or to maintain established institutions. This card can be said to denote the borderline between intuition and unacknowledged desire. If desire plays the greater part then genuine intuition is likely to be stultified. Water of Water—the Nereid

King of Cups

Design

Marseille: A seated king, holding in his right hand a large and ornate cup

Waite: A king seated on a throne which stands on a stone block in the middle of the sea. A fish emblem is pendant from a chain round his neck, repeated as a jumping fish in the background. In his right hand he holds a cup, in his left a lotus sceptre

Aquarian: A king holding a cup firmly in his right hand

Crowley: A naked man in a shell throne drawn over the sea by what could be either a swallow or pigeon. In his right hand he holds a lotus sceptre, inverted

New: King of Pears. A vase with a crown device, cruciform, at the top. On the side of the vase are the following: two white roses, a pear, a stylized scarabaeus beetle with a torch on his back bearing in one pair of legs a red flower and in the other a double-headed axe. At the bottom is the sign for Scorpio

Interpretation

Case: Fair man, calm exterior, subtle, violent, artistic

Crowley: The Prince of the Chariot of the Waters. Rules 20 degrees Libra to 20 degrees Scorpio. The airy part of water. Subtlety, secret violence and craft, intensely secret, an artist, external influences only serve (transmuted) to further his secret designs, without conscience, perfectly ruthless, cares for power, wisdom and his own aims

Douglas: An expansion of the ideas of Waite emphasizing skill, agility and manipulation

G. Dawn: Subtle, violent, crafty and artistic, fierce nature with calm exterior, powerful for good or evil but attracted by evil if allied with apparent power or wisdom. Ill-dignified he is intensely evil and merciless. Air of water, Prince and Emperor of Nymphs and Undines

Gray: Traditional; but concentrating more on Waite than on Mathers

Grimaud: Knowledge and abundance, possessions safeguarded and protected, inalienable riches. Enforced downfall of something that seemed protected, a serious move

Huson: Sensitive or creative man, benefactor, husband, father

Kahn: A red-haired man, a man of good humour, a kind man, making a large offering, a big spender, a sensitive man, an artist. A man who will meet with disappointment, a tutor or teacher, a man in anger

83

Kaplan:	Essentially as Gray
Mathers:	A fair man, goodness, kindness, liberality, generosity. Man of good position, shifty in his dealings, distrust, doubt, suspicion
Papus:	A fair man, a friend, a barrister, judge, ecclesiastic, a bachelor
Thierens:	Honest man, philosophical or idealistic, doctor or professor, teacher, hunter, the Querent's business actions judged or brought to light, hope and promise for the future, some exaggeration or fantasy perhaps, possibly travelling on the sea
Waite:	Fair man, man of business, law or divinity, responsible and disposed to help the Querent, equity, art and science, those who profess science, law and art, creative intelligence. Dishonest, double-dealing man, roguery, exaction, injustice, vice, scandal, pillage, considerable loss. Beware of ill-will on the part of a man of position, hypocrisy pretending to help. Loss
Suggested:	King of Cups, Water, Intuition and Father of the Fool. Father of the Ace of Swords. Those things or people who work to destroy or to establish the institutions having to do with intuition, i.e., schools, churches, occult publishing houses etc. Judgement of this suit. Air of Water

Swords

The last of the suits of the Minor Arcana. It corresponds to air and to thought. In general the attributions to Swords are dark ones. Nearly all the writers cited in this book sense misfortune in the suit as a whole, either in their writings or in Tarot cards designed to their specifications. I think this is a mistake. Each of the suits, each of the Major Arcana, is a two-edged weapon; it can cut or cure. Intuition, generally reckoned to be a good thing, could become a curse if it enabled one to see and not be believed or if it enabled one to see too much. So intellect, the attribution of Swords, has the faculty of cutting both ways.

Case: Trouble, sadness, sickness, death. Unfriendly with pentacles, friendly with cups and wands

Crowley: The powers of air

Douglas: Movement, conflict, progress, the establishment of order

Gray: Generally aggression or strife. Eden Gray also gives for this suit, as for each of the others a detailed explanation of other facets of its meaning: The direction north, the Sylph (an air elemental), melancholy temperament, the Apocalyptic figure of the eagle. The suit for warriors

Huson: Things to do with stress or authority

Kaplan: Strength, strife and misfortune. Fire

Mathers: Very dark people, quarrelling and trouble

Papus: The bull, autumn, the last quarter, evening, maturity, hatred and misfortune. The court cards represent dark people, either wicked or enemies

Waite: (No meaning for the suit as a whole)

Ace of Swords

Marseille: A sword brandished. At its tip is a crown. Nine solar 'Yods' fall to its left, fifteen to its right

Waite: A heavenly hand holding forth a sword upright, the tip of which is crowned. The crown is garlanded with two branches, one of which has red berries. Solar 'Yods' are also in the card. The striking similarity between Waite's design and that of the Marseille Tarot are obvious

Aquarian: A sword, point downward, flanked by two white roses

Crowley: A sword, point upward, the sword crowned (possibly by the sun). The handle of the sword is the double lunar crescent, the two crescents being placed back to back and with full moons between. The handle also incorporates a snake wrapped round it. Near the handle, on the blade, is inscribed, 'Thelema', meaning 'Will' or 'Wish'

New: Ace of Blades

Interpretation

Case: Invoked force, conquest, activity

Crowley: Root of the powers of air. The primordial energy of air

Douglas: Traditional; but with the suggestion that destruction may be necessary to achieve something better

Gray: The traditional aspect of force; but Eden Gray sees that force expressed as justice which maintains the world order, as the equilibrium between mercy and severity

Grimaud: A man forced to use his own strength. Strong action with victory bringing advantage. Violence, murder, sudden death

Huson: Authority and stress

Kahn: Love, affairs of the heart. A love affair with the woman left in the worst way

Kaplan: Traditional

Mathers: Triumph, fecundity, fertility, prosperity. Embarrassment, foolish and hopeless love, obstacle, hindrance

Papus: Commencement of enmity

Thierens:	Initiative, force, masculine activity, seed, germ, commencement in a matter, decision, starting-point, emphasis, fructification, execution, affliction, pain, annihilation of doubt and uncertainty, courage, firmness, integrity, great passion or intense enmity, fury, vehemence
Waite:	Triumph, the excessive degree in everything, conquest, triumph of force, a card of great force in love as well as hatred, the crown may carry a much greater significance than is usual in fortune telling. Disaster. Conception, childbirth, augmentation, multiplicity. Great prosperity or great misery. Marriage broken off (for a woman) through her own imprudence
Suggested:	The prime intellect. If it implies force it is the force of thought rather than the literal force of weapons

Two of Swords

Design

Marseille:	Two curved swords, crossed
Waite:	A blindfolded figure seated beside the sea, its hands crossed and holding two upright swords. Above, a waxing moon
Aquarian:	A blindfolded woman. Two crossed swords
Crowley:	Two crossed swords, the intersection of which is a blue flower
New:	Two of Blades. A lemniscate

Interpretation

Case:	Balanced force, indecision, friendship
Crowley:	The Lord of Peace Restored. The Moon in Libra. Peace
Douglas:	Equilibrium, interplay of opposing forces of creation resulting in life. Strife and dissent uniting to produce truth and beauty. Otherwise traditional
G. Dawn:	Quarrel made up and arranged, peace restored yet with some tension remaining
Gray:	As Waite and Case
Grimaud:	Harmony. Victory without conflict or battle, passive success
Huson:	Temporary amnesty

87

Kahn:	Sanctuary, protection, skill in dealings, guarding one's own interests, care in conversations
Kaplan:	Stalemate, balance, harmony and firmness. But as the negative qualities of these Kaplan chooses duplicity, falsehood, lies, betrayal and dishonour
Mathers:	Friendship, valour, firmness, courage. False friends, treachery, lies
Papus:	Opposition to the commencement of enmity. The enmity does not last
Thierens:	Latent force, magnetism, principle of art, artistic appreciation, virtue, quality, magnetic attraction, affinity, intimacy, affection, sensuality, laziness, dullness, cruelty, unforgiving hatred, passive obstruction
Waite:	Conformity and equipoise, courage, friendship, concord in a state of arms, tenderness, affection, intimacy. Imposture, falsehood, duplicity, disloyalty. Gifts for a lady, influential protection for a man in search of help. Dealings with rogues
Suggested:	The faculty of analysis. The creative power of thought

Three of Swords

Design

Marseille:	Two curved swords, crossed. A third stands, upright, between them
Waite:	Three swords piercing the same heart
Aquarian:	As Waite
Crowley:	Two small swords, one larger sword, their points meeting at the centre of a full blown white flower. Saturn in Virgo
New:	Three of Blades. A triangle

Interpretation

Case:	Sorrow, disappointment, tears, delay, absence, separation
Crowley:	Saturn in Libra. Sorrow. Secrecy, perversion. By implication in his analysis this card is connected with Hecate
Douglas:	Necessary strife and conflict toward the end of the destruction of obsolescence. Wars and disorders generally
G. Dawn:	Unhappiness, sorrow, tears

Gray: Traditional meaning of general troubles of the affections but rather gloomier than Waite and more optimistic than Douglas

Grimaud: Struggle upheld by mental strength ensuring victory over the physical. Gain by force or in battle

Huson: Rupture, delay

Kahn: Sorrow, strife, removal, dispersion. Distraction, confusion, disorder, error, incompatability

Kaplan: Traditional

Mathers: A nun, separation, removal, rupture, quarrel. Error, confusion, misrule, disorder

Papus: Realization of the enmity. Hatred

Thierens: Oppression, worries, being burdened, baffled hopes, troubles, tendency to separateness, rupture and seclusion, pessimism, removal, absence, delay, small talk, bitter and evil thoughts, sickness, alienation, error of judgement, wrong opinion, hatred, aversion, in general . . . affliction. Evil schemes

Waite: Removal, absence, delay, division, rupture, dispersion, mental alienation, error, loss, distraction, disorder, confusion. For a woman the flight of her lover, a meeting with one whom the querent has compromised, a nun

Suggested: The product of thought, books or inventions which depend upon analysis rather than intuition. Reason

Four of Swords

Design

Marseille: Four curved swords, crossed

Waite: The effigy of a knight praying displayed upon a tomb. On the wall three swords hang, point downward. Below him, on the side of the tomb, is another sword

Aquarian: As Waite except that the knight is fully armoured

Crowley: Four swords, the points of which meet in the centre of a lotus. Taken in pairs the swords form a St. Andrew's Cross. Jupiter in Libra

New: Four of Blades. A square

The Devil, *Nineteenth Century French Tarot*

Case: Rest from strife, relief from anxiety, quietness, rest, rest after illness, not a card of death

Crowley: Rest from strife, Jupiter in Libra. Renamed, 'Truce'. A refuge from mental chaos, chosen in an arbitrary manner. It argues for convention (meaning imposed)

Douglas: Similar to Crowley. Cowardice, reluctance to face opposition, exile, banishment, enforced seclusion, imprisonment, failure of nerve, depression

G. Dawn: Convalescence, recovery from sickness, change for the better

Gray: Traditional

Grimaud: A tendency toward mysticism, growing understanding of the ideal, beginnings of a plan, flowering of realization

Huson: Solitude, retreat often caused by health or finance

Kahn: Meditation, intimacies of a dark nature, depressing circumstance, deep thought, recovery, solitude

Kaplan: Traditional

Mathers: Solitude, retreat, abandonment, hermit. Economy, precaution, regulation of expenditure

Papus: Opposition to the hatred. Success against the enemy

Thierens: Solitude, repose, retreat, gathering, collecting, meditation, economy, avarice, hermitage, grave, coffin, precaution

Waite: Vigilance, retreat, solitude, hermit's repose, exile, tomb, coffin. Wise administration, circumspection, economy, avarice, precaution, testament. A bad card. A certain success following wise administration

Suggested: The establishment of thought. Universities. The regulation of thought, by law or by custom

Five of Swords

Design

Marseille: Four curved swords, crossed. In the centre is an upright sword

Waite: A man holding two swords over his left shoulder, a third, point downward, in his right hand. On the ground near him are two other swords. Two figures walk away from him in dejection. An expression of malicious triumph is upon his face

Aquarian: The man bears the swords as in Waite; but the triumph and the other figures are missing. His expression is pensive rather than malicious

Crowley: Five swords of differing hilts, the points of which intersect near the centre of an inverted pentagram of rubies. At the top, the sign of Venus. That for Aquarius, which should also appear on the card, is lacking

New: Five of Blades. An inverted pentagram

Interpretation

Case: Defeat, loss, failure, slander, dishonour

Crowley: Defeat, Venus in Aquarius. Intellect defeated by sentiment (pacifism implied). Possibly treachery

Douglas: Traditional; but with the implication that the disaster must be overcome in order for future progress to take place. Be wary of treachery

G. Dawn: Defeat, loss, malice, slander, evil-speaking

Gray: Traditional

Grimaud: Fierce struggle to penetrate to higher planes, wish to destroy the body in favour of the mind. Defeat, struggle without result

Huson: Loss, affliction, bereavement, defeat

Kahn: Escape from danger, entrapment, partial defeat

Kaplan: Traditional

Mathers: Mourning, sadness, affliction. Losses, trouble

Papus: Opposition to the opposition to enmity. The enemy triumphs at the moment one fancies that the victory is secured

Thierens: Affliction, crisis, bitterness, impotence. Loss in most cases

Waite: Degradation and destruction, revocation, infamy, dishonour, loss. Burial and funerals. An attack on the fortune of the querent. Sorrow and mourning

Suggested: The malice of thought. Mischievous intellect. Perhaps great danger from liars

Six of Swords

Marseille: Six curved swords, crossed

Waite: Two hooded figures seated in a boat which also contains six swords, point downward. The boat is poled by a man

Aquarian: As Waite, basically, except that the figures are lacking. Also, the boatman's pole is tipped with wings

Crowley: Six swords, the points of which intersect at the centre of a circle, within a cross, within a greater circle. Mercury in Aquarius

New: Six of Blades. A hexagram

Interpretation

Case: Success after anxiety, passage from difficulties, a journey by water

Crowley: Earned success, Mercury in Aquarius. Retitled, science. Pure balance of mental and moral faculties

Douglas: Polarity of this card between a solution to immediate problems or moving away from immediate danger, the disappearance of a major hindrance to travel, possibly to peaceful surroundings, to new obstacles after the disappearance of old ones. Travel indicated

G. Dawn: Labour, work, journey (probably by water)

Gray: A journey, in flesh or spirit. The hindrance of a journey

Grimaud: The liberation of matter (a euphemism for murder?). Force or security

Huson: Struggle, turmoil, travel

Kahn: A long journey by sea. A return journey

Kaplan: Journey, with implication of progress. Stalemate, unwished suggestion, no solution at present

Mathers: Envoy, messenger, voyage, travel. Declaration, love proposed, revelation, surprise

Papus: Equilibrium of the opposition. The enemy is rendered powerless at last

Thierens: Arterial system, health, travel (especially water), sensuality and expressions of it, badly aspected it is a serious illness and the probability of the passing-away of the patient

Waite: Journey by water, route, way, envoy, expedient. Declaration, confession, publicity, proposal of love. The voyage will be pleasant, unfavourable issue of a lawsuit

Suggested: The measure of intellect, tests, trials, perhaps lawsuits, perhaps simply evaluation

Design

Seven of Swords

Marseille: Six curved swords, crossed. A seventh sword upright

Waite: A man stealing away from a crusader's camp with five swords. Two others remain, point downward, in the ground behind him

Aquarian: A man walking away with five swords. Two others remain

Crowley: A sword, hilt downward. The hilt combines the motifs of the lotus and the solar disc. Six other swords, point downward. Their hilts are formed from the signs for: the Moon, Venus, Mars, Jupiter, Mercury, and Saturn. The Moon in Aquarius

New: Seven of Blades. Four above, three below. A square superior to an equilateral triangle

Interpretation

Case: Unstable effort, uncertainty, partial success

Crowley: Unstable effort. Moon in Aquarius. Retitled, 'Futility'. The policy of appeasement. (With the note that the success of the policy is in doubt as long as there exist 'violent, uncompromising forces which take it as a natural prey')

Douglas: Powerful opposition to the Querent or great danger. Courage, perseverance, prudence and possibly cunning are required. Cowardice, hesitancy, surrender immediately before victory would have been won

G. Dawn: Untrustworthy character, vacillation, journey by land shown by nearby cards

Gray: Possible failure of a plan, foolish attempt at some kind of theft, arguments, spying, incomplete success, efforts that

94

are unstable. Unforeseen good, good advice or instruction, wishes on the verge of fulfilment

Grimaud: A wish to destroy by material means (armaments) and by mental ones (acts of magic). Ephemeral realizations, disappointment in family or other close relationship

Huson: Hope

Kahn: Hope, death, voided effort. Intimacy, love, close relationship, advice

Kaplan: New schemes, desires on the verge of fulfilment, attempts or endeavours. Hope or confidence. Negative meanings are those of quarrelling or disputes, unsound or unwise counsel

Mathers: Hope, confidence, desire, attempt, wish. Wise advice, good counsel, wisdom, prudence, circumspection

Papus: Success assured to the enemy

Thierens: Meeting the opponent, perhaps fighting but more strategy than fighting is indicated. Using weapons of the enemy, practical ability, science of the arts and crafts, tricks, understanding of practical and material obstacles and of work to be done, the enemy disarmed, arguments, undone, person of technical ability, favours technical professions, success by capability

Waite: Design, attempt, wish, hope, confidence, quarrelling, a plan that may fail, annoyance. (Waite notes that the design of his own card is 'uncertain in its import, because the significations are widely at variance with each other'.) Good advice, counsel, instruction, slander, babbling. Dark girl, a good card, promise of a country life after a competence has been secured. Good advice, probably neglected

Suggested: Perfect wisdom. Maturity. Control of power, control of emotions, control of intuition and control of intelligence summarized

Eight of Swords

Design

Marseille: Eight curved swords, crossed

Waite: A blindfolded figure standing bound, three swords stand on its right, five on its left

Aquarian: As Waite

Crowley:	Six swords horizontal, each different from the others. Two swords vertical, point downward, crossing the others. Jupiter in Gemini
New:	Eight of Blades

Interpretation

Case:	Indecision, waste of energy in details, a crisis
Crowley:	Shortened force, Jupiter in Gemini. Retitled, 'Interference'. The will thwarted by accidental interference
Douglas:	Similar to Waite but with the additional meaning of the end of a period of misfortune provided that opportunities for change are recognized and seized
G. Dawn:	Narrow or restricted, petty, a prison
Gray:	Restriction or imprisonment generally, with the negative (in the context of this card) meaning of release from restriction.
Grimaud:	Heavy and overpowering, despair
Huson:	Criticism
Kahn:	As Waite
Kaplan:	Traditional mostly; otherwise very similar to Eden Gray
Mathers:	Sickness, calumny, criticism, blame. Treachery in the past, event, accident, remarkable incident
Papus:	Partial opposition to this success. The enemy only partly triumphs
Thierens:	Obstacles, conflict, danger, sex problems of a threatening nature, danger of death sometimes, revenge, debt, incident or accident, uncouth female
Waite:	Temporary durance, bad news, violent chagrin, crisis, censure, conflict, calumny, sickness. Disquiet, difficulty, opposition, accident, treachery, what is unforeseen, fatality. Scandal spread in respect of a woman, departure of a relative
Suggested:	Evolution and strength of intellect. Inspiration of intelligence. Genius

Nine of Swords

Marseille: Eight curved swords, crossed. A single sword in the centre

Waite: A figure sits up on a bed, covers its eyes, weeping? Behind it nine horizontal swords. The bedcover is decorated with a design of squares which contain, alternating, red roses with the planetary signs and those for the houses

Aquarian: The figure and swords only are visible. This deck makes the figure definitely a woman

Crowley: Nine swords point downward. They drip blood. Mars in Gemini

New: Nine of Blades. In wheel form, like a buzzsaw, clockwise

Interpretation

Case: Worry, suffering, despair, misery, loss

Crowley: Despair and cruelty, Mars in Gemini. Retitled, 'Cruelty'. Unconscious, primitive instincts, the psychopath, the fanatic. Suggested solutions for dealing with this card: passive resistance, resignation or martyrdom, perhaps implacable revenge

Douglas: Assorted tribulations, most of them arising from the evil doings of others. They can be combated effectively by calculated inaction. As in Waite, Douglas suggests this is the card of the martyr. At best it brings new life out of suffering, at worst complete isolation from all hope or comfort

G. Dawn: Illness, suffering, malice, cruelty, pain

Gray: Suffering generally. The negative aspect of the card is hope for the morrow

Grimaud: Matter struggling towards evolution. Desire to succeed

Huson: Unmarried or unattached person. Unseen complications or adversaries

Kahn: Traditional, generally as Mathers and Waite, but with the negative aspect of the card being total disasters of assorted varieties

Kaplan: Polarized between misery and anxiety on the one hand and doubt or slander on the other

97

Mathers:	An ecclesiastic, a priest, conscience, probity, good faith, integrity. Wise distrust, suspicion, fear, doubt, shady character
Papus:	Certain duration of the hatred
Thierens:	Dogma, dogmatism, ecclesiastic mind, hard judgement, orthodoxy, asceticism, swearing, shyness, miscarriage, shame, false evidence given, a scrupulous mind, conscientiousness
Waite:	Utter desolation, death, failure, miscarriage, delay, deception, disappointment, despair. Imprisonment, suspicion, doubt, reasonable fear, shame. An ecclesiastic, a priest, a card of bad omen. Good ground for suspicion against a doubtful person
Suggested:	Senility

Design

Ten of Swords

Marseille:	Eight curved swords, crossed. Two diagonal swords, one crossing each set of four curved swords
Waite:	A man laying face downward. His back is pierced with ten standing swords
Aquarian:	As Waite
Crowley:	Two hour-glass hilts, two Greek Cross hilts, two four-pointed star hilts, a hilt with scales at the top and a hilt with pentagram and crescent at the bottom. Many of the blades are broken. Sun in Gemini
New:	Ten of Blades. Five above, clockwise; five below, anti-clockwise

Interpretation

Case:	Ruin, pain, desolation, *not* a card of sudden death, end of delusion in spiritual matters
Crowley:	Ruin, the Sun in Gemini. Reason run mad, soulless mechanism, the logic of lunatics and (for the most part) philosophers. Reason divorced from reality. The energy of Swords as a completely disruptive force
Douglas:	Desolation and ruin as in Waite; but Douglas further suggests that this tragedy is on a community rather than an individual level. Positive element of the card suggests cause

for hope, the worst being over. Negative aspect is of false dawn, continuing (or presumably worsening) suffering

Gray: As Waite in the positive or upright aspects of the card. Eden Gray reads the negative or reversed meaning as overthrow of evil forces, a measure of success, courage to rise again, looking for help from higher powers

Grimaud: The beginning of harmony between evolved matter and the things of the mind. Agreement, equilibrium, understanding

Huson: Traditional

Kahn: Tears, jealousy, envy. A party, loss, illness of short duration, in the evening

Kaplan: Positive meanings are pain, etc. as traditional. Negative interpretation is benefit, profit, possibly temporary gain

Mathers: Tears, affliction, grief, sorrow. Passing success, monetary advantage

Papus: Uncertainty in the enemy

Thierens: Karmic results whether benefic or malefic, material limits, physical necessity, authority, official might and power, official persons, due reward and honest profit, merited position, possessions may become a curse, not very beneficient for the parents of the querent or else he does not himself esteem them, a card of worldly position

Waite: Whatsoever is intimated by the design (i.e. death), also pain, affliction, tears, sadness, desolation, not especially a card of violent death. Advantage, profit, success, favour, but all of them transient, power and authority. Followed by the Ace and King of Swords . . . imprisonment, for a girl or wife . . . treason on the part of friends. Victory and subsequent fortune for a soldier in war

Suggested: The total failure of intellect. Insanity. Death. Cerebral degeneracy. Diseases which may affect the nervous system and the brain. Catatonia. Television

Page of Swords

Design

Marseille: A young man resting a sword over his left shoulder

Waite: A young man standing on a windy hill, brandishing a sword

Aquarian:	A young man with a sword
Crowley:	The Princess of Swords. She brandishes a sword, point downward, from a throne set in the middle of storm clouds
New:	Blade Page. A half light/half dark face or mask. A horn, a chalice of blood overflowing, a sword, a victor's wreath. Below is the sign of Gemini

Interpretation

Case:	Vigilant, acute, subtle, active youth
Crowley:	The Princess of the Rushing Winds. The Lotus of the Palace of Air. Rules a quadrant of the heavens around Kether. She represents the earthy part of air, the fixation of the volatile, she brings about the materialization of idea. Her character is stern and revengeful, her logic is destructive, she is firm and aggressive, great practical wisdom, subtlety in material things, cleverness in managing practical affairs, especially if they are controversial. Ill-dignified she is incoherent, displays low cunning
Douglas:	Similar to traditional, with additional negative implications of deviousness, prying, vindictiveness, or treachery
G. Dawn:	Same title as Crowley. Wisdom, strength, acuteness, subtleness in material things, grace, dexterity. If ill-dignified she is frivolous and cunning. Earth of Air, Princess and Empress of the Sylphs and Sylphides
Gray:	A brown-haired, brown-eyed boy or girl. A page in the diplomatic service, possible great understanding or knowledge of diplomacy, messages or spying, grace or dexterity. Negative aspects include imposters, likelihood of exposure, frivolity or cunning, possible sickness. Watch out for the unforeseen
Grimaud:	Defensive and agile intellect triumphing without violence over matter. Defence against fate. Oppression by matter, powerlessness in the face of strong forces
Huson:	A spy or rival, deceit
Kahn:	A friend who gives aid in need. Spy
Kaplan:	Similar to Eden Gray
Mathers:	A spy, overlooking, authority. That which is unforeseen, vigilance, support
Papus:	A child, an enemy, bad news, delay

100

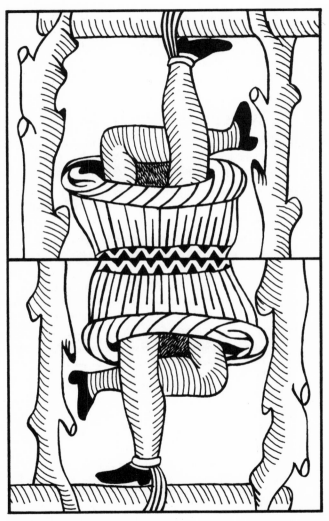

The Hanged Man, from a Grimaud Deck—*The Double Headed
Tarot of Besançon*—in which all the court cards and major arcana
have no reversed positions possible. Early nineteenth century.

Thierens:	Results of studies, examination, policemen, spy, dilettante, sudden events or effects, surprises
Waite:	Authority, overseeing, secret service, spying, vigilance, examination. The evil side of the above. What is unforeseen, unprepared state, sickness. An indiscreet person who will pry into the Querent's secrets. Astonishing news
Suggested:	Messages requiring thought. Disturbing or exciting news. Newspapers. Fire of Air. Hermes as messenger

Design

Knight of Swords

Marseille:	A mounted knight, his sword in his left hand. On his left shoulder is one of the pair, Urim and Thumim. (See The Chariot for explanation)
Waite:	A knight riding furiously, brandishing his sword, through the wind. His clothing is decorated with butterflies and red birds
Aquarian:	A knight, resting his sword on his left shoulder. His helmet is topped with a snake's head
Crowley:	Four wings, issuing from the tip of his helmet, enable the Knight of Swords in this design to fly together with his horse. In his right hand is his extended sword. In his left hand is extended a shorter sword. Below are three birds
New:	Blade Knight. A helmet with purple plumes. A plum. The roman numeral I. The cosmic lemniscate on a shield which is white above, red below. A sword, the point of which forks lightning. An explosion on the horizon.

Interpretation

Case:	Active, clever, subtle, skilful, domineering young man, enmity, wrath, war
Crowley:	The Lord of the Winds and the Breezes. The King of the Spirits of Air. 20 degrees Taurus to 20 degrees Gemini. The fiery part of air, the violent part of motion applied to an apparently manageable element, the idea of attack, activity, skill, subtlety, cleverness, fierce, delicate, courageous, the prey of his own idea which comes to him without reflection. Ill-dignified he is incapable of decision, any action of his is easily thwarted by opposition, the futility that is inadequate violence

102

Douglas:	Traditional
G. Dawn:	Active, clever, subtle, fierce, delicate, courageous, skilful, inclined to domineer and overvalue small things. Ill-dignified he is deceitful, tyrannical, and crafty. Fire of Air. King of Sylphs and Sylphides
Gray:	A dark-haired, brown-eyed young man. Dashing, brave, possibly domineering, clean-hearted, courageous. Possibly the start or end of misfortune. Possibly extravagant, a braggart, a tyrant over anything or anyone too helpless to defend themselves. Ready for a fight. When the Querent card is another possible destruction through the activities of the person represented by this card
Grimaud:	What appears bad is good, troublesome events take a turn for the better, good news. News of a disaster
Huson:	Traditional
Kahn:	Traditional
Kaplan:	Martial bravery generally. Incapacity, impulsiveness, imprudence, conceit
Mathers:	Soldier, skilfulness, capacity, address, promptitude. A conceited fool, ingenuousness, simplicity
Papus:	A young dark man, an enemy, he is also a spy
Thierens:	Military man, one avenging family or other wrongs, wrongs avenging themselves, a surgeon, reopening an old wound, hatred, destruction, extravagance, impertinence
Waite:	Romantic chivalry, skill, bravery, capacity, defence, address, enmity, wrath, war, death when near other cards indicating death. Imprudence, incapacity, extravagance. Heroic action. Dispute with an imbecile. For a woman, struggle with a rival who will be conquered
Suggested:	The defender of intellect. Mental illness from the viewpoint of one trying to help himself or others. Psychoanalysts. Some teachers, social workers. Earth of Air

Queen of Swords

Design

Marseille:	A seated queen with a sword held upright in her right hand

103

Waite: A stern queen, sitting on a throne decorated with butterflies and winged cherubs. Her crown is also decorated with butterflies. She holds firmly upright a sword in her right hand

Aquarian: A queen with a sword. At the hilt of the sword are five full ruddy roses.

Crowley: A queen seated on a cloud. In her right hand hangs a sword, point downward. In her left hand she holds a human head. Her throne is jagged and crowned with the head of a cherub

New: Blade Queen. Two peacocks, a sword, purple irides, a ship, a crown with an eye set into its side. Below is the sign for Libra

Interpretation

Case: Widowhood, mourning, a keen, quick, intensely perceptive, subtle woman, usually fond of dancing

Crowley: The Queen of the Thrones of Air. 20 degrees Virgo to 20 degrees Libra. The watery part of air, elasticity of air and its power of transmission, perceptive, keen observer, subtle interpreter, individualist, swift and accurate at recording ideas, confident actions, gracious and just, graceful, good at dancing and balancing

Douglas: Intelligence, complexity of personality, attention to accuracy/detail, alertness, skill at discernment, independent, versatile, swift to act, ingenious. Negatively can be devious, slanderous, an enemy of subtlety and dangerous qualities

G. Dawn: Intensely perceptive, keen observation, subtle, quick, confident, accurate in superficial things, graceful, fond of dancing and balancing. Ill-dignified she is cruel, sly, deceitful, unreliable, with a good exterior. Water of Air, Queen of the Sylphs and Sylphides

Gray: A brown-haired, brown-eyed woman. Her interpretation combines many features of Waite and Case

Grimaud: Calumnious will, unpleasant advice, slander, evil words. Destruction bearing fruit

Huson: Woman in authority, a widow, dour, sad

Kahn: As traditional, with the added interpretations of sly or crafty, a prostitute

104

Kaplan:	Traditional
Mathers:	Widowhood, loss, privation, absence, separation. A bad woman, ill-tempered and bigoted, riches and discord, abundance together with worry, joy with grief
Papus:	A dark wicked woman, gossip and calumnies
Thierens:	Suffering, afflicted woman, widow, woman of lower sort of character, paid love, sterility, deception, menace, grief, mourning, failure, unemployment, the absence of a woman or the evil influence of one
Waite:	Familiarity with sorrow, not a symbol of mercy nor of power, widowhood, female sadness, absence, sterility, mourning, privation. Malice, bigotry, artifice, prudery, bale, deceit. A widow. A bad woman with ill-will towards the querent
Suggested:	The Queen of Swords, Mother of the Fool and of the Ace of Pentacles. Water of Air. Those things or people who work through the established institutions of intellect to rule them. University administrators, prime ministers and presidents. Politicians. Government

King of Swords

Design

Marseille:	A seated king, sword upraised in his right hand, a sceptre loosely held in his left. On his shoulders are the Urim and Thumim (see The Chariot)
Waite:	A stern king seated on a stone throne carved with a waxing crescent, a waning crescent, butterflies and women. His crown incorporates the design of a winged cherub. In his right hand he brandishes a sword
Aquarian:	A king with his sword over his left shoulder. His shield incorporates a crown
Crowley:	The Prince of Swords. A black king in a chariot drawn by three small winged figures. The king is also winged. It should be noted that the wings are highly stylized. He threatens the three who draw his carriage with his sword
New:	Blade King. A helmet with the German Imperial Eagle brandishing a sword upon it. Over the body of the eagle is a shield, black and yellow, with a burning torch upon it. Below is the sign for Aquarius

105

Case: Distrustful, suspicious man, full of ideas, thoughts and designs, care, observation, extreme caution

Crowley: The Prince of the Chariot of Air, rules from 20 degrees Capricorn to 20 degrees Aquarius. The airy part of air. Intellectual, the mind as such. A pure intellect who destroys as soon as he creates, intensely clever, admirably rational, unstable as to purpose since he knows that each of his ideas is as worthless or worthwhile as the last and the next and thus reduces everything to unreality. Totally impossible to get a grip on such people

Douglas: As the traditional, with the added thoughts that he may be a person who advocates modernity at the expense of tradition. A person who may produce chaos in the name of order

G. Dawn: Full of ideas, thoughts and designs, distrustful, suspicious, firm in friendship and enmity, careful, slow, over-cautious, symbolizes alpha and omega, the giver of Death who slays as fast as he creates. Ill-dignified: harsh, malicious, plotting, obstinate, hesitating, unreliable. Air of Air, Prince and Emperor of Sylphs and Sylphides

Gray: Traditional, except his personification as a mature man with dark hair and eyes

Grimaud: Supremacy, sanctions taken by force can only be controlled by force. Alteration of events by force, threat of conflict, justice enforced by the sword, matters only settled by war. Unremitting conflict

Huson: Man in authority, judge or critic, severe

Kahn: A dark man with good judgement, a professional man, a subtle man. A vicious or crafty man, a dangerous man, a man to be careful of, a ruthless man

Kaplan: Traditional

Mathers: Lawyer, man of law, power, command, superiority, authority. A wicked man, chagrin, worry, grief, fear, disturbance

Papus: A dark , bad man, a soldier, a powerful enemy who must be distrusted

Thierens: General, captain, power, command, cruelty, tyranny

Waite: Perhaps justice, but also the power of life and death, judgement, power, command, authority, militant intelligence, law, officers of the crown. Cruelty, perversity, barbarity, perfidy, evil intention. A lawyer, senator, doctor. A bad man, caution that it's time to put an end to a ruinous lawsuit

Suggested: King of Swords/Air/Thought. Father of the Fool and of the Ace of Pentacles. Air of Air. Those things or people who work to destroy or to establish the institutions having to do with the suit. The changing law, the courts. Revolutionaries, anarchists, a very few politicians

From this section upon the Minor Arcana it can be readily seen that many of the modern commentators (Eden Gray, Paul Huson, Alfred Douglas and S.R. Kaplan) draw heavily upon A.E. Waite and Macgregor Mathers for their interpretations, because the Tarot is a continuing tradition. Even then each of the writers adds something of his own to the originals. The bare bones of explanation which occur in Mathers's book are expanded considerably by A.E. Waite. Eden Gray and Alfred Douglas add vast amounts of detail to Waite. Paul Huson and Yitzhac Kahn employ humour in their explanations, totally lacking in all other commentators except Crowley, whose humour is frequently obscure and at the expense of the reader.

Study of the Minor Arcana as a whole shows more diversity of opinion upon the court cards than upon the numbered cards. Which could be explained by too much reliance on Waite, the lack of illustration on the numbered cards of most decks, or simply a general lack of interest in the numbered cards *vis à vis* the court cards. Eden Gray, particularly, is much more interested in court cards than in numbers, assigning each of them to definite physical characteristics so that they may each be assigned to a particular Querent or to a particular character in the Querent's cartomantic drama.

Of all the writers consulted here, Aleister Crowley alone considers the numbered cards in any great detail. By consulting *777* and *The Book of Thoth* a variety of meanings can be obtained. And his writing is frequently the most original that has been accomplished on the Tarot. Wherein lies its virtue and its danger.

With Crowley all magick was a *now-you-see-it* game. He demands of the believer disbelief. Anything short of it leads to madness. So a reader consults him at his own peril.

The least interesting of the books used in this section is that of S.R. Kaplan, published by U.S. Games Systems, which has received world-wide circulation and is probably the best-known work on the Tarot next to the books of A.E. Waite and Eden Gray, to both of which it is vastly indebted and considerably inferior, containing, at least in the Minor Arcana no original thought.

So much for the minor suits. In the Major Arcana which follow, considerably greater range of opinion will be seen and many more writers, covering in 22 cards all of life: from birth through love, from triumph through death to resurrection and eventual and total victory.

(b) *The Major Arcana*

The Major Arcana are usually numbered from 0 through 21 or from 1 through 22. The odd card is the Fool, the Joker, placed either as number 0 or 21 or 22. This book uses the numbering system of A.E. Waite, wherein the Fool is numbered 0 and the numbers of Strength and Justice (11 and 8 respectively in the Marseille pack) have been interchanged to make Strength 8 and Justice 11.

The Fool

The Fool as an Archetypal figure is, as Jung points out in his study appended to *The Trickster* by Paul Radin, one of the most important symbols of the unconscious mind.

Among other legendary meanings he is the self at the beginning of the journey, he is the fool who has lost his wits, the fool who has, with divine wisdom, abandoned them for something better. He is the trickster whose practical jokes never quite come off, he is Punch or Reynard the Fox or Harlequin. He is the stupid brother (or sister) left at home in the ashes when his older brothers go out into the world and who must eventually rescue them from that world when their wit will not stretch as far as his cunning or his kindness. Do you remember the fairy tales of the fool?

As Tyl Eulenspiegel he was known to medieval man in Germany and the Low countries. As the Fool of God he was known in Russia. As the Juggler of Our Lady he appeared in the France of Charlemagne. Dostoevsky writes about him in the person of Prince Mishkin. Many different writers have written about him in the person of Merlin, the magician at the court of King Arthur. And as Coyote or Raven or simply Trickster he appears in American Indian legend.

To the originator of the Tarot cards The Fool in many of these guises was well known. The legends were already part of his family history. The family being European Man. But he was not entirely a hero of legend. At the royal courts which used the Tarot, where the first cards were painted, he was well known as the Court Jester or Court Dwarf. In Italy the dwarf became for a short time a badge of royalty almost as important as the crown. Par Lagerqvist in his novel *The Dwarf* relates that side of the history of the Fool indelibly.

In the culture of our own time the fool still survives in such varied forms as the circus clown, the Punch and Judy Show, and even the television comedian.

The Fool attends the Mardi Gras in New Orleans, the Carnival in Rio and Fasching in Munich . . . one last outbreak of the unsane before the rectitude of Lent.

He is what we try to forget about ourselves and what, at the same time, we had better not forget: Cinderella in the ashes and Cinderella at the ball. At one and the same time.

In a sense it is the spirit of The Fool which animates the entire Tarot deck. In the earliest deck known he is shown towering over midget human figures, a Giant of Folly and of super-rational sanity. It is with his madness, that of the Fool of God, that the cards are illuminated; for in any reading of the Tarot it is the Fool who asks and the Fool who answers every question.

Design

Gringonneur: A giant fool, half naked in a jockstrap, standing in Gargantuan triumph over four not very distressed people

Bembo: A ragged fool, with feathers or straw in his hair. Both the Bembo and Gringonneur Fools are probably based on European carnival customs of burning or drowning an effigy of the carnival king on the last day of carnival or the first of Lent. In some festivals the effigy was provided by a living person, which led to a few fatal mistakes when the crowd got too enthusiastic. It's likely that this custom bears some relation to that of killing the Solar King at the end of a solar year or that attributed to the Druids of erecting a Wicker Colossus, similar to a scarecrow, with the effigy of a man's head at the top. The hollow interior of the figure was filled with malefactors, prisoners of war and sometimes innocent persons and then the whole figure was burnt as a sacrifice. An illustration of this figure, reproduced from an old print, is to be found in Lewis Spence's *Magic Arts in Celtic Britain,* and on the cover of this book.

Swiss: A court fool in particoloured red, blue and yellow. He is very similar to the Joker in an ordinary playing card deck (or, for that matter, to The Joker in *Batman and Robin*) whose direct ancestor he is

Insight: The Fool setting forth on his journey. He is being attacked by a smiling cat

Marseille: Same basic design as Insight; but the cat has torn away part of his trousers

Italian: The same

Wirth: A wildcat attacking the Fool's left leg. He wears an expression of considerable anguish

Waite:	A young man poses on the edge of a precipice. In his left hand he carries a white rose. His dog barks with joy
B.O.T.A.:	As Waite
Aquarian:	A dreamer. Holds a rod, blooming, on his right shoulder, and in his right hand a white rose
Crowley:	A staring, horned fool, oblivious of a tiger biting his leg, a crocodile behind him, and a landscape littered with occult symbolism
New:	Titled, 'The Nameless One'. A naked figure accompanied by what looks like a dog leaves a field of bones. In one hand he carries an open scroll which he reads. In the other a furled scroll. Over his head a spider hangs

Interpretation

Case:	Aleph. Numeral value 1. Its name is ALP, meaning Bull or Ox. Breath, as in the life principle of all things, breath of the beasts of the field. Fiery or scintillating intelligence, limitless light prior to creation. Colour: pale yellow. Planet: Uranus. Tone: E natural. Originality, audacity, venturesome quest. Folly, eccentricity, inconsiderate action
Christian:	The Crocodile: Expiation. Sichen in the Hebrew Alphabet. Its number is 300. Represents punishment following every error. The slave of material things who is inevitably ruined
Crowley:	Air, the father and mother of manifested existence. The Green Man of Spring, the Holy Ghost, Harpocrates or Parsifal. The bi-sexual Zeus, Dionysus Zagreus or Bacchus. Baphomet (the ass-headed 'god' of the Templars). The Ox. Scintillating intelligence. Bright pale yellow. Meditation on the wind. Topaz. Chalcedony. Aspen. Eagle (Sign of Scorpio) or Man (Cherub of Air). Jupiter. The power of divination. His perfume is Galbanum (a resin from Persian fennel). His weapon is the dagger or fan. An original, subtle, sudden impulse or impact, coming from a completely strange quarter. A bearded ancient, the Spirit of AEther. Related to the Sylphs. Having to do with the respiratory organs. The Mighty and Terrible One or the Beast. Lineal figures of the airy triplicity
Douglas:	Unexpected, unplanned, or challenging influences. Impulses lead to major problems.
Gray:	The dreamer confronted with choices has to act with great care

111

16 | LE FEU DU CIEL

The Ruined Tower (The Fire From Heaven) *Nineteenth Century French Tarot*

G. Dawn:	The Crown of Wisdom, the primum mobile acting through the air on the Zodiac. Krishna, Harpocrates, or Dionysus
Grimaud:	Man progressing towards evolution. Thoughtlessness, lack of colour, carelessness in promises, insecurity
Huson:	Anarchy or the irrational, the divine bum
Kahn:	Traditional, plus a gambler, mishandled intention or the end of a cycle
Kaplan:	All of the drawbacks which a fool could possess
Knight:	Chaos, the spiritually innocent containing within it cosmic racial wisdom
Lind:	The spirit involving to its source
Mathers:	Will, will-power, dexterity. Will applied to evil ends, weakness of will, cunning, knavishness
Mayananda:	The Head (in Buddhist symbolism), the 1000 petalled lotus, AEther, the highest of the five elements of eastern religion. That which comprises *all* possibilities of movement . . . infinite dimensions. It neither begins the series nor ends it, it is omnipresent. That is, it is neither numbered 0 nor 21 nor 22 in the sequence of Major Arcana. 0 here would represent 'centre' rather than number
Papus:	21 in the sequence of Major Arcana. Inconsiderate actions, madness
Sadhu:	Shin, numerical value 300. An arrow in direct but wavering flight
Thierens:	Foolishness and, as well, that which cannot be helped, that which will take care of itself, that over which we have no control. Astrological sign, Earth
Ussher:	Alpha and omega, beginning and end. 0 or infinity, both the void before creation and the accomplishment of the seventh day. Random chance or contingency. The reverse of the Hanged Man
Waite:	The spirit in search of experience. The flesh, the sensitive life. Waite notes that the subsidiary name of this card has been, The Alchemist. (Used in the sense of ultimate folly rather than ultimate wisdom.) Folly, mania, extravagance, intoxication, delirium. Negligence, apathy
Suggested:	The legendary meanings imply the value: the Querent,

113

regardless of sex. This seems a little more likely than a reliance on the court cards of the Minor Arcana for 'dark-haired people with blue eyes' or whatever. His place in the Tarot would be all of the following; before the Ace of Pentacles, after the King of Swords, before The Magician and after The World. He relates to every card in the deck

The Magician

One way of looking at the Tarot deck is to think of the cards of the Major Arcana as falling into pairs. Though this does not seem to have been previously commented upon, a relationship between The Fool and The Magician, The Papess and The Empress, The Emperor and The Hierophant seems fairly obvious. So the legendary meanings of The Magician are those of his obverse twin plus the added attributes of Hermes the Magician. The attributes of carnival mountebank (the quickness of the hand deceives the eye), the old shell game, the juggler, the minstrel, the craftsman in the occult arts, and even, in some decks, the cottage craftsman, perhaps a cobbler

Design

Gringonneur: Missing

Bembo: An unhappy juggler, seated. On a table before him are a covered dish, a glass, a knife and two pennies (?). His left hand holds a rod

Swiss: A fairground mountebank. On the table in front of him are several balls, horns, cups, and an open box. He holds a rod. General suggestion of juggler

Insight: Roughly the same but incorporating a lemniscate

Marseille: The same as Insight

Italian: Similar to Swiss but with two closed boxes

Wirth: The symbols on the table have been replaced by the suits: a cup, a sword, three pentacles or coins. He holds a wand

Waite: A magician stands behind a table. In his upraised right hand is a wand. His left hand is extended downward pointing towards earth. Above his head is the lemniscate. On the table before him are the symbols of the four suits: pentacle, wand, cup, sword. Red roses bloom over him, red roses and lilies bloom before him

B.O.T.A.:   As Waite

Aquarian: As Waite

114

Crowley:	Hermes leering. Above his head the Hindu symbol for male/female, joined, with wings. Lower right, an Ape of Thoth. He plays with the symbols of the four suits. Behind Hermes' head is a snake symbolic of both the Uraeus headdress of the pharaohs and the caduceus of Hermes
New:	Retitled, 'Changer'. A man, dressed as an eastern monk, standing astride a white sphere. His arms are outstretched on either side. In his right hand a lotus, from his left falls water. On his left shoulder a hooded vulture or falcon has sunk its claws into his flesh. Before him, on a blanket, are the symbols of the four suits of the Minor Arcana of this deck: Pears (Cups), Stones (Pentacles), Snakes (Wands) and Scimitars (Swords)

Interpretation

Case:	Beth. Meaning of the letter Beth in English is 'House'. Case connects up House-housebuilding-Freemasonry and thence Hermes-Thoth as housebuilding is an Hermetic science. Mercury. Yellow. E natural. Intelligence of Transparency. The control of forces and things below the self-conscious level. Energy from above, focussed by attention
Christian:	Human will as the earthly reflection of divine will promoting good and preventing evil
Crowley:	House, Mercury, Intelligence of Transparency. The Juggler. Yellow. Thoth or Cynocephalus. Aupu—the Hips. Hanuman or Vishnu as Parasa-Rama. The Swallow, the Ibis, the Ape. His herbs are Vervain, Herb Mercury, Marjolane, Palm. His precious stones are Opal and Agate. His magical weapon is the Wand or Caduceus. His perfumes are Mastic, White Sandal, Mace, Storax and all fugitive odours. His drugs are all cerebral excitants. His magical powers in Western mysticism are Healing, the Gift of Tongues, the Knowledge of the Sciences. His name is The Magus of Power. Crowley comments in *The Book of Thoth* that no true representation of this card is possible as it represents perpetual motion. Lineal figure, the Octagon. Skill, wisdom, adroitness, elasticity, craft, cunning, deceit, theft. Occult wisdom, power, messages or business transactions. Interference of learning or intelligence with the matter at hand
Douglas:	The beginning of consciousness, intellect, strength of will, adaptability or the search for meanings. The negative in-

115

	terpretation is weakness of will (and presumably weakness of intellect)
Gray:	Will generally and the exercise of will, either alone or in harmony with the divine. Weakness of Will, indecision perhaps, or use of power for destructive purposes
G. Dawn:	The Crown of Understanding, beginning of material production, the primum mobile acting through the philosophic Mercury on Saturn. Skill, wisdom, adaptation. Craft or cunning depending on neighbouring cards. Sometimes occult wisdom
Grimaud:	The destiny of man struggling with the undercurrents of the occult. Hesitation, guile, uncertainty, change caused by chance
Huson:	Skill, cunning, dexterity or trickery in application. Hermes Psychopompos leading the Querent into a new area. (Where Hermes is not only the conductor of souls but also the magician)
Kahn:	A magician. Ability with women, agility, wit. Extremes of difficulty, instability or impotence
Kaplan:	Traditional
Knight:	The spirit: receptive to cosmic forces and at the same time activating matter
Lind:	Traditional
Mathers:	Will, willpower, dexterity. Will applied to evil ends, weakness of will. Cunning, knavishness
Mayananda:	Mercury in the highest form. Abstract will
Papus:	A female enquirer. Man seeking for the God in Heaven and, at the same time, the demon below. The creator
Sadhu:	The striving toward unity, initiation
Thierens:	Aries, the Querent, beginnings
Ussher:	Time, seen as an ironic spirit, looking forward. A torch, waved in the void
Waite:	The possession and communication of gifts of the spirit. The divine motive in man. Skill, diplomacy, sickness, pain, loss, disaster, snares of enemies. Self-confidence, will. A physician, a magus, mental disease, disgrace, disquiet
Suggested:	The ambivalence of Hermes: true or false

The Papess

The Papess is a memoir of two medieval legends, that of Pope Joan and the Visconti Papess.

The Visconti Papess, Sister Manfreda, was elected by an Italian religious sect, the Guglielmites. One of their beliefs concerned the sect's founder, Guglielma of Bohemia, who died in 1281 but was to be resurrected in 1300 on the Feast of Pentecost and inaugurate a new age wherein women would be popes instead of men. I n preparation for this very early example of Women's Lib the Guglielmites nominated Manfreda Visconti to be their papess. The burning of Sister Manfreda at the stake in 1300 determined the question in favour of the orthodox and male chauvinist papacy of Rome.

The alternate source, Pope Joan, has exerted an almost tidal influence on the imaginations of Europe. The first popular report of Pope Joan occurs in 1282 in the writings of Martin Polonus. He says that after the death of Pope Leo IV (c. A.D. 855) one John Anglus (surely this should be Johanna Anglus) a native of Metz, was elected to the throne of St. Peter and remained pope (or papess) for two years, five months and four days. She was discovered when, on a procession from St. Peter's to the Lateran, she collapsed in childbirth. At this point the story becomes a little vague. Pope Joan was either torn to pieces by the enraged mob who thought they had been conned (it was, after all, a sacrilege; a woman, pope) or she died of the childbirth. In either case it made a lovely story. Many were only too eager to believe all possible evil of Rome, all possible corruption of the Popes; and the legend of Pope Joan simply confirmed their most delicious fears concerning both. There is, however, one small fly in the telling of it all. After the death of Leo IV only one and a half months elapsed before the consecration of Benedict III. For which coronation elaborate evidence exists. But leaving no time at all for the reign of Pope Joan.

Knowledge of both these legends was certainly available to the early designers of the Tarot. In the case of Sister Manfreda, she has been immortalized in the Bembo Tarot cards which were painted for her distant relative, Bianca Maria Visconti. It is her face which looks so longingly towards Heaven from the Papess card in the Visconti Tarot. That card is now in the Pierpont Morgan Library. And Pope Joan by the nature of her story, became an ecclesiastic joke. She pops up in the writings of many Church Fathers desirous of proving the truth or falsity of the story according to their church; and she appears later on in the novel, *Pope Joan,* by Emmanuel Royidis, translated into English by Lawrence Durrell. And still a third source could have been returning Crusaders, bringing back the story of 'The Fisherman's Wife', from the *Arabian Nights.*

She asked, of a miraculous Flounder, a number of wishes: that she be Empress (granted), then that she be Pope (granted), and finally that she become God. At which point the pious Flounder returned her, by the same miraculous means as before, to the humble cottage wherein she had conceived her first delusions of the grandeur of God.

117

Whichever of the three sources in legend, she continues to exert a strong influence on Tarot design. She is one of the strongest designs in the Major Arcana in both the Waite and Crowley decks, though in both she is more likely to represent the High Priestess of the Eleusinian Mysteries. (See Hierophant, card 5).

Design

Gringonneur: Missing

Bembo: A nun, wearing the triple crown and the habit of the Umiliata Order. She holds a breviary or Bible in her left hand. This is probably the earliest representation of The Papess in the Tarot and dates from about 1450

Swiss: Juno standing with her peacock. In many Southern French Tarots the Papess was replaced by Juno to avoid giving offence to the Church

Insight: A high priestess of Isis, seated on a throne. She holds a partially visible scroll with the legend, 'Tora', (Hebrew for Law). On her breast is a solar cross, at her feet a waxing crescent moon. She is flanked by lotus pillars. On the pillar to her right the word 'Boaz', is partially visible, signifying negation. On that to her left is the word, 'Jachin', or 'Beginning'

Marseille: A seated papess, wearing the triple crown, a book (The Bible) shown open on her lap

Italian: The same

Wirth: Similar to the traditional; but Wirth has added a crescent moon to the crown. Also, she bears the Keys of St. Peter

Waite: A priestess of Isis, the solar cross upon her breast. The waxing crescent beneath her left foot. She sits between the pillars Boaz and Jachin and before a screen decorated with pomegranates. In her lap is a rolled scroll of the Tora. On her head is a crown signifying waxing, waning and full Moon and probably The Triple Goddess as well

B.O.T.A.: As Waite, except that the pillars between which the priestess sits are lotus buds rather than opened flowers to signify her virginity, that is, latent or undeveloped powers

Aquarian: A pensive priestess sits before a curtain figured with pomegranates. In her left hand are several flowers. Two rods stand on her left, signifying Boaz and Jachin

Crowley: Isis enthroned. Isis because she has in her lap the bow and arrows of the Virgin Goddess. On her head the crown of Isis. Between her and the viewer is a screen, before which are grapes, a lotus, crystals, a cone and a camel

New: Retitled, 'Mother'. A nearly naked woman stands astride the two pillars, one light, one dark. In her upraised left hand is a lotus, in her right a lightning bolt. Between her breasts is a seven-pointed star, she is crowned with the double-headed snake. Over her head is the sign of Aquarius

Interpretation

Case: The Hebrew letter, Gimel, meaning Camel. The Moon Uniting intelligence. Memory, the subconscious. Potential

Christian: Truth hidden. Discretion

Crowley: Camel. Luna. Uniting intelligence. The high priestess. Blue. Hathor, the left eye. Chandra. Artemis, Hecate. The dog or almond, mugwort, hazel, ranunculus, moonwort. Moonstone, pearl and crystal. Her weapons are the bow and arrows. Her perfumes are menstrual blood, Camphor, aloes, all sweet virginal odours. Her drugs are Juniper, pennyroyal, and all emmenogogues. Her powers are clairvoyance or divination by dreams. Her name is The Priestess of the Silver Star. The possibility of form, potentially a goddess of fertility. The idea behind form. Lineal figure, the Enneagram. Pure, exalted and gracious influence. Change, alternation, fluctuation, increase and decrease. A liability to be overwhelmed by enthusiasm

Douglas: Inspiration, revelation, divination, intuition. A wise or prophetic woman giving good advice. Emotional instability or enslavement. Lack of foresight, reluctance to take advice giving rise to problems

Gray: Traditional with reversed meanings of conceit, sensuality, superficiality

G. Dawn: The Crown of Beauty. The beginning of soverignty and beauty. The primum mobile acting through the Moon upon the Sun. Change, alternation, increase or decrease. Fluctuation

Grimaud: The occult, intuition. The forces of nature. Safety, power over events, something hidden revealed, certainty triumphing over evil. A card of doors opening

Huson: Intuition reversed by hostility or hypocrisy

119

Kahn:	Traditional with some imaginative additions: Psychic ability, astral projection, possible primeval instincts. Reverse meanings of a virgin, an outgoing woman, a woman with many lovers, a prostitute or vampire. Decadence and cynicism
Kaplan:	Juno. A concentration on the intellectual aspects of the card rather than the intuitive
Knight:	The path of secrecy or silence. Desolation, nothingness, purification. The acceptance of absolute despair
Lind:	Illumination or spiritual enlightenment
Mathers:	Science wisdom, knowledge, education. Conceit, ignorance, unskilfulness, superficial knowledge
Mayananda:	Wise adaptation of solar power. Enlightenment brought to unillumined consciousness. A link card between that which is inmanifest and that which is phenomenal
Papus:	A woman adorned with the attributes of authority and persuasion
Sadhu:	(Nothing)
Thierens:	Taurus. God the Woman or The Divine Mother. The eternal feminine. Constancy, fidelity, repose, stability. Dumbness, laziness, resistance, endurance. Passive opposition. It rules art, the artistic abilities, wealth and the masonic lodge
Ussher:	The formative or the healing. Nature's magic web. Destiny. Moira
Waite:	The spiritual bride and mother. The Queen of the Borrowed Light. The co-habiting glory . . . Supernal understanding and indwelling glory. Secrets, mystery, the future as yet unrevealed. Silence, tenacity, wisdom, science. Passion, moral or physical ardour, conceit, surface knowledge
Suggested:	Teacher in perhaps an occult sense. A guide. She could be playing games

The Empress

Design

Gringonneur:	Missing
Bembo:	A seated Germanic queen, holding her husband's jousting

shield, on which is an Imperial Eagle. The card is further decorated with the three interlocked diamond rings, repeated, of the Sforza family

Swiss: A seated queen, holding a rod in her right hand, her left hand partially raised with the forefinger pointing upwards

Insight: A seated queen in flowing robes. Repeated throughout the card are crosses. A general feeling of abundance

Marseille: A German empress, seated, bearing in her left hand a sceptre surrounded by an orb and cross

Italian: Similar, with the addition of an angel's wings and a second head for the eagle on the shield

Wirth: Throned empress, with angelic wings, her head surrounded by a corona of stars. Her left foot rests upon a crescent moon, waxing

Waite: An empress, seated, wearing a gown decorated with pomegranates. On her head a crown of stars. She holds a rod raised in her right hand. A device on the symbol for Venus with a heart. Ripe wheat in the foreground

B.O.T.A.: Similar, but she bears a heart-shaped shield with a dove upon it in her right hand. In her left a sceptre terminating in an orb. There are no pomegranates visible, but on her left are roses in full bloom

Aquarian: Repeats the ripe wheat, the crown of stars and the female symbol upon her shield

Crowley: The empress seated, with an opened lotus in her right hand. On her head is a Crown of Isis surmounted by a Maltese Cross. On her left is the waxing crescent. On her right, the waning. In the foreground at her left is a shield bearing the Imperial German Eagle. In the foreground at her right is a swan seen upon a nest of cygnets

New: Retitled, 'Feeler'. Shows a priestess standing between two cypresses. In the night sky above her is the sign of Cancer. Her head is crowned by the Ankh. Snakes wrap themselves around her ankles.

Interpretation

Case: Daleth, that through which something passes. Ingress, egress, transmission, diffusion, dissemination. Division. Venus, Hathor. Wisdom and folly. Luminous intelligence. The warm Mother Goddess. Nature

121

Christian:	The supreme power balanced by the eternally active mind and by absolute wisdom. The universal fecundity of the Supreme Being. Nature in labour. Success, provided that productive activity is united with rectitude of spirit
Crowley:	Illuminating intelligence. Emerald Green. Hathor. Freya and Aphrodite. Venus. The sparrow, the dove, the swan. Myrtle, rose and clover. Emerald or turquoise. Her weapon is the girdle. Her perfumes are sandalwood, myrtle, all soft voluptuous odours. Her drugs are all aphrodisiacs. Her magical powers are those governing love philtres. Her name is The Daughter of the Mighty Ones. Implies that the fundamental law of the universe is love. In alchemical terms she is salt, the inactive principle of nature which must be energized by sulphur to maintain the whirling equilibrium of the universe. Lineal figure, the heptagram. Love, beauty, happiness, pleasure, success, completion, good fortune, graciousness, elegance, luxury, idleness, dissipation, debauchery, friendship, gentleness, delight
Douglas:	The Mother Goddess: Demeter, Ishtar. Feelings or emotions (as distinct from intuition, which belongs to the papess or to the suit of Cups). Mother-fixation which can become Kali, the devourer of her own children (or Hecate, the Greek equivalent) . . . thus the maternal and crone aspects of the Triple Goddess in this card, while the maiden aspect is in the high priestess. Fertility, sensuality generally. Reassurance or security derived from the senses. Negative aspects include sterility, maternal tyranny, domestic strife, psychic alienation, poverty or a sense of the universe as impersonal or malevolent
Gray:	Mainly traditional; but including the concept of Isis unveiled, therefore the Maternal aspect of the goddess, as the high priestess is her veiled or maiden aspect
G. Dawn:	The wisdom of understanding. The union of the powers of origination and production. The sphere of the zodiac acting through Venus upon Saturn. Beauty, happiness, pleasure, success, luxury or dissipation
Grimaud:	The passive power of the material world. A force against which one cannot react. A state of affairs that nothing can alter. Delay in the accomplishment of something
Huson:	Traditional with the added implication of mater dolorosa, therefore not only a mother-figure representing abundance but also one who represents sorrow

122

The Chariot from an early Tarot deck

Kahn:	Traditional but including the additional meanings of lust and loneliness, a nymphomaniac, overindulgence or extravagance
Kaplan:	Traditional
Knight:	The Gate of Manifestation. The face to face vision of God, the complete illumination
Lind:	The seed in the darkness of night. Mother goddesses, goddesses of fruitfulness or fertility
Mathers:	Action, plan, undertaking, movement in a matter. Initiative. Inaction, frittering away of power, want of concentration, vacillation
Mayananda:	Astarte: love in physical aspects, Aphrodite: love between mental complements, affection, that love which produces works of art, Hermaphrodite: wisdom and understanding united in cosmic or universal love. The love of master and student in the mysteries
Papus:	(Nothing)
Sadhu:	She reigns with her love over all that has been born, all that is, and all that will be born
Thierens:	Gemini. She represents the sphere of Mercury . . . so this card bears the meaning of messages and writing, news to be heard, instructions to be received. The card of knowledge and universal fecundity
Ussher:	The Corn-Woman. Earth, maternal and material, at the time of Eden, before all culture whether Hebrew or Classic. The matrix of civilizations
Waite:	The fruitful mother of thousands. Fruitfulness, action, initiative, length of days, the unknown, clandestine, difficulty, doubt, ignorance, light, truth, the unravelling of involved matters, public rejoicings, vacillation
Suggested:	The mother of all, Demeter/Kore/Hecate. A giver of rich gifts to those she loves who is also capable of terrible anger and awesome violence. The Maenads who tore to pieces Pentheus

The Emperor

Grigonneur:	A seated emperor. In his right hand, a sceptre. In his left, an orb. Two children kneel on his left
Bembo:	A seated emperor, probably Frederick III. In his left hand, the imperial orb. In his right, a sceptre
Swiss:	As Marseille
Insight:	Seated on a throne embellished with rams' heads. He holds the orb, surmounted by a cross, in his left hand. In his right he bears a sceptre terminating in the Crux Ansata
Marseille:	The emperor, seated in profile. On the side of the throne is the Imperial German Eagle. His legs are crossed in the sign of 4
Italian:	The same as Marseille; but with the Eagle doubleheaded
Wirth:	Similar to the Marseille; but exaggerating the crossed legs in the sign of 4
Waite:	Derived from the Insight Tarot. Seated on a throne embellished with rams' heads. He holds the orb, without the cross, in his left hand. In his right hand, the sceptre which terminates in the Crux Ansata
B.O.T.A.:	Derived from Wirth. The emperor seated in profile. His throne is a cube, on the side of which is a ram's head. The symbol is repeated on his left shoulder plate. Exaggerated sign of 4 as in Wirth. In his right hand, the sceptre with Crux Ansata. In his left, the orb. The zodiacal sign for Aries appears at the top of his helmet
Aquarian:	The emperor upon the rams' head throne. In his right hand, the Crux Ansata sceptre. In his left, the orb without cross. In front of him are lilies
Crowley:	The emperor, seated, legs firmly crossed in the 4, bearing in his right hand the rams' head sceptre. In his left hand is the orb with Maltese Cross. His shield is the Imperial Double Eagle. Behind him, at either side, are rams. At his feet, a lamb, with a circle suggesting a halo and a flag draped casually over its shoulders
New:	Retitled, 'Actor'. He stands before a throne on which is a crown and a two-horned dog. His left foot rests upon the neck of a lion which sleeps beneath him. In his left hand is

125

an orb without cross. There are two rather sinister blue
birds in the card and a pattern of stars upon the ground

Case: Hebrew letter, Heh, or window, wind-door. All the functions of the sense of sight, i.e.: vision, introspection, recon-
naissance, watchfulness, care, vigilance, examination,
calculation, analysis, induction, inquiry, investigation.
Constituting intelligence. Authorship. Invention. Aries,
Mars, the Sun exalted. Scarlet. C natural. Rulership,
government, guidance, leadership, force, strength, energy,
courage, activity, he who sets in order, the ruling mental activity

Christian: Realization. The necessity of a firm will strengthened by the
knowledge of truth and justice. The realization of hope
depends on finding someone more powerful than the
Querent to be of assistance

Crowley: Though he later changed his mind, Crowley gives in 777 the
attribution, Heh, window, as Case and Golden Dawn.
Thus: Aries, Fire, ruled by the Sun and by Jupiter. Constituting intelligence, The Emperor, Scarlet, Isis, Shiva,
Athena, Mars, Minerva. The Ram, the Owl, the Tiger Lily,
Geranium, the Ruby. His magical weapons are the Horns,
Energy, and the Burin. His perfume is Dragon's Blood. His
drugs are all cerebral excitants (as the Magician). Crowley
gives as his power that of consecrating things. (This may
have been interchanged in 777 with the attribution to The
Hierophant, whose power is given as the secret of physical
strength.) Lineal figure, Puer. The Sun of the Morning,
Chief among the Mighty. In *The Book of Thoth*, Crowley
gives Tzaddi as the Hebrew letter for the Emperor. Aries
ruled by Mars, Sun exalted. He connects the Hebrew up
with Sanskrit and thus to such modern words as Caesar,
Tsar, Sirdar, Senate, Senior, Signor, etc. War, conquest,
victory, strife, ambition, originality, over-weening confidence, megalomania, quarrelsomeness, energy, vigour,
stubbornness, impracticability, rashness, ill-temper

Douglas: Douglas's interpretation of this card is not unlike Crowley's
emphasizing temporal power and strength, with the
negative aspects of immaturity or subservience

Gray: As Douglas, with the additional negative meaning of
possibility of being defrauded in one's inheritance

G. Dawn: The Wisdom of Soverignty and Beauty, the originator of them, the Sphere of the Zodiac acting through Aries upon the Sun and initiating spring. War, conquest, victory, strife, ambition

Grimaud: Transient wealth and power. Loss of wealth or authority

Huson: The horned patriarchal god, Herne the Hunter, the Green Man, Cernunnos. (Perhaps, therefore Hercules, as the Cerne Giant at Cerne Abbas in Dorset is cognate with Solar Hercules and there appears to be some relationship between Cerne and Cernunnos and Herne.) Fundamentally a priapic progenitor. (Again, borne out by the Giant.) Paternalism, tyranny, authority, protection, potency, stability, the god-king

Kahn: The emperor reinterpreted as a modern captain of industry. One who is dedicated and disciplined. One who embodies or suffers from a lack of the Roman virtues

Kaplan: Literally traditional

Knight: Natural intelligence, Tzaddi, Aquarius

Lind: Temporal power

Mathers: Realization, effect, development, stoppage, check, immature, unripe

Mayananda: Aries ruled by Mars or Uranus. Sun exalted

Papus: Daleth, the Womb. Domination of spirit over matter, active creation

Sadhu: An engineer, a constructor

Thierens: Cancer. Thierens reasoning for changing the astrological attribution of this card is as follows: originally emperors were chosen by the people. Vox populi, vox Dei. And the people are ruled by Cancer. The representative of the past, memory, tradition, dharma and the motives of the soul. Possibly the physical parent of the Querent. An inner realization of the significance of outer facts

Ussher: Not only Mediterranean patriarchal figures (Jupiter, Zeus *et al*) but also such as Urizen. The Hebrew patriarchy or that of the Dorians taking over from earlier matriarchies. Daleth, the Door. Irish-Duir, the Kingly Oak, Runic Thorn or Thor, the Thunderer . . . opener of Heaven and Earth. Conscious energy

Waite:	Virile power, lordship of thought, stability, power, protection, realization, a great person, aid, authority, will, benevolence, compassion, confusion to enemies, obstruction, immaturity
Suggested:	Jupiter (the crossed legs, 4. The planetary sign for Jupiter is 4.) The father. The father of his people

The Pope or Hierophant

It is likely that this card represents just what it appears to be in the earliest decks, The Pope. But many nineteenth century writers on the Tarot have called it The Hierophant, in an attempt to connect the cards with the worship of Isis in the City of Hermes in Egypt or with the worship of Demeter, the Great Mother, at Eleusis in Greece.

The Hierophant was the High Priest of the Eleusinian Mysteries, the rites of Demeter, which were celebrated at Eleusis and Athens. Virtually nothing is known of these rites as all initiates were under strict vows of secrecy as to what had befallen them; and only The Hierophant knew, in any case, the full ceremonies. According to custom each Hierophant chose his successor and communicated the exact tradition to him orally. Nothing at all was written down.

When it came time for the penultimate Hierophant to die there was no initiate suitable within the 'church' to whom he could communicate his secret. So he chose a Priest of Mithras, a religion which was then in its heyday throughout the Roman Empire. And to him he entrusted the revelation of the Eleusinian Mysteries, naming him at the same time as the new Hierophant. Upon the death of the Priest of Mithras, the last Hierophant, the Eleusinian Mysteries were forever lost. And the last high priest, like some dinosaur that lived beyond its time, died with his words, unspoken, unknown.

So much for the hard story. There is no obvious connection between this legend and the cards designed by Gringonneur and Bembo for the two earliest Tarot decks. But even if these early artists regarded the card as The Pope there are still reasons for considering it as being, as well, The Hierophant. When the Roman Catholic Church took over from paganism it modelled, sensibly, many of its institutions upon those of the old religion. Thus providing for its worshippers a thread of continuity between the old dispensation and the new.

The mystery religions of the Mediterranean, with their worship of the Mother Goddess (The Triple Goddess) and their priesthoods based on Hermes/Thoth were a prime source of inspiration for the early Church Fathers and, presumably, for Christ, himself. And another lesser source of inspiration would have been the sun-worshipping druids of Europe and Britain. For by this time most of Europe, like Judaea, was part of the Roman Empire; and there would have been some interchange of ideas and beliefs.

These mystery religions, whether solar or maternal in foundation were each presided over by a high priest, a final authority in matters of faith. And so, Christ, in St. Matthew, Chapter 16, Verses 18 and 19, says: 'And I say also unto thee, That thou art Peter, and upon this rock I will build my Church; and the gates of hell shall not prevail against it. And I will give unto thee the keys of the kingdom of heaven: and whatsoever thou shalt bind on earth shall be bound in heaven: and whatsoever thou shalt loose on earth shall be loosed in heaven.' Which authority is cited by the Catholic Church for considering Peter, and the apostolic succession of popes which followed him, to be Pope of the Roman Catholic Church as well as Bishop of Rome. His function being, essentially, the same as that of The Hierophant; and the doctrine which confirms him being one which most of the old religions would have incorporated in some form.

So the new mystery religion, Christianity, was born, and with it a new high priest. The Pope. The old mystery religion, that of Eleusis and Ephesus and Stonehenge, lingered on for a few centuries and then was largely forgotten.

Or rather, the form of the religion was forgotten. The substance of it: life after death, embodied in the legends of Isis, Demeter and the sun god (Llew or Lugh), was itself resurrected in the new religion as The Risen Christ.

Perhaps this, then, is the meaning of the card: He is The Pope and The Hierophant: both of them The High Priest of the Religion of the Resurrection. Whether the resurrection involved is that of The Crucified, of the Beloved of the Mother Goddess or of the Sun, doesn't matter much. It is the Phoenix.

Design

Gringonneur:	A seated pope, bearing the keys of Saint Peter, flanked by two seated figures, perhaps cardinals
Bembo:	Seated, his right hand raised in benediction
Swiss:	Jupiter, seated and weary. His eagle is on the sand before him. As with the Papess this card is a substitution to spare the feelings of the Church
Insight:	Seated in front of two lotus-topped pillars. His left hand holds a staff terminating in a triple cross, his right is raised in blessing. Two monks (again, perhaps cardinals) petition him
Marseille:	The same
Italian:	Similar, but hand on breast
Wirth:	Similar to Marseille
Waite:	Similar to the traditional design; but with the following changes: the garments of the monks are patterned, one with red roses, one with white lilies. The pillars are decorated in a pomegranate (or grape) motive. A 'W' device surmounts the crown.

129

B.O.T.A.:	As Waite, but lacking the 'W' atop the crown. And the throne bears devices indicative of the winged sun or Taurus the Bull
Aquarian:	The pope seen wearing a stylized version of the triple crown. In the left foreground are the crossed Keys of St. Peter. In the right foreground is the Papal Cross.

Crowley: The Hierophant, seated. His throne is decorated with elephants' heads. Behind him partially around him is a bull. At the four corners of the card are the four Evangelical Beasts of the Apocalypse: the Angel, the Eagle, the Bull and the Lion. In his right hand he carries a rod terminating in a triple circle which should probably be regarded as a combination of the Holy Trinity, the Keys, the Triple Cross and the Phallus. The Crowley deck is frequently ambiguous in its meanings (deliberately so). For example, regard the 'benediction' of the card: the forefinger and middle finger of The Hierophant's *left* hand extended *downward* in a gesture which totally reverses the normal meaning of the card. That same gesture has an even stronger demotic meaning now than it possibly did when Crowley designed the card. At the Hierophant's feet is a standing figure of Isis (?) bearing in her left hand a bow or crescent moon, in her right, a staff. Behind his head is a pattern of nails derived from the Kabbalistic value of the card. On the breast of the Hierophant is an upright pentagram in which is inscribed a running figure

New: Retitled, 'Speaker'. A naked figure standing on a narrow land bridge over turbulent water. In his right hand he holds up a dark circle. In his left, a golden key. His heart is visible in splendour. From his mouth lightnings fork. In back of him a volcano erupts

Interpretation

Case: Vau, meaning nail or hook. Hearing is the sense attributed to Vau, and particularly the interior sense of hearing. Triumphant and eternal intelligence. Taurus ruled by Venus, the Moon exalted. The Voice of the Hierophant giving verbal form to the Vision of the Fool. Revelation, (with the implication of that which is *not* revealed, as well). Latent powers and energies, secretiveness and reserve, the powers of the subconcious, memory and recollection in their highest manifestation. Red-orange. C sharp or B Flat. Case gives us a definition for Hierophant, 'revealer of sacred things'. Intuition as a subconscious response to reason

Christian: The master of the Arcana or occult intelligence

Crowley: Nail, Taurus/Earth, Earth ruled by Venus and the Moon, Triumphal or Eternal One, The Hierophant, Red-Orange, Apis, Osiris, Shiva (Sacred Bull), gives success in Hatha Yoga, Asana and Prana-yama, Venus, the Bull as Cherub of Earth, the Mallow, the Topaz. His weapon in magic is the labour of preparation. His perfume is storax. His drug is sugar. His magical power is the secret of physical strength. (As noted under The Emperor, this is probably a confusion and should read, 'The Power of Consecrating Things'.) Amissio. The Magus of the Eternal. The uniting of the Microcosm with the Macrocosm (in the sense of uniting terrestrial and universal worlds). Stubborn strength, toil, endurance, placidity, manifestation, explanation, teaching, goodness of heart, help from superiors, patience, organization, peace

Douglas: Traditional meanings, adding the concept of 'Pontifex' or Bridgemaker, one who links the outer world of the flesh and substance with the inner one of spirit and trans-substantiality

Gray: Traditional, but pointing out that the card shows the linking of man to God through the inner voice. Can indicate openess to new ideas, unconventionality, the inventor, the hippie, possible predisposition to superstition

G. Dawn: The Wisdom and Fountain of Mercy. The Sphere of the Zodiac acting through Taurus upon Jupiter. The Magus of the Eternal Gods. Divine wisdom, manifestation. Explanation, teaching, occult wisdom. Resembling The Magician, The Hermit, and The Lovers in some respects

Grimaud: The occult power of man. A secret revealed, religious or scientific vocation. A delayed project, a late vocation

Huson: Zeus, Kronos, Ouranos. Traditional implications of the card plus possibly an adviser of the Querent's: psychoanalyst, father-confessor, rabbi

Kahn: Traditional emphasizing the teaching propensities of the figure. Additionally someone who can accomplish practical affairs of a mysterious or deceptive manner

Kaplan: General paternal characteristics, in an emotional, sexual

131

and social sense. Orthodoxy. The reversed meanings are exact reversals of these characteristics

Knight: One mediating power from higher to lower levels

Lind: Traditional

Mathers: Mercy, beneficence, kindness, goodness. Over-kindness, weakness, foolish generosity

Mayananda: The exoteric magical method of instruction. The creative will expressed. The dispenser of welfare, well being, riches, political and social virtue

Papus: Breath, The ram, March. The universal life

Sadhu: Enlightened will power, active authority

Thierens: Leo. The heart. Sanction in the sense of inner consent rather than outer law. Self-centredness and natural authority

Ussher: Aries, the sacrificial ram. (Thus, Ussher incorporates ideas of the king as an annual sacrifice, and, by extension, a scapegoat.) The codifier to the source of power. (The Emperor.) The priest seen as one of two media of Truth, Art and Religion. Ussher's suggestion of sacrificial ram and thus the connection between the priest (as killer) and the king (as annual sacrifice) which would seem to follow from it is ingenious. It not only completely delineates power, both temporal and heavenly or spiritual; but it also indicates the pairing which occurs between the emperor and the high priest. They are bound together, each necessary for the other and ultimately the same figure, just as the papess and the empress are identical

Waite: The ruling power of external religion, the power of the keys, exoteric orthodox doctrine and the outer life which leads to the doctrine. The sum of theology in its most rigid forms but also all things that are righteous and sacred. The channel of institutionalized (as distinct from natural) grace. Marriage, alliance, captivity, servitude, mercy and goodness, inspiration, the man to whom the Querent has recourse. Society, good understanding, overkindness, weakness

Suggested: High Priest of the Mysteries, exoteric and esoteric. The last high priest

The Lovers

Gringonneur:	Three pairs of lovers, promenading. The central pair appear to be quarrelling. In the heavens are two Cupids taking aim with bows and arrows
Bembo:	Cupid, blindfolded, standing on a pedestal. Before him is a pair of lovers, probably Francesco Sforza and Bianca Maria Visconti, the lady for whom these cards were designed. 'Love' in this card and in the previous version refers specifically to 'Courtly Love', a concept which owes its origin to Provençal poetry of the twelfth century and the works of the Roman writer, Ovid. From these sources it develops in the writing of Boccaccio and Margaret of Navarre. The themes are literally 'Courtly': the books were to be read at royal courts. Not surprisingly a disproportionately large number of the characters were noble
Swiss:	Two lovers, Cupid aiming from the heavens; and the scene observed by an old man leaning on a staff
Insight:	A young man, apparently choosing between an older and a younger woman. Cupid, again taking aim, is here set against the sun in glory
Marseille:	As Insight
Italian:	As Insight; but with Cupid blindfolded
Wirth:	As above
Waite:	An angel blessing Adam and Eve. Eve stands before the Tree of the Knowledge of Good and Evil, on which is wrapped the smiling snake. Adam stands before a tree of flames. (The flame design reappears in Card 15, The Devil.)
B.O.T.A.:	As Waite
Aquarian:	Two lovers shown with iris flowers in bud
Crowley:	A king and queen join in marriage before an arch-druidical figure whose hands are raised over them in blessing. She wears the crown of Isis, he, a traditional king's crown. They are attended by two naked boys, one black carrying a club, and one white carrying flowers. The Queen offers a chalice with a dove upon it with her left hand. The king holds in his left hand a spear. Their right hands are joined. Below is a winged egg, wrapped round with a snake. Below right, an

133

The Chariot, *Waite Tarot*

eagle. Below left, a lion. Both of these heraldic animals are plainly laughing

New: Retitled, 'Unity'. A man and woman on the periphery of a circle, hands and feet just touching. Within the circle is ocean and two fish (dolphins?). Two ladders: one white, one brown: at either side. Moon at top shown in all four quarters. At the bottom the following , left to right: sword, pentagram, ripe corn, an ibis standing upon a tortoise, and a pear tree

Interpretation

Case: Zain, Hebrew letter meaning 'sword' or 'weapon'. Thus diversity, contrast, antithesis, distinction, discrimination, perception, acuteness, sharpness, etc. Smelling is the sense attributed. Gemini ruled by Mercury. Orange, D natural. Disposing intelligence

Christian: The two roads. The struggle between the passions and conscience

Crowley: Sword. Gemini. Air. Saturn and Mercury ruling air. Disposing one. Various twin deities: in Egyptian mythology, the twin Merti, Castor and Pollux, Apollo the Diviner. The magpie. Orchids, hybrids. Alexandrite, Tourmaline, Iceland Spar. His weapon is the Tripod. His perfume is wormwood. His drugs are ergot and those used to produce abortions. His powers are those of being in two or more places at the same time and prophecy. Albus. The Children of the Voice. The Oracle of the Mighty Gods. The Brothers or Lovers. Analysis followed by synthesis. Openness to inspiration, intuition, intelligence, second sight, childishness, frivolity, thoughtfulness divorced from practical consideration, indecision, self-contradiction, union in a shallow degree with others, instability, contradiction, triviality, the highbrow

Douglas: Choice or discrimination, the traditional meanings, or the failure thereof

Gray: Traditional meanings

G. Dawn: The understanding of beauty and production of beauty and sovereignty. Saturn acting through Gemini upon Sol. The Children of the Voice Divine. The Oracles of the Mighty Gods. Inspiration (passive and in some cases mediumistic). Motive, power and action arising from inspiration and impulse

135

Grimaud:	The thought of physical love. Card of union, marriage. Many unions, perhaps, thus infidelity. A choice to be made
Huson:	Choice; but also a possible change in someone's lovelife
Kahn:	Love, love affairs, divorce, dissatisfaction, choice generally
Kaplan:	Choice, sacred versus profane love, unhappy loves, necessity for trial and testing
Knight:	Nothing
Lind:	Virtue versus vice
Mathers:	Wise dispositions, proof, trials surmounted, unwise plans, failure when put to the test
Mayananda:	He who is enamoured. More than choosing. By seeing the central figure transforms himself and what he sees, as distinct from that kind of seeing which is *perception*, where that which is seen is clearly distinct from that which sees
Papus:	Vau, the Eye, all that relates to light and brilliancy. The Bull. Reunion, antagonism, with all their consequences. The choice between submitting to the passions and conquering them and becoming an initiate
Sadhu:	Vau, an eye and an ear. The enamoured one. Choice or decision
Thierens:	Virgo. The nervous system and everything acting as an organ. The eye included as an organ. The law of duality, of 'good' and 'evil'
Ussher:	Wisdom versus pleasure. Pleasure being the likely winner as the choice is up to a youth and pleasure is appropriate for his age
Waite:	The card of human love, exhibited as part of the way, the truth and the life. A mystery of the covenant and Sabbath. Attraction, love, beauty. Trials overcome. Failure, foolish designs. Marriage frustrated and contrarieties of all kinds
Suggested:	The choice between mother and wife, wealth and love, age and youth, wisdom and passion

The Chariot

From Roman times it was customary to exhibit in triumphal parades the captives and spoil of conquest in Germany and Gaul and Britain. The idea being that the more magnificent the spectacle, the more political bonus points would accrue to the general, who would probably cash them in when he tried to become Emperor. Even then the tradition was of incredible age. According to Curtius, Plutarch and Diodorus, Alexander the Great made a triumphal progress through Carmania (now Persia) in a sort of double-sized chariot, filled with his intimate friends and loaded with flutes and food and wine. It is supposed that Alexander did this, if it happened, in imitation of the Dionysiac revels or triumphal marches of Dionysus through Asia after his conquest of India. Thriambus (Triumph) was one of Dionysus' titles. And, from there the connection between Triumph (Dionysus) and Triumph (Alexander) and Triumph (Roman) rises. The tradition continues down through the Tarot cards and Trionfi to such varied forms of expression as the 137 Woodcut designs by Hans Burgkmair and others for a projected triumph of the Emperor Maximilian the Great. A more grotesque example of the triumphal chariot is the funeral car of the Duke of Wellington. Which may provide an added dimension to the card

The legendary significance of the chariot probably lies in the chance that it gives every beholder, whatever his circumstances, to win. A very human card and possibly connected in meaning with The Wheel of Fortune

Design

Gringonneur: What appears to be the statue of a warrior, possibly the actual warrior, drawn in a triumphal car by two spirited horses

Bembo: A seated empress in a chariot drawn by two winged white horses. She holds the orb in her left hand

Swiss: Divided in two parts. In the upper, a king is looking out from under a canopy. In the lower, two horses pull an empty chariot in two directions at once

Insight: A king borne in a triumphal car. He is armoured and his shoulder plates are fashioned to resemble the Urim and Thumim

Marseille: As above, but one horse is red, the other blue

Italian: As Insight

Wirth: As Insight; but with the following changes: The triumphal car is drawn by sphinxes, the canopy is embellished with stars, the winged solar disc appears on the chariot

Waite: Similar to Wirth, except: The lingam and yoni appears on the front of the chariot. On the king's breast is a radiant square. An eight-pointed star on the crown

B.O.T.A.: Similar to Waite, except: The king's crown incorporates

137

several pentagrams instead of the hexagram. The device on his breast is a square figured with three Tau Crosses. His sceptre, in his right hand as traditional, ends in a variant of the lemniscate combined with the lingam and yoni

Aquarian: Wearing the shoulderplates, a pentagram upon his head

Crowley: A fully armoured knight (including closed vizor) with a rapidly rotating disc. On his head is a crab. The chariot is drawn by four fabulous beasts

New: Retitled: 'Victorious One'. A warrior with one sandal leads a gentle white beast and a savage dark one away from a chariot. Over his head flies an Eagle with arrows in both claws. His unshod foot is winged. A pair of dice in the foreground shows three faces on each die. Any two corresponding faces total seven. Behind him a flock of birds bearing a curtain in their beaks and containing wild beasts, possibly wolves or horses

Interpretation

Case: Cheth, meaning field and the fence enclosing it. Speech. Intelligence of the House of Influence. Cancer ruled by the Moon. Jupiter exalted. The breast, the chest (a fence of bones) and the stomach. Psychic, receptive sign. Tenacious memory. Orange-yellow. D sharp or E flat. Victory

Christian: Zain, meaning sword or weapon. The domination of spirit over nature, the priesthood and the empire, the submission of the elements and forces of nature to intelligence and the labours of man. Go towards the future with courage reinforced by the knowledge of doing right

Crowley: Cheth, fence. Cancer, water. Mars ruling water. Intelligence of the House of Influence. The Chariot. Amber, Kephra, Apollo the Charioteer, Mercury. The Crab, the Turtle, the Sphinx. The Lotus. His weapon is the Furnace. His perfume is Onycha, one of the ingredients of an incense burned in mosaic ritual. His drug is watercress. His power that of casting enchantments. Populus and Via. The Child of the Powers of the Waters. The Lord of the Triumph of Light. Cancer, the sign into which the Sun moves at the summer solstice. Triumph, victory, hope, memory, digestion, violence in maintaining traditional ideas, the 'diehard', ruthlessness, lust of destruction, obedience, faithfulness, authority under authority

Douglas: Traditional

Gray:	Traditional
G. Dawn:	Understanding acting upon severity. Saturn acting through Cancer upon Mars. Child of the Power of the Waters. Lord of the Triumph of Light. Triumph, victory, health, success. They may not be stable or enduring
Grimaud:	The material currents which carry man along. Unexpected news, conquest. News spread abroad by word of mouth, a timely good word, slander. Bad news, a card which is not strong itself but asserts authority upon other cards
Huson:	Struggle. The outcome may be determined, ranging from victory to disaster, according to the surrounding cards
Kahn:	A card of balance and imbalance, accomplishment and failure, stamina and weakness
Kaplan:	Trouble or adversity, possibly in the past. Generally traditional
Knight:	Nothing
Lind:	The Magus, having apparently completely mastered his animal pasions, is now ready to move ahead to the second stage of development. No indication from this card on its own as to whether the outcome will be successful or not
Mathers:	Triumph, victory, overcoming obstacles, overthrown, conquered by obstacles at the last moment
Mayananda:	The chariot of the incarnation. That which is fixed and concrete, Adam Kadmon, the higher self or reincarnating aspect of the ego. It cannot presently be said that any thoroughly satisfactory ideas about this card have been promulgated
Papus:	A conqueror advancing in a cubical chariot. The man who has vanquished and directed the elementary forces
Sadhu:	Victory
Thierens:	Libra, the self embodied, marriage, contract, body and bodily existence, organization, achievement, cooperation
Ussher:	War, ruthless power, will in application, the conquering Sun of May
Waite:	Triumph in the mind. Triumph over nature. Succour, providence, war, triumph, presumption, vengeance, trouble, riot, quarrel, dispute, litigation, defeat

Strength

The early cards show a woman opening or closing the jaws of a lion or, in some cases, a male figure (possibly Hercules) beating a lion with a club. During the Middle Ages the lion was an alchemical symbol for the sun, for gold, and for sulphur. In a sixteenth century alchemical text which is presented as a dream, the dreamer is required to subdue a lion in order to be admitted to the followship of a group of scholars. At first, he approaches the lion (an old one) and attempts to stroke it. Then he wrestles with it and eventually kills it. The scholars approve his effort but give him the added task of restoring the lion to life. By now it has been dissected into red blood and a large quantity of white bone. Other medieval connotations would be as the Lion of St Mark, one of the Apocalyptic Beasts or as the Cherub of Fire, and yet another would be as Samson or Androcles

Design

Gringonneur: A seated woman breaking a pillar

Bembo: Hercules armed with a club, beating a lion which appears to be trying to slink away, its tail between its legs

Swiss: Hercules with a lion. Hercules appears to be wrestling with it and has discarded his club. Conceivably a reference to Androcles and the Lion

Insight: A woman, wearing a hat with the lemniscate incorporated into its brim, opening the jaws of a lion

Marseille: The same

Italian: The same

Wirth: The same

Waite: As above, except that she is closing the lion's jaws. She is crowned with flowers and the lemniscate hovers above her head. A garland around her waist

B.O.T.A.: As Waite, except that she is again opening the jaws. The flowers round her waist are connected with a garland round the neck of the lion thus implying some relationship other than domination pure and simple

Aquarian: A stern knight with his dog. A motif of arrowheads or spearpoints

Crowley: Retitled 'Lust'. A woman riding a seven-headed beast. A representation of Crowley's scarlet woman, Babylon the Great. (Rev. 17, v. 3-6)

New: Retitled, 'Deliverer'. A woman is being sacrificed by fire before a lion over whose head hovers the lemniscate, also in fire. Left, a serpent rising from a cubical box. Right, a man drinking what appears to be blood from a chalice

Interpretation

Case: Strength. Teth, meaning snake. Serpent power or cosmic electricity, regeneration, reincarnation, and immortality. Taste is the sense, digestion the function. Leo, ruled by the Sun, Neptune exalted. Yellow, E natural. Intelligence of the Secret of all spiritual activities. The titles 'Strength' or 'Force' allude to the fiery life power which is the source of all human action

Christian: Cheth. The Tamed Lion: Strength. The principle of all strength, spiritual or material. Moral or organic force

Crowley: Serpent. Leo, fire. The Sun and Jupiter ruling fire. Intelligence of all the activities of the spiritual Being. Strength. Yellow, greenish. Sekhet, Basht and others. Horus. Vishnu in his Nara-Singh avatar. Demeter borne by lions. Venus repressing the fire of Vulcan. The lion, Cherub of Fire. The Sunflower, The Catseye, His Weapon is preliminary discipline. His perfume is Olibanum. His vegetable drugs those used for expelling wind and tonics. His power is that of Taming Wild Beasts. Fortuna Major and Fortuna Minor. The Daughter of the Flaming Sword. Lust. Crowley changed the name of this card to Lust to imply not only strength but the joy of strength exercised. Vigour and the rapture of vigour. It would seem that the attribution is introduced with some mischief aforethought and should be so regarded. Other meanings: Courage, strength, energy and action, a grand passion, resort to magick, the use of magickal power

Douglas: Spiritual strength, courage enough to take risks, defeat of unworthy impulses. Reconciliation with external or internal enemies. The opposites of any of these

Gray: Spiritual strength, much as Douglas. The negative possibilities include domination by the material, fear of the unknown. Abuse of power

G. Dawn: Fortitude. Mercy tempering severity. The glory of strength. Jupiter acting through Leo upon Mars. The Daughter of the

Flaming Sword, Leader of the Lion. Courage or strength. Power not arrested as in the act of judgement, but passing on to further action, sometimes obstinacy

Grimaud: Force. The mind can always dominate matter. Events overcome by willpower. The situation mastered with right on your side. Events or people overcome you, you become the victim of superior forces

Huson: A card providing good counsel: a time to be firm, courageous, steadfast. Negative possibilities are stubbornness or obstinacy

Kahn: Hanging tight. Consolidation of energy, coming to a reasonable assessment of oneself in relation to the world. Grasp on reality, a workable alternative, truthful direction, discovering of centre, the sacred urge, help from friends or loved ones. Negative meanings include: Decadence, addiction, disaster, friend or lover who will cause harm or unhappiness, loss of reputation, perversity, putrefaction, deprivation

Kaplan: Traditional meanings of this card combined with many of the traditional implications of the pope and emperor

Knight: A test of what has happened so far in personal evolution. Acceptance of both fact and responsibility

Lind: The enchantress. Lind notes that Papus gives Mars as the astrological affinity of this card. Case gives Leo. Several others have given Aries or the Sun. After pointing out the futility of trying to force astrological attributions onto the Tarot he gives his own choice, Virgo. The reconcilement of two (or from the above) many sides of ones nature

Mathers: Power, might, force, strength, fortitude. Abuse of power, overbearingness, want of fortitude

Mayananda: Dichotomy resolved. Leo with the Sun exalted. Generation (the Sun or Leo) kept in exact balance with disintegration (lunar forces)

Papus: Strength and vitality

Sadhu: Kaph. Mars. Force. The spirit of inner strength, will exercised

Thierens: Aquarius. Union and friendship with that which we have mastered, with people who are able to respond to our

The Ace of Pentacles, *Schaffhouse Tarot*

emanations of thought or to whose emanations we are able to respond

Ussher: Renewed youth or legendary feats. Mars. Wisdom as power, weakness as strength, innocence as generative virtue

Waite: Innocence and strength residing in contemplation. Fortitude connected with the divine mystery of union. Power, energy, action, courage, magnanimity, complete success, honours. Despotism, abuse of power, weakness, discord, disgrace

Suggested: Great danger

The Hermit

Design

Gringonneur: A hermit carrying an hourglass

Bembo: A hunchback carrying an hourglass

Swiss: A monk carrying a lantern

Insight: The same

Marseille: The same

Italian: The same

Wirth: The same except that he shields the light with his cloak. Additionally, there is a nearby snake in the act of striking, though not at the hermit

Waite: As traditional, except that the light is from a hexagram-star within the lantern

B.O.T.A.: As Waite

Aquarian: As Waite, except that the star is eight pointed

Crowley: As Waite, except that the star is sixteen pointed. In his right hand the hermit carries an egg wrapped with a snake. He is accompanied by a three headed dog (Cerberus, guardian of the Underworld). He walks through a field of ripe wheat. Another symbol in the card is indecipherable in my deck

New: A blindfolded man prays to a volcano or possibly to a woman fleeing. She abandons his nakedness, an open book, and a bouquet of flowers as she hurries toward a distant city

144

Case: The Hermit. Yod, meaning the hand of man. The open hand. Touch, coition. Virgo ruled by Mercury and Mercury exalted. Intelligence of will. Self-training in the right interpretation of experience, in concentration, in the manipulation of subconsciousness leading to eventual union with God, that is, I am

Christian: Thela. The Veiled Lamp: Prudence. Silence is golden

Crowley: Hand. Virgo, Earth. Earth ruled by Venus and the Moon. Intelligence of will. Green, yellowish. Isis as Virgin. Attis, Ceres, Adonis. Any solitary person or animal, a virgin or anchorite. The snowdrop, lily or narcissus. The Peridot. His weapons are the lamp and wand, except for its virile force. The bread. His perfume is narcissus, his drugs are all anaphrodisiacs. His magical powers are invisibility, parthenogenesis and initiation. Conjunction. The Prophet of the Eternal, the Magus of the Voice of Power. Illumination from within, secret impulse from within, practical plans based upon inner knowledge, retirement from participation in current events

Douglas: The start of the journey towards spiritual perfection. A councillor, retreat from the world, a need for caution, patience, discretion and silence. Refusal to listen, foolhardy reliance on ones own resources, stupid rejection of sagacity. Suspicion of others' motives or of innovation.

Gray: Traditional interpretation of the card as that of The Hermit, either the Querent or someone instructing him. Negative readings include the tendency on the part of the Querent to remain an eternal Peter Pan

G. Dawn: The mercy of beauty, the magnificence of sovereignty, The glory of strength. Jupiter acting through Virgo upon the Sun. The Magus of the Voice of Light. Wisdom sought for and obtained from above. Divine inspiration (but active, as opposed to that in The Lovers). With the Hierophant and the Magician one of the three Magi among the mystical cards

Grimaud: The inner life. Secret which shall be revealed. Great delay in the revelation of a secret

Huson: Saturn, bringer of old age, the god who confers longevity as well. Planning, manipulation or delays caused by unreasonable caution, fear, stubbornness, opression or even deceit

145

Kahn:	The summit, perspective, circumspection, preparation, precautionary measures, care, isolation, separation, solitude, correct choice, a man beyond desire for personal gain who has the vision to benefit the world, awareness, scrutiny, a corner on the market. A rogue, a wise man in action in the world, an arch-criminal, the search, the hunt, the quest
Kaplan:	Inner wisdom or truth and the search for them. Negative indications are those of immaturity, rashness, overprudence or total lack of prudence
Knight:	The Quest of the Holy Grail, linking spirit with individuality. The focusing point of the whole being of man in manifestation. The hidden, cosmic mind of man which serves to guide and inspire the soul in all its ways
Lind:	The realization of a balance between material and spiritual. Necessity to continue working to maintain that balance and to progress
Mathers:	Prudence, caution, deliberation, over-prudence, timorousness, fear
Mayananda:	The House of the Master . . . 'Where I am, there you may be.' Very important to initiatory experience
Papus:	Teth, a roof, a place of safety, a protection. Safety and protection ensured by wisdom or circumspection
Sadhu:	Teth, Leo. Enlightenment in all three worlds. Protectors, initiation, prudence
Thierens:	Sagittarius. Ideas, perspectives, spiritual or moral influences. Teachers, legal authorities and guides
Ussher:	Teth, a serpent or twisted power
Waite:	A card of attainment, 'Where I am, there you may be.' Prudence, circumspection. Treason, dissimulation, roguery, corruption. Concealment, disguise, policy, fear, unreasoned caution
Suggested:	Loneliness, pilgrimage, a teacher, inner wisdom. Concentration of total faculties on one small area in order to force growth. That which meditates, which is observed meditation or which observes meditation

The Wheel of Fortune

A description of the concepts embodied in this card occurs in *The Death of King Arthur*, written by an unknown French writer in about A.D. 1230-1235. In the account King Arthur is dreaming that he is seated atop a high wheel, where he has been placed by a beautiful woman. She asks him what he can see; and he replies that he can see the entire world. At which point she pushes him to the ground, saying that earthly pride being what it is, everyone has to fall.

The wheel, as it occurs in Arthur's dream, is an exact description of a modern day Ferris Wheel, and is very similar to the concept of the Wheel of Fortune as it appears on the cards.

An important element in representations of the Wheel of Fortune is the legend *Regnabo, Regno, Regnavi, Sum sine regno*. Which, translated from the Latin, is: 'I shall reign, I reign, I reigned, I am without reign.' And the context within which this legend is displayed (frequently animals or monsters dressed as humans) is usually sufficient to indicate the artist's contempt for earthly glory. In other words, *Sic transit gloria mundi*. So the element of savage mockery in this card harks back to The Emperor and The Chariot

Design

Gringonneur: Fortune standing astride her wheel. In her right hand she holds a sceptre, in her left, an orb. Through the centre of the wheel a country scene and castle are visible

Bembo: Fortune blindfolded, seated in the centre of her wheel. At the top is a cherub with an ass's ears and the legend, *Regno*. Two other figures, one ascending, and one descending, bear the legends: *Regnabo* and *Regnavi*. At the bottom there is an old man, on hands and knees, with the legend, *Sum sine regno*.

Swiss: Blind Fortune, naked except for strategic drapery, cranking a wheel which appears to stand on the edge of a precipice. Beneath the wheel is a blooming rose tree. At the top of the wheel are a young couple, the man blissfully ignorant of danger, the girl looking over her shoulder in alarm. At the lower right is the falling figure of a man who has been turned off

Insight: Three monkeys riding on a wheel: one crowned on top, one rising, one falling. Clockwise movement of the wheel

Marseille: The same crowned monkey, with a sword. The direction of the wheel is counterclockwise

Italian: A crowned monkey with one wing, standing astride a wheel.

147

A dog or wolf ascending at three o'clock on the wheel. (According to tradition this figure is Typhon)

Wirth: A wheel, surmounted by a sphinx armed with a sword. The base of the Wheel rests in a boat. Around it twine two snakes, symbol of Hermes. Ascending the wheel at three o'clock is a dog bearing the caduceus. Descending, at nine o'clock, is a demon with a pitchfork. Wirth apparently intended these figures to signify Anubis and Typhon

Waite: A wheel, surmounted by a smiling sphinx, holding a drawn sword over her left shoulder. On the wheel are the letters, T-A-R-O; and, interspersed between these letters, are the Hebrew letters Yod-Heh-Vau-Heh, or Jahweh, Jehovah. Tetragrammaton, the unmentionable name of God. Additionally the symbols for mercury, sulphur, salt and water (Aquarius). At the four corners of the card are the four Apocalyptic Beasts, the Cherubs of the Four Elements. On the right, Anubis rising. On the left, Typhon descending in the form of a snake. (Anubis is associated with Hermes Psychopomp)

B.O.T.A.: As Waite

Aquarian: Similar to Waite except that both beasts are rising and both are snakes. A winged bull and winged lion, the two other apocalyptic beasts missing. The sphinx and Anubis are not represented

Crowley: Typhon descending at the right of the wheel. The symbols of royal authority in his hands. The Ape of Thoth ascending at left. The sphinx, with drawn sword, ignoring everything from her perch atop the wheel

New: Retitled, 'Royal Maze'. A black horse and white horse holding up a circle divided into a pattern of circles and squares. Additionally the following: A lemniscate, a torch, a sailboat, a cup filled with blood or wine. Three interlocked rings at the top of the card

Interpretation

Case: Kaph, a curve. Wealth and poverty. Jupiter ruling Sagittarius and Pisces, exalted in Cancer. Violet. B flat or A sharp. Intelligence of conciliation or rewarding intelligence of those who seek. Rotation, cyclicity, sequence, whirling motion, simultaneous ascent and descent, evolution and involution, fortune, destiny, chance, fate, necessity, probability

Christian:	The active principle that animates all beings, ruling authority, good or evil fortune. 'Remember, son of earth, that ability depends on the will; if your will is to be accomplished, you must be daring; and to dare successfully you must be able to keep silence until the moment comes for action. To possess knowledge and power, the will must be patient; to remain on the heights of life—if you succeed in attaining them—you must first have learned to plumb with steady gaze vast depths'
Crowley:	Palm. Jupiter. Intelligence of conciliation. Wheel of Fortune. Violet. Amoun-Ra. The left ear. Brahma, Indra. Zeus. Jupiter or Pluto. The Eagle. Hyssop, oak, poplar, fig. Amethyst, lapis lazuli. His weapon is the sceptre. His perfume is saffron, all generous odours. His drug is cocaine. His magical power is that of acquiring political and other ascendancy. The square and rhombus. Lord of the forces of life. Fortune. Attributed to Jupiter, planet of greater fortune. Kaph. Not just good fortune but also luck, the incalculable factor. Change of fortune, generally good as the fact of consultation implies anxiety or discontent
Douglas:	The traditional meaning of chance, generally seen as external to the Querent
Gray:	To the traditional meaning of blind fate, Eden Gray adds the possible reading of the law of Karma, what you do comes home to roost
G. Dawn:	The mercy and magnificence of victory. Jupiter acting through Jupiter direct upon Venus. The lord of the forces of life. Good fortune and happiness (within bounds); but sometimes also a kind of intoxication with success, if the cards near this bear this out
Grimaud:	Evolution. Events moving towards change. The outcome is inevitably happy. Possibly the transformation will be made with difficulty
Huson:	Nothing
Kahn:	Stability, ease, grace, benefit, money, control of life force, earnings gained in a compatible manner or with a minimum of effort or by luck. Hard work, poverty, difficulty, day-to-day existence
Kaplan:	Traditional
Knight:	Within the Querent, the pattern of destiny evolving

149

Lind:	The working out of Karma
Mathers:	Good fortune, success, unexpected luck. Ill fortune, failure, unexpected ill-luck
Mayananda:	The creative essence in motion
Papus:	Yod, the forefinger extended as a sign of command. The idea of command or supremacy. The idea of duration and of the eternal action of time
Sadhu:	Yod, testament in which are flowing all mental principles and currents. The mill of transformation which pulls us implacably in a painful process which is to refine us. Fortune. Virgo
Thierens:	Fortune, good or bad. Capricorn. The authorities to which the querent is subject but also his own actions, deeds, manifestations, and the position in the world which he occupies. Karma in the strict sense. Fortune. The fruits of former words
Ussher:	Chance and fate, end and beginning
Waite:	The perpetual motion of a fluidic universe and the flux of human life. Destiny, fortune, success, elevation, luck, felicity, increase, abundance, superfluity.
Suggested:	The relation between this figure and the solar wheel has not, I think, been commented upon elsewhere. It *does* represent the Sun and therefore is connected with the suit of Pentacles as a whole and particularly with the Ace and Six. Who reigns, who reigned, who is to reign and who is without reign

Justice

The blindfolded figure of Justice as it appears in the eleventh card is based on the Greek Titaness, Themis. Statues of her, seated or standing, with sword upraised in one hand and scales of truth in the other, grace porticoes of halls of justice, throughout Europe and America. She was one of the planetary guardians of Jupiter, and also a guardian of the infant Zeus, protecting him from his father, Cronos. She had the gift of prophecy and succeeded Mother Earth at Delphi. Later she resigned the shrine in Apollo's favour. Her worship was probably as a Triple Goddess: Anthea (flowery), Hyperea (being overhead, as in the sense of midsummer), and Pitthea (pine goddess, in whose honour Attis/Adonis would have been annually sacrificed). In her persona as Mother Goddess she corresponds to Isis; and in her capacity as Justice she corresponds to Maat, the Egyptian goddess who was either wife or female equivalent of

Thoth. Both as Themis and as Maat she is concerned with 'weighing' truth. For to the ancients, as well as to our own society, it was something that could be measured, even if light as a feather.

Design

Gringonneur:	Justice seated, scales in left hand, upraised sword in her right
Bembo:	Same
Swiss:	Standing, otherwise same
Insight:	Seated
Marseille:	Seated
Italian:	Seated
Wirth:	Seated
Waite:	Traditional; but with a square device ornamenting her crown and a further square, enclosing a circle, used to fasten her cloak
B.O.T.A.:	Similar to Waite; but the crown is a variant of that of Isis; and the cloak fastening is a Tau Cross
Aquarian:	Similar in all major respects to Waite and Marseille
Crowley:	Justice standing with a drawn sword pointing downward between the scales. The hilt of the sword incorporates lunar motives. In the pans of the scale are, on her right, the Greek letter, alpha; on her left, the Greek letter, omega. The sword is a replica of that previously seen on the Ace of Swords
New:	Retitled, 'Donor'. A woman, drawn sword hanging from around her neck, holds up two pillars, one in either hand. Black in her right hand, white in her left. Two hands coming from the sky above her. Her sword just piercing a heart between her feet

Interpretation

Case:	Lamed, to teach or to instruct. An ox-goad. Its function is work or action (in the sense of the great work). Karma. Libra ruled by Venus, Saturn exalted. Green, F sharp or G flat, faithful intelligence
Christian:	Absolute justice, attraction and repulsion, Man's narrow and fallible justice
Crowley:	Ox Goad, Libra, Air. Saturn and Mercury ruling Air.

151

Faithful intelligence. Justice. Emerals Green. Maat. Yama, Themis, Minos, Aeacus, Rhadamanthus. Vulcan. The elephant. The aloe. The emerald. Her magical weapon is the Cross of Equilibrium. Her perfume is Galbanum. Her drug is tobacco. Her magical powers are those of justice and equilibrium. Puella. The daughter of the lords of truth. The ruler of the balance. Crowley renames the card, adjustment, in *The Book of Thoth* and in the Thoth Tarot. The equilibrium of all things. The feminine counterpart of the Fool. Th e act of adjustment, suspension of action pending decision; lawsuits or prosecutions. Marriage or marriage agreements, treaties

Douglas:	Conscience reminding the conscious mind of the existence of the unconscious. Judgements, arbitration, vindication of truth. Injustice of various kinds, legal tangles, expensive lawsuits
Gray:	Equilibrium through the love of the Great Mother. Justice. Mercy advised and excessive severity contraindicated
G. Dawn:	The severity of beauty and sovereignty. Mars acting through Libra upon Sol. Daughter of the Lord in Truth. The Holder of the Balances. Eternal Justice and Balance. Strength and Force arrested as in Judgement. Legal proceedings, a court of law, a trial at law
Grimaud:	Equilibrium. Trial, rehabilitation, honesty, justice performed, loss, unjust condemnation
Huson:	Advice to weigh a situation carefully. Balance, equilibrium, natural balance, Dharma. An arbitrator. Negatively it is imbalance, bias, prejudice, an unfair or corrupt arbitrator
Kahn:	Cosmic law, means by which man apprehends the universe, occult studies, secret societies, divinatory arts, regulating forces of the universe, Kharma, legal contracts, licenses both practical and mystic, illegal activity, ruthless people, crime
Kaplan:	Traditional meanings plus virginity, violence
Knight:	Karmic adjustment
Lind:	Divine (without the blindfold) Justice. Everything weighed in the balance
Mathers:	Equilibrium, balance, justice. Bigotry, abuse of Justice, Over-severity, inequality, bias

152

Mayananda:	(Nothing)
Papus:	Heth, a field. Cancer. Equilibrium in all its forms
Sadhu:	Balance. Law, Karma
Thierens:	Scorpio. Avenging justice, with its emphasis upon vengeance rather than justice. The faculty of desire, higher and lower. Sexual experience. Occult and psychic experience (where traditionally sex is sublimated). Transmutation. The card of sorrow as well as that of deeper satisfactions. The secret or the hidden
Ussher:	Reason for its own sake, spiritual growth possible, cancer, the equalization of all individual manifestations of will
Waite:	Equity, rightness, probity, executive, triumph of the deserving side. Law, legal complications, bigotry, bias, excessive severity
Suggested:	The complementary card to 10, The Wheel of Fortune. The wheel is the card of fate or luck, random factors that one can do little but roll with. Justice is exactly a card of justice absolute, titanic justice

The Hanged Man

As far as I know Paul Huson and Alfred Douglas were the first to point out the significance of The Hanged Man and his connection with Odin.

In the translation of *The Words of the High One* by Paul B. Taylor and W.H. Auden, from The Elder Edda, there occurs the following:

'Wounded I hung on a wind-swept gallows
For nine long nights,
Pierced by a spear, pledged to Odin,
Offered, myself to myself;
The wisest know not from whence spring
The roots of that ancient rood.

They gave me no bread, they gave me no mead;
I looked down; with a loud cry
I took up runes; from that tree I fell.'

Gallows, rood, and tree are all Yggdrasil, the World Tree, the ash which is rooted in the Underworld and which supports Heaven. Yggdrasil was known as 'Odin's Horse'; and it was Yggdrasil that sheltered the remnant of mankind at the time of Ragnarok, the Twilight of the Gods, when everything else perished.

Yggdrasil means, literally, Yggr's Tree, Yggr being another name for Odin. And from Yggr you get Ogre; and first thing you know it's Jack and the Beanstalk. By custom hanged men were considered to have been sacrificed upon Yggr's Tree (the gallows) to Odin. After death they became members of his band, riding with him in the storms. So the tree is a place of sacrifice, of safety, a gallows, and a place of visionary experience.

In the Edda, Odin is offering himself to himself; there is no suggestion of coercion. At the end of nine nights he descends, having taken up runes, or, in other words, having *learned* runes, words of power

Later in the poem, Odin says, referring to his runes

'I know a twelfth: if a tree bear
    A man hanged in a halter,
I can carve and stain strong runes
That will cause the corpse to speak
    Reply to whatever I ask.'

Necromancy, or divinatory power working through the dead. He is talking about his twelfth rune. The Hanged Man is always the twelfth card of the Major Arcana.

Perhaps coincidence; but The Hanged Man is never shown suffering. He is either expressionless or in the middle of some beatific vision which lights up his face. There is a suggestion of suffering in the sacrifice of Odin; but it is clear that the suffering is voluntary and that it has a purpose; initiation or the acquisition of knowledge.

Hanging featured in another belief in medieval times. The Hand of Glory. Thieves would obtain the hand of a man hanged for murder. They would then either render the hand to tallow and make candles or burn the hand, itself, as a candle. Burning a hand-candle in a house was said to make the thief invisible or to cause the occupants of the house to fall asleep. Thieves were, of course, under the protection of Hermes. And Hermes has been equated with Odin.

So much for the connections between Hermes/Thoth, Odin, and The Hanged Man. They are tenuous, at best; but they embody an explanation of the meaning of the card that makes considerably more sense than has been advanced before.

One further note—in some representations of the Hanged Man his legs form a figure 4—thus relating to the Emperor.

Design

Gringonneur:	A man hanging, by one foot, from a frame. He holds a small but heavy bag in either hand. There is no indication of suffering
Bembo:	Similar, except: his legs are crossed in an informal four, his hands are hidden behind his back and possibly tied, again, no sign of suffering
Swiss:	Similar

154

Insight:	Similar, but smiling
Marseille:	As traditional
Italian:	As above
Wirth:	As above
Waite:	The Hanged Man dangling from a Tau Cross of living trees, his head surrounded by a beatific penumbra
B.O.T.A.:	As Waite, except the older 'U' form for the gallows. Crescent moons decorate his tunic. (These are an adaptation of the pockets on the Marseille Tarot)
Aquarian:	As Waite, except that the cross is a standard design, formed of living wood
Crowley:	The Hanged Man with arms outstretched and nailed, as is one leg. The other leg, by which he hangs, is loosely held by a reversed Ankh, implying an effort of will rather than punishment. A snake wrapped round his leg, near the Ankh. His head haloed (?). Another snake at the bottom of the card
New:	Retitled, 'The Hanging Man'. A man standing, legs astride, sunset or sunrise visible behind him. His left foot upon a castellated tower, his right, braced against a globe on top of another building. From his left arm hangs a naked man, tied by his hands. From his right hangs, reversed, a naked woman. It is not made clear how she hangs. A girdle of living serpents around the central figure's waist. On his chest, the letter 'A'. A red lotus or tulip growing from his head. As he might well be after all this, the man is crying

N.B. It is worth noting that only in the Gringonneur, Swiss, Waite and B.O.T.A. decks is The Hanged Man hanging by his right leg. In the others it is his left

Interpretation

Case:	Mem, literally meaning 'Seas', but generally, water. Neptune, pale blue, G sharp or A flat. Suspended mind
Christian:	The sacrifice. Violent death. The revelation of the law, the teaching of duty, sacrifice
Crowley:	Water. Cold and moist. Stable intelligence. The Hanged Man. Deep blue. Asar as hanged man. Isis, Poseidon, Neptune. Eagle, snake, scorpion. Lotus. All water plants. Beryl or aquamarine. His magical weapons are the Cup and Cross

155

The Ace of Cups, *Schaffhouse Tarot*

of Suffering, the Wine. His perfumes are onycha (one of the perfumes used in incense for mosaic ritual) and myrrh. His drugs are cascara and all purges. His magical powers are the great work, talismans, crystal gazing. His linear figures are those of the watery triplicity. His name is Spirit of the Mighty Waters. The spiritual function of water in the economy of initiation. A baptism which is also a death. Enforced sacrifice, punishment, loss (fatal or voluntary), suffering, defeat, failure, death

Douglas: The ability to adapt to changing circumstances. Flexibility of mind. Willingness to submit oneself to the dictates of the inner self and cast aside practical considerations when the time is right. Wisdom and guidance from the unconscious. Over-reliance on the concrete mind. Materialism. A warning of impending psychic disorder through an inability to accept the reality of the unconscious. An inner struggle ending in defeat

Gray: In spiritual matters . . . wisdom, prophetic power. A pause in one's life, suspended decisions. Self-surrender leads to transformation of personality. Material temptation conquered. Arrogance, preoccupation with the ego, resistance to spiritual influences, absorption in physical matters, wasted efforts, false prophecy

G. Dawn: The severity of splendour. Execution of judgement. Mars acting through water upon Mercury. The Spirit of the Mighty Waters. Enforced sacrifice, punishment, loss. Fatal and not voluntary. Suffering generally

Grimaud: That which is up is like that which is down. (A variant on 'As above, so below'.) A bad card, always indicating the abandonment of something, destruction, renunciation, uncertain projects. A card of second rank which has no strength. When enclosed by others the influence is destroyed. It can also mean bound by fate. Possible success on a plan of sentimental nature, but a doubtful success without enjoyment or pleasure. Lack of frankness, reticence, hidden plan, hypocrisy

Huson: Wisdom, often occult and intuitive, attained through sacrifice. Psychological constriction. An ill-conceived sacrifice or a loosening of strictures. The turning point in the psychic life and coming to grips with the unconscious. The means by which the descent into the underworld is made

157

Kahn:	A person of high spirituality, sacrifice of one's own interests for a spiritual or artistic gain, suspension of will, annihilation of being thereby becoming wedded to the primal will, gate to awareness of universal truth and cosmic reality, the first stage of unfolding, intuitive experience, timing, survival through intuition and faith, priest, prophet, magician, doing the bidding of higher forces, slow reconstruction of attitudes and awareness, keeper of the temple. Tact, reserve, finesse, escape from danger, ability to talk oneself out of trouble, tactful handling of enemies, sudden disappearance, disguise, false pretext, pretending, blending into one's surroundings in order to escape detection, a criminal who escapes, winning confidence through tact
Kaplan:	His face expresses repentance rather than suffering. Life in suspension, reversal of both mind and one's way of life. Transition, abandonment, renunciation, changing of life's forces, sacrifice, readjustment, regeneration, rebirth, improvement, sacrifice which may have to be undertaken in an effort toward a goal which may not be reached. Lack of sacrifice, unwillingness to make necessary effort, failure to give oneself, preoccupation with ego, false prophecy
Knight:	Utterly unselfish cooperative effort for the good of the whole, the exchange of something for something better, the values of the higher world are the reverse of the lower
Lind:	Voluntary sacrifice, the incarnation of spirit in matter, the quickening of nature by an exterior spiritual force. The winter solstice
Mathers:	Self-sacrifice, sacrifice, devotion. Bound: selfishness. Unbound: partial sacrifice
Mayananda:	Baptism and transition, sacrifice in the sense of making holy or whole. Scorpio. Evolution. The dark night of the soul as an inevitable prelude to direct vision of the sun
Papus:	Lamed, the arm, a sign of expansive movement. Punishment or violent death, voluntary and involuntary. Libra. Absolute submission to the divine. Equilibrated force
Sadhu:	Lamed, an arm or hand outstretched, an open hand. Sacrifice. The messenger from above to below, service.
Thierens:	The Hanged Man. Pisces. Loss to the outer world, handing over the results of one cycle to the following one. Waste, spoil, mishap. The consciousness opened to inner truth

Ussher:	The crucified God, an ordeal, Libra, lamed, a goad or pointed instrument
Waite:	It should be noted that (1) the tree of sacrifice is living wood; (2) that the face expresses deep entrancement, not suffering; (3) that the figure as a whole suggests life in suspension, but life not death. It is a card of profound significance, but all the significance is veiled. Wisdom, circumspection, discernment, trials, sacrifice, intuition, divination, prophecy. Selfishness, the crowd or body politic
Suggested:	Initiation. Not under any circumstances a card of death. A card of the greatest strength, fortune

Death

This card retains its image and its number throughout the history of the Tarot. Its likely origin is in the Black Death which swept Europe in 1348 and which became a popular image for artists and writers in the centuries that followed. As an image it has a unique attraction within the Tarot deck. It is a totally democratic design. The closest card to it, The Wheel of Fortune, is primarily concerned with the problems of being royal: I reign, I reigned, I shall reign, I am without reign. Of the four figures, only the last is a 'commoner'. And, if the wheel can be said to turn for all men equally, it is plain that on the wheel some are more equal than others.

But the card of death shows all men: king, bishop, woman, child: harvested by the same sure scythe. That such a design, concerned with the democracy of death, should arise from a period that was anything but democratic seems appropriate

Design

Gringonneur:	Death on horseback, trampling his victims
Bembo:	A skeleton, standing with a bow
Swiss:	Death harvesting
Insight:	Death harvesting a crop of heads, hands and feet
Marseille:	The same
Italian:	Similar
Wirth:	As Marseille
Waite:	Death in black armour riding a white horse. He carries in his left hand a flag on which is a white rose on a black field. In the field through which he rides are a dead King, a

curious child, a despairing woman and a praying bishop. The sun is rising

B.O.T.A.: As Marseille, but with rising sun

Aquarian: Similar to Waite, but only the bust of death, the flag, and the rising sun are visible

Crowley: Death with a scythe. Also on the card: a scorpion, a snake, a fish, a lily, a laughing eagle and shades of the departed

New: Retitled, 'The Renewer'. A hooded man stands within a large crown. He presents a skull to a man kneeling before him. From outside the crown a woman pleads with death. A circle of stones in the background containing a golden chalice. The sun seen behind cloud

Interpretation

Case: Nun, meaning fish. As a verb, to sprout or grow. Fertility, fecundity, productiveness, generative power. Motion, to walk. Change, transformation, modification, variation. Change as the basis of modification. Scorpio ruled by Mars with Uranus exalted. Greenish-blue, G natural. Imaginative intelligence

Christian: Creation, destruction and renewal. The ascent of the spirit into the divine spheres. The transformation of human nature upon reaching the end of its organic period

Crowley: Fish. Scorpio, water, Mars ruling water. Imaginative intelligence. Death. Green-blue. Typhon, Khephra. Kundalini. Ares, Mars, scorpion, beetle, lobster or crayfish, wolf. Cactus, snakestone. His magical weapon is the pain of the obligation. His perfumes are Siamese Benzoin, opoponax. His magical power is necromancy. His geomantic sign is rubeus. The Child of the Great Transformers. The Lord of the Gates of Death. Transformation, change (voluntary or involuntary), logical development of existing conditions, but perhaps sudden and unexpected. Apparent death or destruction

Douglas: Major change, perhaps apparently by chance, which is the logical result of what has gone before. A clean sweep necessary for further growth

Gray: Transformation, change, destruction followed by rebirth. Disaster, revolution or other forms of violent change. Negative meanings imply stagnation, lack of change

G. Dawn: The sovereignty and result of victory. Sol acting through

Scorpio upon Venus, Osiris under the destroying power of Typhon afflicting Venus. The Child of the Great Transformers, Lord of the Gates of Death. Time, ages, transformation, change involuntary. Sometimes, but rarely, death and destruction

Grimaud: Symbol of movement and steady advance. Death. The end of something. Illness or shock but a fatal outcome can be avoided. Can mean death whose effects do not stop at death alone, but continue on beyond in evil deeds

Huson: Death, literally. Profound change in the psyche. The initiate stripped of masks

Kahn: Elements of sudden change common to other writers, but also the interpretation of escape from danger, escape from a tricky legal situation, escape from some kind of imprisonment, escape from the persecutions of parts of the Querent's unconscious mind. Change and liberation

Kaplan: As Eden Gray plus the literal meaning of Death

Knight: Literal plus regeneration or life force

Lind: Death of the old, ridding oneself of fleshly desires

Mathers: Death, change, transformation, alteration for the worse. Death just escaped, partial change, transformation for the better

Mayananda: Transformation. Death and resurrection, reincarnation. The dark night of the soul

Papus: Mem, a woman, the companion of man. Being in unlimited space. Destruction preceding or following regeneration

Sadhu: Mem, a woman. No astrological sign. Immortality and permanency in the Essence (God). Transmutation of forces. Death and reincarnation

Thierens: Saturn. Otherwise similar to Waite and Papus

Ussher: The frontier between time and eternity, future and past. Mem, meaning water

Waite: Change, transformation and passage from lower to higher. End, mortality, destruction, the loss of a benefactor for a man, many contrarieties for a woman, failure of marriage projects for a maid. Inertia, sleep, lethargy, petrifaction, somnambulism, hope destroyed

Death in all forms. Resurrection is not in this card except in the sense, 'You die that you may live'. But if the resurrection comes at all it is in another card: perhaps Ace of Wands. The Fool, Judgement, Seven of Swords, Three, Six or Seven of Cups, Ace or Eight of Pentacles

Temperance

This is, for me, one of the least successful of Tarot designs. It is a survival from the earliest decks, from the period when variant decks proliferated and artists must have found it difficult to be innovative in their thinking. The opportunity to revise the card was missed by Wirth and Waite; and it remains essentially what it has been since the beginning, wishy-washy. The original meaning is probably Temperance, that is, cutting wine with water

Design

Gringonneur: A woman seated, pouring liquid from one vase to another

Bembo: The same, standing

Swiss: The same as Bembo, now become an angel

Insight: As above

Marseille: As above

Italian: As above

Wirth: As above

Waite: Similar. An angel stands beside a pool, one foot in the water. From the pool a path leads to the mountains and the sunrise. Beside the pool are yellow irides. On her breast a triangle within a square. On her head is a solar symbol

B.O.T.A.: As Waite, but the angel is pouring from a vase into the pool with her right hand. In her left hand she holds a torch reversed from which descend 'Yods'. The triangle and square upon her breast are replaced by a heptagram, and above it the Hebrew letters for Tetragrammaton. The irides are replaced by two of the Apocalyptic Beasts: the lion and the eagle

Aquarian: A stylized angel

Crowley: A two-headed woman with many breasts pouring liquid with her left hand into a cauldron which she stirs with a bunch of twigs. From the cauldron a white lion and a red eagle drink. Around a circle behind her is the Latin Inscription: Visita Interiora Terrae Rectificando Invenies,

162

Occultum, Lapidem. Which translates: 'Examine the inner parts of the earth. By refining, you will discover the hidden stone.' A pattern of bees and snakes on her gown

New: Retitled: 'Reverser'. A woman standing in a desert holding aloft in her right hand a cone formed of blue liquid and resting her left hand upon a cone formed of red liquid. Above her is a yellow sun with the silhouette of a hawk before it

Interpretation

Case: Samekh. Tent-peg or prop. Wrath (or quivering or vibration). Vibration as the basis of manifestation. Sagittarius ruled by Jupiter. Colour, blue. Tone, G sharp or A flat. Tentative intelligence or intelligence of probation

Christian: The solar spirit: initiative. The perpetual movement of life, the combination of ideas that create morality, the combination of the forces of nature

Crowley: Prop. Sagittarius in fire. The Sun and Jupiter ruling fire. Intelligence of probation or tentative one. Temperance, blue, Nepthys, Vishnu in his Horse Avatar. The hunters Apollo or Artemis, Diana as Archer. The centaur, horse, hippogriff and dog. The rush. The jacinth. Her weapon is the arrow (swift and straight application of force). Her perfume is lign-aloes (obtained from a Mexican tree). Her magical power is transformation. Her geomantic sign is Aquisitio. The Daughter of the Reconcilers, the Bringer Forth of Life. Retitled in *The Book of Thoth*, Art. Combination of forces, realization , action based upon accurate calculation, the way of escape, success after elaborate manoeuvres

Douglas: Literally temperance, mixing of opposite ingredients in proper proportion. The implication is that this mixing takes place internally, within the Querent, that it is a matter of self-adjustment rather than, as with many of the cards, an external force or person which is involved. The negative aspects of the card have to do with inept handling of potentially beneficial situations

Gray: Combination, management, working together, modification. Negatively, the opposite of these

G. Dawn: The beauty of a firm basis. The sovereignty of fundamental power. Sol acting through Sagittarius upon Luna. Daughter

163

of the reconcilers, the bringer forth of life. Combination of forces. Realization, material action, effect either for good or for evil

Grimaud: In every act of renewal, nothing is done abruptly but all is in proportion and moderation. Reflection, decision which is not immediate. Consideration of arguments pro and con. Combines well with Justice, a card of equity. Fickleness and hesitation will be annulled

Huson: Combination, unification, reconciliation. Short-term stalemate followed by resolution. Ill-advised partnerships, concessions, arbitration

Kahn: Distillation, reduction to the simplest ingredient, simplicity. Recklessness, extravagance, perplexity

Kaplan: Frugality, discipline, moderation, patience. Discord, hostility and the negative aspects of moderation, *et al*

Knight: As Crowley with additional interpretations of the reconciliation of evolutionary and incarnationary vehicles of man, individuality and personality. The higher life manifested in the outer world, the life of experience manifested in the higher world

Lind: Purification of the soul. The past, flowing through the present and into the future

Mathers: Combination, conformation, uniting. Ill-advised combinations, disunion, clashing interests

Mayananda: Temperance. Art as symbolic language, mantra or the word. Sagittarius

Papus: Nun, the offspring of the female, a son, a fruit of any kind, all things produced. Augmentation. Scorpio. Combination of different fluids. Individualization of existence

Sadhu: Nun, Scorpio. A foetus. Deduction, harmony of mixed elements, reversability of processes. Pursuit of harmony of the astral constitution

Thierens: Mercury. Distribution. The nervous system. The post office. Reflection and reproduction

Ussher: Rhythm and measure returning to normal after death. The supernatural. Nun, the fish, dweller in the water. Scorpio, the dragon, regenerated as the eagle. (Ussher makes the

The Fool, *Insight Tarot* based on the Marseille Tarot

same connection as Crowley of scorpion/snake or worm/eagle.)

Waite: That which tempers, combines and harmonizes the psychic and material natures. Economy, moderation, frugality, management, accommodation. Things connected with churches, the priest who will marry the Querent. Disunion, competing interests.

Suggested: Economy with one's assets, dilution of strong waters, care with the combination of elements which produce the Philosopher's Stone.

The Devil

The combination of all the European legends concerning the Devil (Antichrist) or the Devil (survivals of pre-Christian gods). In some decks (Marseille, for example) his horns suggest Cernunnos. In other decks he is made bisexual and half goat to suggest Baphomet. He is always the personification of evil; but the inflections which he takes depend upon personal interpretation: evil is desirable or damnable, it is external or internal. A mirror image of The Pope. Typhon

Design

Gringonneur: Missing

Bembo: Missing

Swiss: The Devil triumphing over a damned, weeping soul

Insight: The Devil, hermaphroditic, standing on a platform, his sword in his left hand. Two demons chained to the front of the platform

Marseille: The same

Italian: The same, except that the sword has become a club in his right hand

Wirth: The goat-headed god, torch in his right hand, candle in his left

Waite: A claw-footed devil perched on a black pedestal. His right hand raised, the first and second fingers together as are the third and fourth. The sign of Saturn in his palm. Goat's horns, between which is an inverted pentagram. His left hand holds a torch, inverted, which has fired the tail of his male captive. On the right of the Devil is the woman, whose tail incorporates the pomegranate as part of its design. Both captives are loosely chained and horned. Waite has in-

166

tended an obvious connection between this card and VI, the lovers

B.O.T.A.: As Waite, with the following important changes: The planetary sign for Mercury on The Devil's belly, just below his navel. The breasts are one, square, and one, round, to emphasize the concept of his bisexuality

Aquarian: Stylized design incorporating the inverted pentagram, the inverted torch, and the full moon

Crowley: Highly stylized, incorporating mainly an erect phallus with testicles, the Goat God, and a staff terminating in the Winged Solar Disc and serpents. The Goat God has, in the centre of its forehead, the Wisdom Eye fully dilated. A number of visual puns testicles/cells, genetic symbols/(Chinese?) diagrams

New: Retitled, 'Thinker'. Two figures, a black man and a white woman, strain to dislodge a man seated in full lotus position from the top of a burning tree. A snake coils around the trunk of the tree

Interpretation

Case: Ayin, meaning eye and foundation. The limitations of the visible, sensation. Mirth. Capricorn ruled by Saturn with Mars exalted. Blue-violet or indigo. A natural. Renewing intelligence

Christian: Typhon, Fate. Predestination, Mystery, the Unforeseen, fatality

Crowley: Eye. Capricorn ruling Earth. Venus and the Moon ruling Earth. Renovating intelligence. The Devil. Indigo, Nepthys, Lingam and Yoni, Pan, Priapus (erect Hermes and Bacchus). Vesta. Goat, Ass, Indian Hemp, Orchis Root, Thistle, Black Diamond. His magical weapon is The Secret Force, the Lamp. His perfumes are Musk, Civet and Saturnian perfumes. His drug is orchis (Satyrion). His magical powers are the Evil Eye and the (so-called) Witches' Sabbath. His geomantic sign is Cancer. The Lord of the Gates of Matter. The Child of the Forces of Time. Blind impluse, irresistibly strong and unscrupulous, ambition, temptation, obsession, secret plan about to be executed; hard work, obstinacy, rigidity, aching discontent, endurance

Douglas: Having to do with the unconscious mind generally and its potential dangers

167

Gray: The positive (or upright position of the card) indicates black magic, illness, improper use of force, bondage to material things, discontent, sensation without understanding. The negative (or reversed) meanings are the dawn of spiritual understanding, loosening the chains of slavery to material things, hesitation, conquering of self interest or pride

G. Dawn: The Sovereignty and Beauty of Material Splendour. Sol acting through Capricorn upon Mercury. Lord of the Gates of Matter. Child of the Forces of Time. Materiality, Material Force, Material Temptation, sometimes obsession, especially when coupled with the Lovers

Grimaud: A forceful card which has no meaning in the abstract. Triumph. Not a good card in the physical sense for it signifies triumph obtained by wicked means, by scheming. Fortune acquired by fraud or trickery. The overpowering of others by unscrupulous means, bringing about the destruction of others. Punishment inevitably following. Inverted has a very evil basis with most harmful effects

Huson: Fate in its most tyrannous aspect. Possibly a happy event, depending on other cards. The Querent has absolutely no choice

Kahn: The police, meddling persons, exposure, adultery, a forceful person, force, insanity, seducer, sadism, sordid behaviour, thief, killer, rapist, secret police, insidiousness, double-dealing, act of fate, bigamist, crystallization, robber, voodoo, black magic, forced to do something, sexual deviation, strange or sudden disappearance

Kaplan: Death, misery, disaster, bondage, violence of all forms. The ending of these, the conquering of oneself

Knight: The apprehension of God by the intellect resulting in, possibly the intellect perceiving God as being a distorted vision of itself, hence the Devil

Lind: Pan, instinctive behaviour or folly

Mathers: Fatality for good. Fatality for evil

Mayananda: Capricorn (Saturn negative). The third eye. The opacity in man of the third eye, the Eye of Siva, brought about by the development of the physical at the expense of the spiritual

Papus: Samech, an arrow making a circular movement, the image of the year. Sagittarius, the mysterious astral force. Destiny, fatality, the Dragon of the Threshold

168

Sadhu:	Samech, an arrow flying around in a circle. Sagittarius. Logic, Nahash (the Serpent which tempted Eve). Fate
Thierens:	The Devil. Mars. Sex problems, in nature in every sense and kingdom, but particularly the animal kingdom and animal passion both for preservation of the body and that of the race. Energy, desire, lust, war, struggle, difficulties, pain, loss, exercise, training. The struggle for existence
Ussher:	The subhuman, the libido or anarchy
Waite:	The Dweller on the Threshold Outside the Mystical Garden (Eden). Ravage, violence, vehemence, extraordinary efforts, force, fatality, that which is predestined but is not for this reason evil. Evil fatality, weakness, pettiness, blindness
Suggested:	An evil external force; brace yourself. Internal force which cannot be ignored, learn to deal with it or be destroyed by it. In most readings this card is probably less a card of Evil, *per se*, than it is of paralytic fear, with all that it implies. It can be a card of great personal danger

The Tower

The origins of this card are uncertain. It is usually referred to as 'The House of God', a medieval term for hospital; but the connection between a hospital and the image of the tower destroyed by fire, lightning, or solar fire is lacking. Possible origins are: the Tower of Babel (which provided inspiration for many medieval artists), the Gates of Eden as Adam and Eve were driven forth (as shown in one Minchiate deck of the sixteenth century), the destruction of Sodom as referred to in Chaucer's *Canterbury Tales,* the liberation of St. Paul from prison, or as a general reference to Saturn destroying cities (also mentioned in Chaucer). An additional possibility is as a reference to the Millennium (literally A.D. 1000; but the date tends to shift) when there will be 1) a new order 2) the second coming 3) destruction of the world (cf. The Papess). In all of these variants on The Tower the implication of divine super-rational destruction is paramount as it is on every Tarot deck which I have seen.

Design

Gringonneur:	A tower, apparently blasted by lightning
Bembo:	Missing
Swiss:	As the Gringonneur except one figure has fallen, one is falling
Insight:	As above

Marseille:	As above
Italian:	As above
Wirth:	As above, except that the lightning comes from the sun
Waite:	Similar to the traditional, except that Waite has changed the customary hailstones falling or drops of solar fire to 'Yods' indicating a divine origin for the fire. The symbol is repeated ten times on the right and twelve on the left
B.O.T.A.:	As Waite
Aquarian:	A tower struck by lightning. It is aflame from the upper windows and standing beside the sea. A full moon
Crowley:	A house seen falling beneath an Eye in the centre of heaven. A great serpent with a lotus crown. A dove bearing an olive branch. Flames, from the fanged mouth of Hell
New:	Retitled, 'Citadel'. Background, a series of white concentric arcs resolving to a white star figure at the top of the card. Below that star are a series of circles containing the following symbols: Snake, man and woman joined, a torch, a lion, the T'ai Chi, a book. A winged staff with roots on the right and an upright sword with a crown round its point at the left

Interpretation

Case:	Peh, the mouth as an organ of speech. The power of utterance. Mars ruling Aries and Scorpio, exalted in Capricorn. Scarlet. C natural. Grace and sin or beauty and ugliness are attributed by Qabalists. Active or exciting intelligence. Case notes that it refers traditionally to the Tower of Babel
Christian:	The Lightning-Struck Tower: Ruin. The punishment of pride, the downfall of the spirit that attempts to discover the mystery of God, reversals of fortune
Crowley:	Mouth. Mars. Exciting intelligence. The House of God. Scarlet. Horus. Ares, Mars. The horse, bear, wolf. The plants absinthe and rue. Ruby, any red stone. His magical weapon is the sword. His perfumes are pepper, dragon's blood, all hot pungent odours. His magical powers are works of wrath and vengeance. His geomantic figure is the pentagram. The Lord of the Hosts of the Mighty. The manifestation of cosmic energy in its grossest form. Crowley thinks of this card as total destruction, but destruction in

170

order to obtain 'perfection' which is nothingness according to the doctrine of Yoga. Quarrel, ruin, combat, danger, destruction of plans, sudden death, escape from prison

Douglas: The force of destiny, possibly self-induced

Gray: Divine will attempting to break down man's stubbornness. Change or catastrophe. Freedom gained at great cost, false accusations. imprisonment, oppression

G. Dawn: Victory over Splendour. Venus acting through Mars upon Mercury. Avenging force. Lord of the Hosts of the Mighty. Ambition, fighting, war, courage in certain combinations: destruction, danger, fall, ruin

Grimaud: Imaginary creations produced by the desires of man. A very powerful card. A plan brought to an abrupt halt, liberation from prison, a dramatic turn of events or an unexpected shock, Downfall. Prevails over almost all the cards; but World weakens its influence

Huson: That which is dead renewed by fire, baptism by fire, cataclysm which may be turned to either good or evil result. Not total ruin but rather catharsis

Kahn: More or less traditional interpretation with the addition of miracles, high magic

Kaplan: Traditional

Knight: God, as a solar flare, speaking directly to the individual. Possibility of tremendous benefit to the person properly balanced to receive it; but if the person is too strong it will leave him unmoved, if he is too weak it will consume him

Lind: Destruction from Heaven punishing one who has sold his soul to the Devil. Freedom from the flesh

Mathers: Ruin, disruption, overthrow, loss, bankruptcy. Reversed, the same but only partially

Mayananda: A transitional condition, always unpleasant. Mental obstruction or active opposition to the operation of wisdom. Preparation through destruction for a new birth

Papus: Ayin, material sense. Degenerated it is all that is crooked, false, perverse, and bad. Capricorn. The invisible or spiritual world incarnated in the visible and material world. The material fall of Adam. Divine destruction, the fall, the visible world

171

Sadhu:	Ayin, meaning 'a material tie' or bond, a connection in a state of tension. Logic, in establishing one thesis, eliminating others. The confirmation of the life of one form while destroying another by the use of an astral current. The destroyed or fulminated tower
Thierens:	Uranus. The renewal of the form or of embodied life by the force of Heaven. The relation between the macrocosm and the microcosm, both feeding on each other. Rupture, sudden disillusion, disenchantment, intuition, help from above and clear insight in relation to vanity and sham projects, illusion and meaningless formalism
Ussher:	Lucifer. Faust. The fall as a result of the intellect and its misuse more than as a result of sensual curiousity. Cosmic jokes. Fate or the incalculable factor
Waite:	The ruin of the House of Life when evil has prevailed therein, the rending of the House of a False Doctrine. Intellectual destruction. Misery, distress, indigence, adversity, calamity, disgrace, deception, ruin. Unforeseen catastrophe. Reversed, the same in lesser degree. Oppression, imprisonment, tyrrany
Suggested:	Inspiration, sudden illumination. Do not pass Go. Do not collect two hundred dollars. Go directly to Hell. God having his little joke on you

The Star

In its traditional form The Star is imprecise as to its significance. A kneeling woman is pouring liquid from pitchers held in either hand. She pours one stream on to water and one on to land. Fortunately, most of the legendary meanings of stars are still current in Western belief, among civilized as well as 'savage' peoples.

Jung recalls, in Symbols of Transformation, the Mithraic saying: 'I am a star that goes with thee and shines out of the depths.' And many of the meanings attributed to stars involve, in some way, the quality of movement: the Star of Bethlehem guiding the Three Wise Men, the order of stars and their function in primitive as well as scientific timekeeping, the forces of the spirit struggling against the forces of darkness, the force of the universe expanding and thus implying the mystic centre.

The connection between stars and shooting stars is, in many cultures, this; each man's soul is represented by a star in the heavens. At his birth a new star comes into being; and that star waxes and wanes in the skies according to his fortunes upon earth. At his death his soul is seen falling as a meteor.

A similar legend turns up in Sparta. Every eight years the Ephors of Sparta (a group of five magistrates who supervised the king) gathered to observe a moonlit night sky. If they saw a meteor it was taken as a sign that the king had somehow offended the gods. His suspension followed, until such time as he had purged the offence at the Oracle of Delphi or that of Olympus. This may have been a hangover from an earlier custom of killing the king if a meteor was seen on the night of the Eighth Year.

The other meanings of stars are as symbolic of the collective unconscious, as the Sentinels of Heaven, as Angels (just as falling stars are believed to be, by some, devils), or as the spirit, i.e.: Star of Hope, Star of Wonder.

Design

Gringonneur:	Missing
Bembo:	A gowned woman, standing, her upraised left hand cupping the light of a star. Eight pointed
Swiss:	A woman kneeling on the shore. She holds a vase in either hand, one of which she is emptying into the ocean. There are seven stars, each having six points
Insight:	A woman kneeling on land, a vase in either hand, emptying the contents of both out upon the ground. Eight stars, each having five points
Marseille:	A woman, kneeling on the shore. Pours one vase into water, one on to land. Two small stars with seven points, five small stars with eight points, one large star with fifteen points
Italian:	Similar, but the colour of the two liquids differs
Wirth:	Similar, but a bird, present in both the Italian and the Marseille, is here replaced by a butterfly
Waite:	Similar to traditional except that there are eight stars, each having eight points. Seven are white, the eighth and central star is yellow
B.O.T.A.:	Similar
Aquarian:	A peacock perching on a bush in flower. A ten-pointed star
Crowley:	A Titaness in an icy landscape. With her right hand she pours out liquid upon a globe. With her left she pours out ice. In this Arctic climate there are roses and butterflies. She is naked. The symbolism of the card is simpler than that of many other Crowley cards and, inversely/appropriately more thought provoking
New:	An aged face, haloed, with an eight-pointed star, looks down on a walled city. Light streaming from his eyes. On

the right a chalice empties itself on to a rainbow. On the left
a cock crows

Interpretation

Case: Tzaddi, meaning Fish-Hook, that which draws up the Fish
(Nun, Death) out of the water (Mem, the Hanged Man). A
quest for realization. Meditation, Aquarius ruled by Saturn
and Uranus, Violet, A sharp or b flat. Natural intelligence

Christian: The Star of the Magi: Hope. Immortality, the Inner Light
that illuminates the Spirit

Crowley: Crowley gives two Hebraic attributions: in *777* it is Tzaddi
(as Case and, probably, Mathers and Waite); in *The Book
of Thoth* and in *The Book of the Law* he says, He. Further
correspondences from *777*; Aquarius, Air, Saturn and Mercury ruling air, natural intelligence, the star, violet. Nuit,
Athena, Ganymede, Juno, Man or Eagle. Olive, coconut,
artificial glass. Her magical weapon is the Censer, her perfume is Galbanum, her vegetable drugs are all diuretics,
her magical power is astrology, her geomantic sign:
Tristitia. The Daughter of the Firmament, the Dweller between the Waters. Hope, unexpected help, clearness of
vision, realization of possibilities, spiritual insight, error of
judgement, dreaminess, disappointment

Douglas: Hope, potential fulfilment, possibilities in the future.
Restriction, rigidity of mind or soul, self-doubt

Gray: Traditional plus additional suggestion of giving spiritual
gifts or great love. Pessimism or doubt, illness of the mind
or body

G. Dawn: The Victory of Fundamental Strength. Venus acting
through Aquarius upon Luna. Hope. Daughter of the Firmament. Dweller between the Waters. Faith, unexpected
help, dreaminess, deceived hope

Grimaud: Harmony, based on the psychic and spiritual in all its forms.
Satisfaction, love of humanity in all its beauty. The
destiny of the feelings which animate the being. A powerful
card but easily neutralized. Harmony broken in the destiny
of the seeker. Physical harmony of short duration

Huson: Traditional

Kaplan: Traditional

Knight: Heh, window. Aries the Ram. Most authorities read this

The Devil, *B.O.T.A. Tarot*

card as either Tzaddi or Phe. Only Crowley, in some of his writings, and Knight concur in Heh as a possibility

Lind: Hope

Mathers: Hope, expectation, bright promises. Hopes not fulfilled, expectations disappointed, or fulfilled in a minor degree

Mayananda: The supernal power as divine fire or life, 'The Food of the Gods'. "One of the chief difficulties of the Taro."

Papus: Phe, Speech. Mercury. Immortality, hope, the Force which dispenses the Essence of Life

Sadhu: Phe, a throat with a tongue. Mercury. Hope, intuition, natural divination.

Thierens: Venus, ruler of the signs Taurus and Libra. Benefit, well doing, organization, cooperation, love, beauty, peace, etc. Laziness, indolence, rest, weakness

Ussher: Traditional

Waite: Hope, immortality and inner light, Truth unveiled, pouring on the waters of the soul some part and measure of her priceless possession. The Great Mother communicating to those below in the measure that they can receive her understanding. Loss, theft, privation, abandonment, hope, bright prospects. Arrogance, haughtiness, impotence

Suggested: A window through which the Querent can see himself. A card of potential, whether positive or negative depending upon the cards which lie near it. The soul meaning of Star may, after all, be the closest to what it is

The Moon

Of all the Tarot symbols The Moon is probably better known today than any other. The term 'lunatic', for example, which derives from the Latin for Moon and means, literally, affected by the Moon. For several hundred years any direct connection between the Moon and insanity has been dismissed as superstition. Yet, from what policemen and social workers have told me, there is a correlation between phases of the Moon and cycles of insanity/violence

The word 'month' comes from Moon. As, possibly, does the term 'menstruum', meaning menstrual fluid or the ambience in which the transmutation of a base metal can take place.

In New Guinea it was customary to hasten the passage of the months by throwing stones and spears at the Moon. And wives would sing to the New Moon while their husbands were out hunting. When the Moon appeared they would rejoice in the sign that their husbands were safe and well; for the Moon that shone on them also shone upon the hunters.

Peruvian women at one time prayed to the Moon for safe childbirth. In Italy, Diana, the Moon Goddess, was thought of as being particularly the ruler of the Harvest Moon. In Asia Minor and Greece she was called Pasiphae or Europa. Throughout Europe it was customary until recent times to plant as the Moon waxed and to reap as it waned. As dew and moisture were thought to come from the Moon custom demanded that house-timbers be cut when the Moon was waning and the timber was therefore drier.

Sacrifices to the Moon were foods, perfumes, wines, and in some cases, people. In Albania a slave-priest of the Goddess was sacrificed each year after having spent the preceeding thirteen months in being feasted and fattened. The manner of his death was this: a spear was run through him, piercing his heart. The attitude in which he fell was then carefully observed by the high priest, who interpreted it as being an oracle of the goddess. in Turkey, too, Moon sacrifice was practised, the victim being chosen because he or she resembled the Moon. Perhaps an albino. In Borneo albinoes were believed to be the children of their father, the Moon, and their mother, a mortal. Thus emphasizing in popular myth their appearance.

Moon worship survived in Italy until at least the mid-nineteenth century. Moon myths concerning the Moon and its influence upon business are still current in parts of Germany. And as a symbol the Moon is, even in a Space Age, she who moves the tides of ocean and, perhaps, of men.

Design

Gringonneur: Two scholars (?) measuring the night sky and performing computations in an open book. A waning crescent

Bembo: Diana shown standing with a broken bow in her left hand. In her upraised right hand is a waning crescent

Swiss: A young man, his dog at his side, serenading a girl who gestures from a balcony. In the sky an equatorial crescent moon. At the bottom of the card is a shellfish, perhaps a lobster or a crayfish, flanked by two smaller shellfish

Insight: An equatorial crescent. Below it are two dogs, one of them howling. The other has his paw upraised over the legend 'MA'. A lobster emerging from a pool at the bottom of the card

Marseille: Similar to the above except that the Moon is shown in splendour and the text is missing

Italian: A crescent equatorial Moon, otherwise as Marseille

Wirth: Similar to Marseille except that the artist has here combined the waxing, waning, and full aspects of the Moon. This is suggested in some earlier decks, traditional in some

177

later ones, but it appears to be used explicitly for the first time here

Waite: Based on Wirth and Insight. One of the dogs has become a wolf; and the legend is missing

B.O.T.A.: As Waite; but wolf features exaggerated

Aquarian: A waxing crescent moon

Crowley: The Moon, so stylized that it could be an eye, crescent in such a manner as to suggest the equator. In the foreground are two dark towers, each with a lighted window. Before each tower is the figure of Anubis. Each figure carries in its left hand the planetary symbol for Venus (the sign for woman) with its implied pun in this context of the Solar Ankh. Each Anubis figure is accompanied by a jackal (another representation of Anubis). At the bottom of the card, so placed as to imply the other side of the world or the Underworld, is the beetle, Khephera, with the Solar Disc in his front mandibles

New: Retitled, 'Reacter'. A naked child holding aloft keys. At the end of a long passage behind him is a waxing and waning crescent set against a background of the Full Moon

Interpretation

Case: Qoph, the back of the head. The states of consciousness prior to full control. (Hence unconscious/subconscious contrasted with conscious mind and intuition/vision contrasted with intellect.) Sleep is the function. Pisces, ruled by Jupiter and Neptune. Violet-red, B natural. Corporeal intelligence

Christian: Twilight: deceptions. The abysses of the infinite. The darkness that cloaks the spirit when it submits itself to the power of the instincts, deceptions and hidden enemies

Crowley: The back of the head. Pisces, water. Mars ruling water. Corporeal intelligence. The Moon. Crimson (ultra violet). Khephra (as Scarab in Tarot Trumps). Vishnu in his Matsya Avatar, Poseidon, Neptune, the fish, the dolphin. Plants: unicellular organisms, opium. Pearl. Magical weapons: The Twilight of the Place and The Magic Mirror. Perfume: Ambergris. Drugs: all narcotics. Magical powers: Bewitchments, Casting Illusions. Geomantic sign: Laetitia. The Ruler of Flux and Reflux. The Child of the Sons of the Mighty. Illusion, deception, bewilderment, hysteria, even

178

madness, dreaminess, falsehood, error, crisis, the darkest hour before the dawn, the brink of important change

Douglas: Intuition, generally. Particularly necessary to save the querent from some crisis. Lack of nerve

Gray: Intuition, possible bad luck for a lover of the querent. Imagination restrained by practicality, peace achieved at a high price. Avoid risks

G. Dawn: The victory of the material. Venus acting through Pisces upon the cosmic elements, deceptive effect of the apparent power of material forces. Rule of Flux and Reflux. Child of the Sons of the Mighty. Dissatisfaction, voluntary change, error, lying, falsity, deception

Grimaud: Illusion. Scandal, denouncement or a secret revealed

Huson: Gentle inner force leading to fluctuation, small errors, fertility or fulfillment. Promise

Kahn: The soul, the spirit, danger to either

Kaplan: Deception, trickery and related meanings

Knight: Qoph, Back of the head, Pisces, the Fishes, Ruler of Flux and Reflux, Child of the Sons of the Mighty. Instinctive man, the primitive, nature red in tooth and claw lurking in the primeval racial past

Lind: Traditional

Mathers: Twilight, deception, error. Fluctuation, slight deceptions, trifling mistakes

Mayananda: The Gate of Resurrection. The soul ascending through the unconscious toward rebirth

Papus: Tzaddi, a term, an aim, an end. Aquarius. The final step of the descent of the spirit into matter. The end of physical materilization , the end of divine materialization

Sadhu: Tzaddi, Roof. The most ominous of all the arcana. (He means the Major Arcana.) Twilight, dusk, occult hierarchy, hidden enemies, hidden dangers in general

Thierens: The Moon. The life of the soul, feelings, sentiments, changes wrought in existence by them, water and the female element in general, a woman, women in general, the passing of everything, uncertainty, dreams, exhibitions, plays, the lower class of people

179

Ussher:	Power ideology or the guilt complex. (By extension, Superstition.) Dread of the irrational
Waite:	Hidden enemies, danger, calumny, darkness, terror, deception, occult forces, error. Instability, inconstancy, silence, lesser degree of deception and error
Suggested:	Feeling and intuition. The sum of the two suits: Wands and Cups: and all they stand for. That which is hidden and in that sense Female. That which is past, that which is yet to come. Regret or longing. The card of that which is yet to be born. The intangible and the unreal. Unreal in the sense of being non-physical. The dark half of the T'ai Chi

The Sun

Almost all primitive religions are based either upon this symbol or upon a Sky God who incorporates within his being a solar component. The Sun is usually thought of as masculine, as the Moon is usually feminine. Even so, there are reversals of the roles, for example in Japan, where the sun goddess was said to be incarnated in the person of the Mikado.

The basic solar symbols are the Circle, usually with a dot in its centre; a circle with a human face; or a Solar Wheel, which is a wheel with two diameters at right angles to each other. Other possibles are some variant upon the Eye, as in The Eye of Ra, the Eye of Varuna or the Eye of Ahuramazda. And the Eye sees, and seeing reflects on what it has seen. Which may be the origin of the belief in the Sun as All-Seeing, or All-Wise.

As the God of the Ressurection the Sun comes more easily than his sister, the Moon. For one thing, his death is whole; he vanishes over a specific observable period of time, eclipsed by a known horizon. While the Moon is nibbled away by mice, devoured by some Typhonic monster, over the last fourteen days of her cycle. In some sense her death is more real than that of the Sun, who is reborn in every sunrise.

Sun religions tend to be masculine in their priesthoods, equating solar energy with masculine energy impregnating a passive and feminine Earth. The parallel is taken even further by such solar gods as Osiris, who suffer mutilation and death, only to be reborn, thus proving resurrection. In the case of Osiris, however, his dismemberment at the hands of Set was so complete that Isis was unable to find his masculinity. Legend has it that her reconstruction of Osiris included a prosthetic device to replace that which had been lost. And, still later, the erect phallus became a symbol of Osiris, the solar god. Just as it did in India where it was symbolic of Siva, the generative and destroying part of the Hindu Trinity. So also in Rome, where Bacchus was a phallic deity; and in the Near East where Baal was worshipped as an erect pillar. In Britain the phallic Solar God survives in the figure of the Cerne Giant, Helith or Hercules.

180

Because of the numerology and the arrangement of the figures in The Chariot, The Devil and The Sun, these cards are probably related.

Design

Gringonneur: A woman standing with a spear behind her. Her hands appear to be bound in some way. Above her the Sun in Splendour

Bembo: A cherub bearing aloft the Sun, represented as a disembodied head

Swiss: Two lovers off by themselves. The girl holds an open book. Above, the Sun in glory

Insight: A naked child smiling from the back of a white horse. He carries in his left hand a long banner on a pole. Behind him is a walled garden with sunflowers visible above it. Above, the sun in glory

Marseille: Two children standing in front of a wall. Above them the Sun in Glory

Italian: As above

Wirth: As above, except that here they are a little older and one is a girl

Waite: Similar to the Insight deck

B.O.T.A.: Based on the Marseille Tarot. Two children, a boy and a girl, standing in front of a wall. Each has one foot in a small circle and the other in a larger concentric circle

Aquarian: The Sun in splendour

Crowley: The Sun surrounded by the Signs of the Zodiac. Below are two winged figures dancing

New: Retitled, 'Doer'. An Eye in Midheaven, dilated. In the foreground a man is standing presenting to the viewer the open pages of a book. In his left hand he holds a ribbon which is tied loosely to the right forefoot of a black horse. Over his head a white horse (almost like a white bull) rears. The man is unconcerned. At the bottom left a skull with flowers growing from it

Interpretation

Case: Resh, the Head and Face of Man. The Sun, exalted in Aries, ruling Leo. Fruitfulness and Sterility. Collecting or Collective Intelligence

Christian:	The Blazing Light: Earthly Happiness. The Supreme Heaven, Sacred Truth, Peaceful Happiness
Crowley:	Head. Sun. Collecting Intelligence. Orange. Ra, Hathor. The Right Eye. Helios, Apollo. The lion, the sparrowhawk. (Lion being cherub of fire.) Sunflower, laurel, heliotrope. Chrysoleth. His Weapon is the Lamen or the Bow and Arrow. (The Spear?) Olibanum, cinnamon, all glorious odours. Alcohol is his drug. His magical power is the Red Tincture, the Power of Acquiring Wealth. The Lord of the Fire of the World. Glory, gain, riches, triumph, pleasure, frankness, truth, shamelessness, arrogance, vanity, manifestation, recovery from sickness but sometimes sudden death
Douglas:	Success generally, possibly after a period of danger or doubt. Misjudgement ending in disaster, exposure of fraud or trickery, fantasy substituting for success
Gray:	Happiness of all kinds: material, emotional, creatively, freedom. Negative meanings have to do with future troubles, clouds on the horizon
G. Dawn:	The Splendour of the Material World. Mercury acting through the Sun upon the Moon. Lord of the Fire of the World. Glory, gain, riches. Sometimes also arrogance. Display, vanity, but only when with very evil cards
Grimaud:	Universal radiance. Elements of triumph and success in whatever circumstances one finds oneself. Very powerful, in no case influenced by cards around and which can be applied to all cards
Huson:	Abundant joy
Kahn:	Traditional positive aspects. Negative aspects include distinct imperfections in an otherwise powerful and fertile circumstance, perversion or sterility, unused powers, divorce, lack of money, discoveries which must be guarded
Kaplan:	Traditional
Knight:	Enlightenment
Lind:	Spiritual victory over the flesh. Naked innocence. The regenerated soul illuminated by divine light
Mathers:	Happiness, content, joy. Reversed: these in a minor degree
Mayananda:	The Lord of the Aeon. Renewal, a change of outlook and a

new point of view incident upon cosmic cycles and the opening of the Third Eye: a turning of the attention from the physical person to the mental individual and the possibility of reincarnation and life in the higher bodies

Papus: Quoph, a sharp weapon. Awakening of the spirit, the body of man renewed, the material world commencing an ascension towards God

Sadhu: Quoph, an Axe. Fruitful truth, human virtue, gold of the philosophers

Thierens: The positive or masculine elements in general, power and function of will and concentration, great benefit and mighty protection in spiritual as well as mundane matters. The spiritual centre of man, the centre of importance. The heart and the solar plexus

Ussher: The super-rational, the freedom of the harmonized personality, regained innocence, renewal out of chaos. Self expression

Waite: The transit from the manifest light of this world to the light of the world to come. Consciousness in the spirit. Material happiness, fortunate marriage, the same in a lesser sense

Suggested: Sensation and thought. All of the attributions of the two suits: Pentacles and Swords: and all that they stand for. That which is manifest and in that sense male. That which is present, here, now. The tangible, the real. In all senses this card is the complement of the preceding card, neither being, of itself, good or evil. Both are statements of things as they are. The evil and the good are what you make of them. The light half of the T'ai Chi

Judgement

The legendary meanings of this card are numerous and derive from almost all religions. Its components are (1) The Last Judgement; (2) Resurrection; and (3) (to a lesser extent) Initiation, Purification, or Baptism. The sources of the tradition are Christian, Eleusinian, Mithraic, Egyptian, and Judaic. Additional parallels may be found in North American Indian beliefs and in Alchemical writing.

Of all the Tarots, this card is one of the least ambiguous.

Design

Gringonneur: Angels seen blowing the last trumpets. The dead rise from the grave

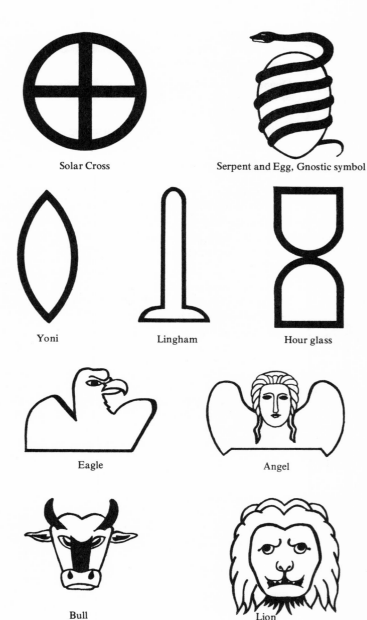

Solar Cross

Serpent and Egg, Gnostic symbol

Yoni

Lingham

Hour glass

Eagle

Angel

Bull

Lion

Bembo:	As above, except that God himself is seen in the Heavens
Swiss:	As Gringonneur, except only one angel
Insight:	As Swiss, except the trumpet has a flag with cross on it attached
Marseille:	As above
Italian:	As above but lacking flag
Wirth:	As above, but again with flag
Waite:	As Insight
B.O.T.A.:	As above
Aquarian:	The Angel only, blowing a trumpet
Crowley:	Retitled, 'The Aeon'. The body of the goddess, Nuit, forming an Omega. Below her the winged disc and an oval form so connected as to imply the Ankh. The product of their union is represented two ways simultaneously: As the child, Horus (Harpocrates), and as Ra Heru Khuti or Harmachis, the falcon-headed God. The Hebrew letter, Shin, bearing three foetal humans, is at the bottom of the card, superimposed on a very stylized sign for Libra
New:	Retitled, 'Knower'. A man standing, one foot in each of two pools which together form the lemniscate. The left is a pool of fire, the right is a pool of water. In his right hand he holds an egg. Above his head is a winged solar disc with rays of light emerging from it at the top and the bottom to form a cross with the wings

Interpretation

Case:	Shin, tooth (probably a serpent's fang). Fire is the element attributed to Shin. Pluto and Vulcan (as yet hypothetical between Mercury and the Sun.) Perpetual Intelligence. Scarlet. C natural. Judgement or the Last Judgement. Completion, decision, termination
Christian:	Rasith. The Awakening of the Dead: Renewal. Change which is the end of all things, Good as well as evil
Crowley:	Tooth. Fire. Hot and dry fire. Perpetual Intelligence. The Angel or The Last Judgement. Glowing Orange Scarlet. Horus, Agni, Yama, Hades, Vulcan, Pluto, Lion. Red Poppy, hibiscus, nettle. Fire opal. Weapon: The Wand or Lamp, Pyramid of Fire. Perfumes: Olibanum, all fiery

185

odours. Mineral Drugs: Nitrates. Magical Powers: Evocation, Pyromancy. Geomantic figures: those of the fiery triplicity. The Spirit of the Primal Fire. The Aeon. (Crowley changed the name of the twentieth trump when he came to design his deck.) For the symbolism relating to this the reader is referred to *The Book of the Law*. Final decision in respect of the past, new current in respect of the future. Always represents the taking of a definite step

Douglas: Substantially as Waite

Gray: As Waite

G. Dawn: The Splendour of the Material World. Mercury acting through Fire upon the Cosmic Elements. (Almost identical to the attribution in Trump 19, The Sun.) The Spirit of the Primal Fire. Final decision, judgement, sentence, determination of a matter without appeal on its plane

Grimaud: The call of a man to a higher state. His tendencies and desires to raise himself above the physical plane. Fame of an intellectual order and having a good influence. Fame or glory but only transient and of short duration

Huson: A card of resolution or completion. The final determination of something with the suggestion of something else to follow. Reluctance to come to a conclusion or determination

Kahn: Confrontations, meetings, eyeball to eyeball, etc. Difficult task, pressure, court proceedings, divorce, act of will

Kaplan: Traditional

Knight: Shin, tooth. The way of evolution, the middle way. Man evolved to the point of being able to control Sun and Moon, thus individuality and personality

Lind: Eternal life. The secrets of the ages revealed

Mathers: Renewal, result, determination of a matter, postponement of a result, delay, matter reopened later

Mayananda: The Aeon. The Inner Fire, the self judged by the Universal Self

Papus: Resh, the Head. Saturn. Return to the divine world, life renewing itself by its own motion, the vegetable world

Sadhu: Resh, the human head, Saturn. Divine Attraction, the Way of Reintegration, Astral Transformation

186

Thierens:	Jupiter. Ideals, religious, social or other ideas, aspiration, deliverance from narrow thought
Ussher:	Existence turned to essence, consciousness brought forth from unconsciousness by the power of the Word, revealing the logical syntax of Being
Waite:	The accomplishment of the great work of transformation. Change of position, renewal, outcome. Total loss through lawsuit. Weakness, pusillanimity, simplicity, deliberation, decision, sentence
Suggested:	Judgement, choice, initiation into nirvana or choosing to stay on earth. Resurrection from a dead time . . . if at the beginning of a spread what follows is indicated in the cards. If at the end of a spread if postulates change from the cards which precede it but without indicating what the change will be. When this is a card of goals attained it is the achievement of one summit only to realize the existence of another. A pivotal card

The World

The four beasts usually on this card: Angel, Eagle, Bull and Lion: represent the four evangelists or the four elements. The figure at the centre is occasionally a hermaphrodite, signifying the completion of the great work, i.e., manufacturing 'gold'. But in most cases the central form is that of a woman dancing, a very pensive expression on her face, particularly in the Marseille pack. In almost all books this card is interpreted as triumphant, which interpretation may refer to the oval wreath which surrounds the dancing figure. But, as Crowley implies in *777* and *The Book of Thoth,* the wreath could as easily be a funereal sign

On the whole an ambiguous card of unsatisfactory design.

Design

Gringonneur:	Missing
Bembo:	Two cherubs holding aloft the image of a walled city
Swiss:	A woman holding a piece of cloth strategically. She is surrounded by a wreath of leaves and berries. At the top of the wreath is an eagle, below left is a bull, below right is a lion. Two birds sang at the top, on the left and right
Insight:	Similar; but she bears a wand in either hand, the wreath is flowered, the angel (sylph) is included and the birds are omitted

187

Marseille:	As above except that the wreath is plain. All the beasts are haloed except the bull
Italian:	Similar; but lacking a wand in the right hand and haloes on the beasts
Wirth:	Similar; but bearing two wands, both in her left hand
Waite:	Traditional
B.O.T.A.:	Similar to Waite but the rods are replaced with tight spirals, possibly signifying energy
Aquarian:	Fully clothed, bearing in her right hand a flower in bud
Crowley:	Retitled, 'The Universe'. Stylized version of the traditional design. She dances with a crescent moon in her right hand. Her hair is shaped to resemble a ram's horns. From a cosmic eye issues forth a serpent with whom she dances, at the same time keeping one foot firmly upon its head
New:	Retitled, 'Virgin'. She dances as Siva, her right leg forming the sign of 4. In her right foot she holds a rod. In the four corners of the card are: an inverted cup, a face . . . half black and half white, a zebra with lightning, and an apple

Interpretation

Case:	Tav, Signature or mark. He comments that the 'mark' is a Greek Cross. He further points out that the related Tau Cross was used by the Egyptians both as a letter (Tav or Tau) and as a device for measuring right angles and the depth of the Nile. Salvation from death, eternal life, final seal and witness to the Great work of liberation. Saturn, co-ruler of Aquarius with Uranus, ruler of Capricorn, exalted in Libra. Indigo or blue-violet, A natural. Dominion and slavery. Administrative Intelligence. Cosmic consciousness or Nirvana, final Union
Christian:	The Crown of the Magi: The Reward. Thoth (letter). The reward of free spirits, that they participate with the Divine Omnipotence, etc.
Crowley:	Tau (as the Egyptian letter, presumably meaning both letter and symbol). Saturn. The Universe, Indigo. Brahma, Athena, Saturn, Crocodile. Ash, cypress, hellebore, yew, nightshade. Onyx. His magical weapon is a sickle. Perfumes: Assafoetida, scammony, indigo, sulphur: all evil odours. Lead (drug). Magical power: Works of malediction and Death. Geomantic sign, the triangle. The Great One of

the Night of Time. Crowley seems of two minds on the card. He defines it as the completion of the Great Work. But he also implies that the great work is negative. idiotic, and (from some of the correspondences) ultimately malicious. In *The Book of Thoth* he retitles it, The System. It is likely that he means this in its most pejorative sense. The matter of the question itself, synthesis, the end of the matter, may mean delay, opposition, inertia, patience, perseverance, persistent stubborness in difficulty. Crystallization of the whole matter involved

Douglas: Traditional

Gray: Completion, travel, arrival at a state of cosmic consciousness. Success. Success yet to be won, fear of change or travel, lack of vision

G. Dawn: The Foundation of the cosmic elements and of the material world. Luna acting through Saturn upon the Elements. The Great One of the Night of Time. The matter itself, synthesis, world, kingdom, usually denoting the subject of the question and therefore depending entirely upon the surrounding cards

Grimaud: The perfection of man. The individual. The intellectual element in man, the personal element in woman. Triumph or negation according to the surrounding cards

Huson: Prize or reward. Longed-for goal, magus-mind, monetary recompense. The best card in the deck. A sense of permanence, cosmic time

Kahn: Symbol of attainment, a dangerous situation

Kaplan: Traditional

Knight: Tau, Saturn, Great One of the Night of Time. 'Administrative Intelligence . . . so called because it directs and associates the motions of the seven planets, directing all of them in their proper courses'

Lind: The ecstatic soul, fully conscious of its divine origin

Mathers: Completion, good reward. Evil reward

Mayananda: The Universe, or Universal Rebirth to 0. The Tau Cross or Saturn. Victory. A sign of blessing. The unity of positive and negative forces. The four directions of space, the four elements with Aether at the centre making the fifth. That which is created or nothing. (He implies, therefore, 'That

189

Lemniscate

Eight-pointed star (Octagram)

Seven-pointed star (Heptagram)

Octagon

Hexagon

Swastika (Right hand)

Gnostic Sun

Sun

Sun

Waxing Crescent

Waning Crescent

Urim (Moon in the first quarter)

Cup

Sword

Wand

which is created nothing'. Which would accord with Eastern thought)

Papus: Perfection. The absolute, containing in itself God, Man and the Universe

Sadhu: Than, the breast, the all-accepting bosom. Metaphysical Absolute, Adaptation of the Great Operation, Omnipotence of Nature, The Magic Crown or the World

Thierens: Neptune. Cosmic conditions to which we are subject, but which at the same time present us with what we need for sustenance. Tau, the womb, a sign of reciprocity, the image of that which is mutual and at the same time of abundance and perfection

Ussher: The angelic state to which man comes. Beauty, love and happiness arising from the communion of souls. Eternity, the eternal morning of him who kisses joy as it flies

Waite: The perfection and end of the cosmos, the secret which is within it, the rapture of the universe when it understands itself in God. Assured success, recompense, voyage, route, emigration, flight, change of place. Inertia, fixity, stagnation, permanence

Suggested: The World, the weight of the world. Not a card of endings, a card of results which will tend to be physical. Can be a sign of reward or punishment, even imprisonment; but it is always a sign of the Karmic Law, as you sow . . .'Like many of the Tarot cards, The World is ambiguous

In this section on the Major Arcana it will be noted that not all of the cards are prefaced with a historical description. For many of the cards it is simply that they are so common to European cultural heritage as to make commentary unnecessary. Examples of this are The Emperor and The Empress, loosely modelled on Zeus and Hera or Jupiter and Juno. In the instance of other cards the description prefacing the delineation of the design has been lacking or sketchy because of a lack of sympathy on the part of the author with that particular card. Temperance is one such card, that comes to mind. And in yet other instances the historical origin of the card is probably a redundant moral or alchemical one which is better illustrated by another card.

Ouspensky in his short book on the Tarot has commented on the possibility of pairing the cards of the Major Arcana for further insight into their meanings. Little needs to be said concerning this as the pairs are obvious when they occur in the cards as they are at present ordered. For examples: *The Fool and The Magician, The High Priestess and The Empress, The High Priestess and The*

191

High Priest, The Emperor and The Pope, The Lovers and The Chariot, Strength and Temperance, The Hermit and The Hanged Man, The Wheel of Fortune and Justice, The Hanged Man and Death, Death and Judgement, The Devil and The Magician, The Devil and The Hermit, The Tower and The World, The Emperor and The Star, The Moon and The Sun, The Moon and The High Priestess, The Sun and The High Priest, The World and The Fool. These pairs often reveal opposing characteristics of the same thing, such as its male and female qualities. When they occur together or in proximity in a reading a powerful vortex exists which should be taken into account. For the Major Arcana are, individually, indicative of power. When they occur in pairs or groups that strength can be magnified or annulled, depending upon the combination.

4 *Methods of Divination*

To begin divination the reader must first choose the Tarot deck with which he will be working. The best way to do this is to go into any store which carries a variety of Tarot packs and look at as many as possible. Concentrate on the pictures; and one deck will stand out as being particularly attractive and rich with familiar symbols. Buy it without quibbling about the price. The issue is not how much the cards are going to cost but whether they will work in a sensitive situation. To haggle over the cost of a deck of Tarot cards is roughly analogous to buying 'cut-price' life preservers. A wise man might question the reality of such a 'bargain'.

Having chosen your deck familiarize yourself with it. Memorize the pictures, getting a feeling not only of the individual designs but of the entire sequence as well. When you are not using the cards keep them in whatever place you reserve for your most personal possessions: love letters, baby shoes, a lock of hair. Sleep with them under your pillow. You can even, if you are a traditionalist, consecrate them to your use according to one of the rituals in *Mastering Witchcraft* by Paul Huson or similar books. This treatment of the cards is far from being facetious, as it might appear on the surface. The more you identify yourself with your deck of cards, *by whatever means,* the more you are likely to be able to obtain results through using them. So, as they are a personal possession, keep them safe. Except when you are actually doing a reading let no one handle your cards. And under no circumstances let anyone else attempt readings with them.

Once you are familiar with the cards choose several methods of divination and learn them. Two kinds of divination are possible and you will require systems to handle both. One kind answers simple yes or no questions; and the other kind gives a fuller picture of the querent's future. Yes or no questions would normally be answered by a spread such as the Celtic or the Traditional Gypsy Method while a life reading would include all 78 cards.

Having chosen a system, memorize the meanings of the cards and their play within the system. Both must become as nearly automatic as possible to allow your intuition full freedom to work. To get caught in the middle of a reading in a panic; what card goes where; will totally blast your concentration.

When you start feeling easy about the cards and the method try doing some practice readings for yourself. These are practice only; normally no Tarot reader does his own readings. There is a reason for this: the question should be

193

known only to the querent. The reader may need to know the general area of enquiry or even the accuracy of a reading up until a certain point; but he should not know the exact question, nor does he need to fully understand the answer. The message is not for him, it is for the querent. The reader is simply a vehicle; and, just as a car does not need to ask questions of the driver as to destination and purpose, the reader does not need to *know* the origin or purpose of the enquiry. Such knowledge will only prejudice the reading.

To begin hand the querent the full Tarot deck, face down. Let him concentrate silently for a few minutes on the question. The cards are then shuffled by the reader and cut three times by the querent, using his left hand. The deck is now ready for use in any of the following spreads.

The Celtic Method

Select the Fool (Significator) and place it on the table in front of you. Then:

(1) Turn over the first card, placing it on top of the Significator and saying: 'This covers him.' This card indicates the general atmosphere which surrounds the querent and the question.

(2) Turn over the second card, placing it across the first and the significator and saying: 'This crosses him'. This card indicates any contrary influences which may oppose the Querent or the question.

(3) Turn over the third card, placing it above the others and saying: 'This crowns him'. This card designates the Querent's ideal hope in the matter.

(4) Turn over the fourth card, placing it below the central pile and saying: 'This is beneath him'. This card is the foundation of the question.

(5) Turn over the fifth card, placing it to the right of the central pile, saying: 'This is behind him'. This card represents the past of the Querent.

(6) Turn over the sixth card, placing it to the left of the central pile saying: 'This is before him'. This represents the future of the Querent. It is important to note that cards five and six deal with the Querent while card four deals with the question.

(7) Turn over the seventh card and place it to the right, and a little below the cross that has been formed by the first cards, and saying: 'This answers him.' This card gives the answer to the question.

(8) Turn over the eighth card, placing it immediately above the seventh, and saying: 'This strengthens him.' This card represents people or forces which may assist the Querent in the matter.

(9) Turn over the ninth card, place it directly above the eighth, saying: 'This defines him.' This card defines the Querent on all levels: Sensation, feeling, intuition, and thought.

(10) Turn over the tenth and final card, placing it directly above the ninth and saying: 'This ends it.' This card totals all the other cards and is read as if

St Andrew's Cross

Tau Cross

Maltese Cross

Swastika (Left Hand—Nazi)

Greek Cross

Ankh

Sun in Glory

Moon in glory

Equatorial Crescent

Thumin (Moon in third quarter)

Papal Cross

Keys of St Peter

Crowley's Signet

Yod

Tetragrammaton, Yod-He-Vav-He

all the cards progressed toward it in the manner of a story. Card ten gives the final outcome, after the question has been asked and answered and taking into account what is known of the Querent and his background.

This method is one of the simplest. In it, as in the other methods described in this book, all progressions are taken to be from right to left (the reverse of the way you are now reading). The reasons for this are not particularly polymorphous and perverse: the majority of Tarot systems appear to read from right to left, the Hebrew alphabet (with which as expressed in the Kabbala some commentators have found correspondences) reads from right to left, and most important it takes longer in a civilization oriented left to right.

Which brings us to pace. Tarot readings, like those from the I Ching, should be done as slowly as possible, concentrating upon each card and upon its relationship to the cards next to it in the sequence as well as upon the sequence as a whole. By so doing you allow intuition to manifest itself.

Twenty-one Card Gypsy Method

This spread is adapted from Paul Huson's book, *The Devil's Picturebook*.

Having removed the significator, The Fool, and placed it face up upon the table, the rest of the deck is then fanned-out, face down. The Querent draws 21 cards at random and hands them to the Reader. The remaining 56 cards are discarded and play no part in the reading.

The pack of twenty-one is then, still concealed, dealt in a semicircle formed from seven piles, from right to left. The cards will then appear similar to the schematic pattern below:

G	F	E	D	C	B	A
7	6	5	4	3	2	1
14	13	12	11	10	9	8
21	20	19	18	17	16	15

The Fool

The piles are read from right to left, as dealt, with each triplet being read as one picture. Individual meanings of the stacks are as follows:

A: The Querent's present psychic state;
B: His present home life;
C: His present desires, hopes, his question;
D: His expectations in the matter;
E: What he does *not* expect (the kicker);
F: His immediate future;
G: The long term results of the matter.

With this method, as with the Celtic, the reading will benefit by the use of a

deliberate pace. Which will free the Reader's mind to work with the patterns of
the cards to produce an answer.

MacGregor Mathers' Third Method

This spread is adapted from MacGregor Mathers' book, *The Tarot*. Though first
published in 1888 it is still one of the best concise guides to use of the cards.
This layout is the most involved that Mathers gives. It utilizes the entire 78 card
deck and takes several hours to perform properly. Slow hours.

The Significator, The Fool, should be removed from the deck and placed face
upwards upon the table. The remainder of the cards should then be shuffled
and cut as above. They are then dealt, one at a time, face downwards:

	33, 32, 31, 30, 29, 28, 27, 26, 25, 24, 23,		
	66, 65, 64, 63, 62, 61, 60, 59, 58, 57, 56,		
22	55,	44,	11
21	54,	43,	10
20	53,	42,	9
19	52,	41,	8
18	51,	40,	7
17	50,	39,	6
16	49,	38,	5
15	48,	37,	4
14	47,	36,	3
13	46,	35,	2
12	45,	34,	1

The Fool
significator

The remaining 11 cards, 67 through 77, are placed face down under the
significator to be used in the 11th and final step of the reading.

Cards 1—11 and 34—44 represent the past
Cards 23—33 and 56—66 represent the present
Cards 12—22 and 45—55 represent the future

Procedure

(1)   Turn over the first card and 'read' it, following it with the second and on
      up to the 11th, in sequence. Then turn over card 34, continuing onward
      through card 44. This represents the Querent's past and should be read as
      a sequence;

(2)   Perform the same action with cards 23—33 and 56—66 for the present;

(3)   Perform the same action yet a third time with cards 12—22 and 45—55 for
      the future;

(4) Pair 1—34, 2—35, 3—36, and so forth . . . reading the pairs together for the past;

(5) Pair 23—56, 24—57, 25—58, etc., reading them for the present;

(6) Pair 12—45, etc., reading them for the future;

(7) Second series of pairs: 1—44, 2—43, 3—42, etc . . . reading for the past:

(8) Pair 23—66, 24—65, etc . . . reading for the present;

(9) Pair 12—55, etc . . . reading for the future;

(10) Third series of pairs: Place card 1 on 66, 2 on 65, 3 on 64 etc., working through the entire deck until you have a pack of cards, face up, with the card which has been in position 33 on top. Deal them, counterclockwise, in a large circle, with the Fool and his dummy cards in the position of twelve o'clock. 33 will, therefore, be immediately to the right of the Fool (toward one o'clock); and 66 will be the last card (between eleven and twelve o'clock.) Pair and read as follows: 33 acting upon 66, 34 acting upon 1, 32 acting upon 65, 35 acting upon 2 etc., through to the final pair, 17 acting upon 50. A diagram representing this step is below:

Significator

66 33
1 34
65 32
2 35
64 31
3 36
63 30
4 37
62 29
5 38
61 28
6 39
60 27
7 40
59 26
8 41
58 25
9 42
57 24
10 43
56 23
11 44
55 22
12 45
54 21

```
13 . . . . . . . . . . . . . . . . . . . . . . . . . . . . 46
53 . . . . . . . . . . . . . . . . . . . . . . . . . . . . 20
14 . . . . . . . . . . . . . . . . . . . . . . . . . . . . 47
52 . . . . . . . . . . . . . . . . . . . . . . . . . . . . 19
15 . . . . . . . . . . . . . . . . . . . . . . . . . . . . 48
51 . . . . . . . . . . . . . . . . . . . . . . . . . . . . 18
16 . . . . . . . . . . . . . . . . . . . . . . . . . . . . 49
50 . . . . . . . . . . . . . . . . . . . . . . . . . . . . 17
```

The whole of this step requires a great deal of space as well as time. For the above layout somewhere in the region of nine square feet and up to a half hour. The final step in the whole reading is number 11, considerably less.

(11) The entire deck of 66 cards is shuffled, then cut, three times, alternating the shuffle with a single cut. The reader then selects a single card from the pack and places it with the eleven cards, 67 through 77. The cards are dealt out, counterclockwise, beginning with the selected card at a position analogous to that of eight o'clock on the clock dial. The next card goes, face up, in the position of seven o'clock, and so on, around the circle to the position nine o'clock. The 12 cards are read in a sequence, as a coherent story winding up at the central card, the Fool. Which concludes the reading.

A brief explanation of the 12 Houses (as this part of the reading is based on the Zodiac, the zodiacal meanings are used) follows:

eight o'clock	Deals	with money
seven o'clock	Deals	with kindred and journeys
six o'clock	Deals	with inheritance
five o'clock	Deals	with children
four o'clock	Deals	with sickness
three o'clock	Deals	with Marriage
two o'clock	Deals	with Death
one o'clock	Deals	with Long journeys
twelve o'clock	Deals	with Honour
eleven o'clock	Deals	with friends
ten o'clock	Deals	with enemies
nine o'clock	Deals	with Life and health

This arrangement concludes with the most important House, that of Life. It seems appropriate in a Life Reading.

Planetary Arrangement

This 78-card spread uses the entire deck and is based upon the arrangement of the I Ching trigrams made by Fu Hsi.

The cards are shuffled and cut as in preceding methods, then one card is removed and placed face down, underneath the Fool, which is placed on top of it, face up. The remaining cards (76) are then dealt into four equal piles, *A*, *B*, *C*, and *D*, dealing from the right. Thus

D	C	B	A
19 Cards	19 Cards	19 Cards	19 Cards

The *A* pile is then divided into two piles, one about 36 inches above the other, one at 12 and one at 6. That which is at 12 has 10 cards, being the first dealt, and that at 6 has nine.

The *B* Pile is then dealt to 1 : 30 and 7 : 30, beginning at 1 : 30.

The *C* Pile is then dealt to 3 : 00 and 9 : 00, beginning at 3.

The *D* Pile is then dealt to 4 : 30 and 10 : 30, beginning at 4 : 30.

You will then have:

Ch'ien

≡≡≡

The Sun

Tui   Sun

☱   ☴

Jupiter   Venus

Li   K'an

☲   ☵

Mercury   *The Fool*   Saturn
                        hidden card

Chên   Kên

☳   ☶

Mars   Uranus

K'un

☷

The Moon

The two remaining planets, Pluto and Neptune, are read thus:

Pluto: Ch'ien: ≡≡≡ The hidden card and

Neptune: K'un: ☷ The Fool.

The cards are read in a sequence of 10 pictures in the following order:

(1) Ch'ien   (5) K'an
(2) K'un   (6) Li
(3) Sun   (7) Kên
(4) Chên   (8) Tui

         (9) K'un
         (10)   Ch'ien

In this reading there will be three complementary influences working together: those of the trigrams, which are the basic trigrams on which the 64 I Ching hexagrams are based; those of the planets working on the cards over which each of them rules; and, finally, the pattern of the cards themselves.

Procedure

(1) Turn over the pile at Ch'ien (12 o'clock). Fan the cards out from right to left, reading them in the same direction. This position deals with primal strength, untiring power, self expression and the health of the body. Discard the pile;

(2) Turn over the pack at K'un (6 o'clock). Fan the cards as above and read. This position deals with response, fluctuation, devotion, submission. It is as totally 'feminine' as Ch'ien is 'masculine'. Discard these cards;

(3) Turn over the pack at Sun. Fan and read as above. This position deals with love, sex, relatedness, harmony, physical creation or recreation. Discard;

(4) Turn over Chên. This position deals with movement, excitement, struggle, fire, war, hate. It is not as heavy, however, as

(5) K'an, a position of great malevolence, destruction without passion, limitation, perhaps imprisonment or death;

(6) Li: Communication, inspiration, intuition. Light-giving therefore possibly Promethean;

(7) Kên is a contradictory placing, having the attributions of Keeping Still, resting, listening and at the same time those of revolutionary disruptive change. The tension produced by these two opposites governs the cards;

(8) Tui is a position of great joy, pleasure, complacent satisfaction, production, feasting;

(9) K'un, The Fool, who is in a position of impressionability, intellectual and intuitive submission to

(10) Ch'ien, the hidden card which governs the entire reading. In this position Ch'ien has the meaning of elimination, renewal, regeneration, resurrection, eternal strength, life, as well as the tension arising from the opposing concepts of farthest out (Pluto being the farthest planet) and furthest in (in the mind, Pluto being the ruler of the Underworld and of Life after death).

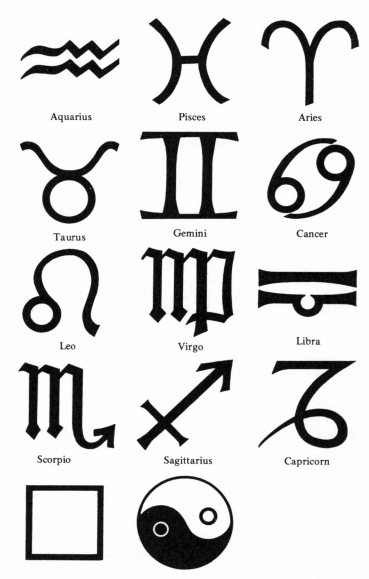

Aquarius

Pisces

Aries

Taurus

Gemini

Cancer

Leo

Virgo

Libra

Scorpio

Sagittarius

Capricorn

Square (The world world order)   T'ai Chi

(11) Meditate on the progression of hexagrams formed from this wheel:
12: P'i: Standstill or Stagnation
42: I: Increase
63: Chi Chi: After Completion
41: Sun: Decrease
11: T'ai: Peace

In this arrangement steps 9 and 11 will be the same in all readings.

The Crowley Divination

This spread is adapted from Crowley's book, *The Book of Thoth*.

Cutting and shuffling are performed as in earlier methods; but the Significator, The Fool is left in the pack of 78. The Querent meditates upon the question, then the pack is dealt as follows:

(1) Cut the pack to your left;

(2) Cut each of the packs so formed to your left;

(3) These four stacks, from right to left, represent Yod-Heh-Vau-Heh.

(4) Find The Fool. If he is in the Yod pack the question relates to work or business. If he is in the first Heh pack the question relates to marriage, love, pleasure, sex. If he is in the Vau pack it relates to loss, scandal, disputes, troubles in general. If he is in the second Heh pack the question relates to money or purely material matters. Tell the Querent the subject of his question. If he agrees proceed further. If he disagrees abandon the divination;

(5) If right, spread out the pack containing the Significator, face upwards. Count the cards from him towards the left, including the Significator as the first card. Values as follows:

Knights, Queens and Kings: 4
Pages: 7
Aces: 11
Small cards: as face value
Trumps: Elemental: 3
Planetary: 9
Zodiacal: 12

The Elemental Trumps are: The Fool, The Hanged Man, and Judgement

The Planetary Trumps are: The Magician, The Papess, The Empress, The Wheel of Fortune, The Tower, The Sun and The World

The Zodiacal Trumps are: The Emperor, The Pope, The Lovers, The Chariot, Strength, The Hermit, Justice, Death, Temperance, The Star and The Moon

Make a story out of the cards, the beginning of the matter;

(6) Pair the cards on either side of The Fool and read them, then the next pair out and so forth. These pairs fill in details omitted in step five;

(7) Ask the Querent if the story so far is reasonably accurate. If not, stop the reading;

Step II

(8) Shuffle, cut and deal into 12 stacks, representing the 12 Astrological Houses;

(9) Make up your mind in which of the piles you should find the Significator.
> 1: Life and Health
> 2: Money
> 3: Kindred and journeys
> 4: Inheritance
> 5: Children
> 6: Sickness
> 7: Marriage
> 8: Death
> 9: Long Journeys
> 10: Honour
> 11: Friends
> 12: Enemies

Turn over that stack and search for it. If it is not there, try a related House. If it is not there either, then abandon the divination.

(10) If you have located the Significator satisfactorily then perform the operation as before, first counting, then pairing. This represents the development of the question;

Third Operation

(11) Shuffle, cut, and deal as in the previous step, into 12 stacks representing the 12 zodiacal signs. Meditate on the stacks and attempt twice only to divine the location of The Fool, according to which of the signs would normally accommodate the question, e.g.:
> 1: Aries: Anger
> 2: Taurus: Beauty
> 3: Gemini: Learning
> 4: Cancer: Rest
> 5: Leo: Prominence
> 6: Virgo: Labour
> 7: Libra: Affection
> 8: Scorpio: Sexuality, birth, death, psychic areas, passion
> 9: Sagittarius: Travel
> 10: Capricorn: Old age, cold, responsibility
> 11: Aquarius: Eccentricity, occultism
> 12: Pisces: Sleep, mysticism, psychism

204

If the Significator is not found after two tries, abandon. If it is then spread and read, pair and read again, as before. This process represents further development of the question;

Fourth Operation

(12) Shuffle and cut as before. Find the significator and place him upon the table. The 36 cards which immediately follow him form this reading (the remaining 41 being set aside until the final step). Deal out the thirty-six cards in a wheel around the Fool, beginning at 12 o'clock and proceeding in a counterclockwise direction. Then count and read, pair and read as previously;

Fifth and final Operation

(13) Take up the entire deck again, replacing The Fool in it. Shuffle and cut as before. Then deal out the cards in the form of The Tree of Life, as below:

```
              1
     3                 2

     5                 4

              6
     8                 7


              9

             10
```

The 11th card will then go on 1, 12 on 2 etc.

(14) The positions with their correspondences are as follows:

1: KETHER:
The Crown. The Fool, Neptune, the highest internal quest

2: CHOKMAH:
Wisdom. The inner intellect, the universe, Uranus, personal initiative

3: BINAH:
Understanding. Outer intellect, Death, Saturn, trouble

4: CHESED:
Mercy. Inner emotion, The Emperor, Jupiter, financial success, prosperity

5: GEBURAH:
Judgement. Outer emotion, The Tower, Mars, enemies, wars, revenge

6: TIPHARETH:
Beauty. The essential self, the Watcher, The Hanged Man, The Sun, splendour

7: NETSACH:
Eternity. Involuntary processes, The Empress, Venus, love, passion, sex

205

8: HOD:
Reverberation, voluntary processes, The Magician, Mercury, wheeling and dealing, communications, politics
9: YESOD:
Foundation. Personal Ego, The High Priestess, The Moon, intuition and feelings, the soul
10: MALKUTH:
Kingdom. The body, The Wheel of Fortune, Pluto (?), the home, physical appetites

(15) Locate the significator in one of the piles. Keep searching until you find it. Discard all the other stacks as they will not be needed. Spread out the stack containing the Fool, count and read, pair and read as before. This reading gives the final result and answer to the question.

The Churchyard Spread

This spread is suitable for answering a question which the Querent has clearly formed within his mind. The result will be an answer or a further definition of the question which will enable the Querent to sort out the answer plus the answer to a second question which applies to or defines the first but which was unknown to the Querent at the beginning of the reading. With the end result that the total answer can be described as: 'Not only . . . but also'.

The Fool, for Significator, is first separated out from the deck. The remaining 77 cards are then shuffled three times, then the Querent cuts the deck three times from right to left while concentrating upon his primary (that is conscious) question. Upon restoring the deck the Reader counts off the top twelve cards, discarding for the remainder of the reading the other 65.

Into the twelve insert the Fool and again shuffle the cards three times. The Querent then cuts the cards, three times as before from right to left. The cards are then dealt out from right to left in a fan shape. Face up. The position of the Fool is of importance here because it indicates the end of one question and the beginning of the other, the secondary or unconscious question.

If the Fool should fall at the beginning of the spread it indicates that the question thought of is not substantial issue. If at the end of implies that the primary question is the only one to be considered at that particular time. Otherwise the reading is straightforward as in any other method.

Repetition of note concerning reversed cards
At the beginning of the section on the Minor Arcana I suggested that reversed cards be ignored. Opinion concerning them is very much split: some Readers avoid them because of their imputed pessimism, others insist upon having them in any spread (to the extent of deliberately using a shuffle that will insure their presence in all spreads), others ignore the reversal (arguing that the symbolism is pretty much the same no matter which way the cards fall) and other writers

give alternative meanings, upright and reversed, for all cards. In Section III where some meanings are contradictory within one interpretation it is usually because the writer has allowed for reversal within his method and therefore paradox.

I would personally incline towards ignoring reversed cards except possibly in the case of cards where the design includes pentagrams and therefore a possibility of reversed pentagrams. Instead, Readers might consider each card as fluctuating between poles of light and dark or positive and negative, thus giving a card its final interpretation in any particular spread according to the surrounding cards and the total aspect of the layout.

5 Systems Design

As noted throughout the book the Tarot has changed often since its invention. There are variant decks, interpretations and methods. All of which point out the central truth of the Tarot: it is *not* the cards or the system. It is the facility which they afford a receptive mind to use them in divination to evoke an already formed answer in the Querent's mind. The important term here is 'divination', used instead of possible alternatives such as 'clairvoyance' or 'fortune-telling'. Both terms are much too emotive; and the Tarot is not an emotive discipline. Intuition does play a part; but it is that same intuition which is employed in water-divining, an eminently practical activity as many water-diviners in semi-desert situations, such as some of the Greek Islands, will testify. The water-diviner does not manufacture the water by any miraculous means, he simply knows if it is there and precisely where. So with the intuitive Tarot reader. The answer already exists, the answers are already complete in all their possibilities. The Reader and the Querent locate them; and it is for the Querent to understand them.

So, having learned the systems and memorized the cards I suggest you do what many writers on the Tarot have done: design your own deck, incorporating those symbols and images which have meaning for you and which will help you to remember, to communicate with your unconscious mind. Designs do not have to be professional, they do not have to be commercially printed, they do not even have to make 'sense', provided that they work for you.

Potentially the Tarot has an immediate advantage over the I Ching and Astrology in that there is considerably more opportunity to develop creative as distinct from passive intuition. Aleister Crowley's adventures with Tarot design and systems of interpretation illustrate this. As do the decks mentioned below:

The Morgan Tarot	This deck, from 1970, bears no relation to the traditional. There are 87 cards, printed black on white, and owing much to 1967 and psychedelic art. They display a great deal of humour (rare in Tarot cards); and are effective in readings. Some of the cards from this Tarot are reproduced in this book.
The Grand Etteilla	No date. Probably late eighteenth century and possibly designed by Alliette, the Barber and occultist. They are

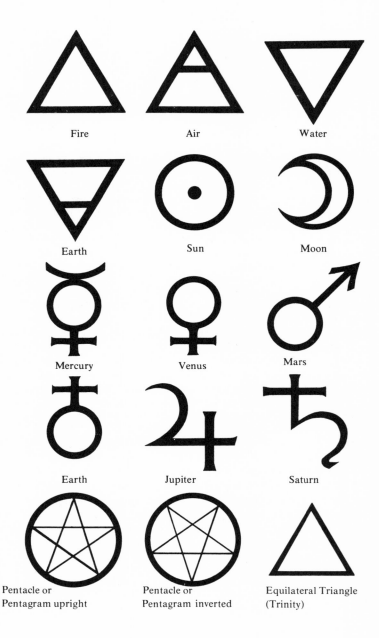

Fire   Air   Water

Earth   Sun   Moon

Mercury   Venus   Mars

Earth   Jupiter   Saturn

Pentacle or
Pentagram upright

Pentacle or
Pentagram inverted

Equilateral Triangle
(Trinity)

referred to as being 'The Egyptian Gypsies Tarot'. Some of the cards have, in addition to their designs, astrological attributions printed upon them. Beautiful designs with little relation to the standard deck. 78 Cards.

The Astrological Tarot   Georges Muchery, no date. 48 Cards, printed in colour on very heavy card plus 312pp book. A system based on astrology, 36 of the cards being the decans (division of each of the 12 zodiacal signs into 3 divisions of 10 degrees each) and the remaining 12 cards being: The Wheel of Fortune, Waxing/Waning Moon, the Ascendant, The Sun, The Moon, Mercury, Mars, Venus, Jupiter, Saturn, Uranus, and Neptune.

Galgal, The Master Game   56 Black and white cards based on the Kabbala and astrology.

The Jesus Deck   48 beautifully designed cards, reminiscent of the Aquarian deck. To be used for meditation and inspiration. Each suit is named after an Apostle.

I Ching Cards   An efficient design that takes advantage of interest in the I Ching and in forms of divination employing cards such as the Tarot. Most ingenious.

The John Upton Deck   From a private collection. These cards consist of 22 Major Arcana in felt pen and collage, highly coloured, and 56 Minor Arcana in collage, primarily black and white. Material used includes pictures from comic books, advertisements for pornography, original drawings, engravings, war pictures, advertisements. Beautifully done.

Bill Griffiths Deck   78 cards hand silk-screened on card in colours. The designs bear little relationship to the originals and the total effect is one of a nice personal statement.

From the way that Tarot systems have proliferated over the past few years it would seem likely that more people will be designing their own decks, devising their own interpretations and systems.

A good thing. The mystery lies not in the cards but in the heads of the people who use them. Anything that helps to lighten the mystery and make it understood will be useful. There's too much mystery. Too many experts. Too many books on the Tarot.

6 Glossary of Terms and Symbols Relating to the Tarot

This section attempts to give some of the basic meanings or attributions behind symbols and terms used in the Tarot systems considered here. The significance of each card is much more easily understood when the reader bears in mind these symbolic meanings.

Above   Heaven or God.

Absinthe   A liqueur containing wormwood. (*Which see*)

Adam Kadmon   Adam is symbolic of primal energy, first man and woman. Adam Kadmon is symbolic of the world soul.

Adonis   A Phoenician god, whose history parallels that of Horus and, in some ways, that of Kore.

Aeacus   One of the three judges of Tartarus (the Greek afterlife). Ruler in life of the island of Aegina, builder with Apollo and Poseidon of the Walls of Troy. He keeps the Keys of Tartarus (possible reference from Keys of St Peter?) and arbitrates quarrels between the Gods.

Agate   Worn as a protective stone against: Spiders and Scorpions (red); Disease in the Eye (green); Evil Eye (brown). The Brown Agate additionally makes a warrior victorious, protects against all poisonous reptiles, wins love, gives riches, happiness, health and long life.

Agni   Indian God of Fire, both Celestial and Hearth. He is represented as both a bull and an eagle. Creator of the Sun and Stars.

Air   Masculine element. Ranked in elemental cosmogonies as either the primal or terminal element, the highest.

Albus   A geomantic sign meaning White Head, Wisdom, Sagacity or Clear Thought. Relates to the Astrological Sign of Mercury. It is Watery, Cancer, 12.

Alexandrite   A variety of Chrysoberyl. Shows green by day and red by artificial light.

Alligator   Connections with Water and with Serpents or Dragons as well as Death.

Almond Tree   Sweetness, delicacy, possibly virginity.

Aloe   Used in spells to bring about restriction.

Amber   Aligned with the Sun, it protects against evil fortune and attacks from witches.

213

Amethyst	A protection against sorcery if the names of the Sun and Moon were inscribed on it. The amulet was then tied to the neck with the hairs of a peacock and the feathers of a swallow. Amethyst was also used as a protection against drunkeness, gout, poison, and outbursts of temper. It was said to improve memory, make its wearer gentle and amiable, and to give pleasant dreams when placed under the pillow.
Amissio	A Geomantic Sign meaning Loss or That which is taken away. A bad figure. It corresponds to Venus, Fire, Libra and 8.
Amon-Ra	A combination of two Egyptian Gods: Amon, a male fertility God, and the much older Ra, a Sun God.
Angel	Symbolic of hidden forces, heavenly power or wrath, messages from heaven, sublimation of earthly desires.
Ankh	A symbol of life, sometimes represented in association with the Phallus. Also known as the Crux Ansata. It is a form of Tau Cross, the Greek capital letter 'T', with a circle or loop attached at the top.
Anubis	The Jackal or Dog-Headed God of the Egyptians. He was a conductor of souls (like Hermes and Thoth) and inventor of the process of mummification.
Ape of Thoth	Thoth (Egyptian Hermes) is sometimes represented as an Ape and is sometimes accompanied by Apes. Like many other sacred animals in Egypt, the bodies of Apes were often mummified.
Aphrodite	The 'Foam-born' Greek Goddess of Desire. She is associated with Doves and Sparrows. Through the anger of Aphrodite Adonis was born; and through her magic girdle and its power they subsequently became lovers. Her soul duty was to make love.
Apis	The reincarnation of the Egyptian God, Ptah, in Bull form. Ptah was the protector of artisans and artists and inventor of the arts as well as being a builder, designer and smelter of metals. He is usually represented as a mummified figure, with only his hands free. As the Bull he was called, 'The Renewal of Ptah's Life'. He had to bear the following markings: black hide, white triangle on his forehead, a vulture with outstretched wings on his back, crescent moon on his right flank, a Scarabaeus Beetle on his tongue, double hairs in his tail. Each of his movements was sacred; and the people of Memphis thronged daily to watch him exercise. His movements would then be interpreted as oracular. The death of the Apis Bull was an occasion for national mourning, Pharaoh, himself, officiating at the funeral. The body would then be embalmed in much the same manner as that of a High Priest.
Apollo	Greek Sun God, patron of the Pythian Games, prophecy, and music. He was guardian of the flocks of the Gods until Hermes stole them. At which point, according to Robert Graves, Apollo delegated the responsibility for watching them to Hermes. Apollo is also concerned with Medicine, being the father of Aesculapius,

214

the 'Father of Medicine'. He preaches moderation: 'Know Thyself' and 'Nothing in Excess'.

Apple   Symbolic of earthly desires, fruitfulness, fecundity, ripeness, that which is most desired or desirable. Cognate myths are those of Atalanta, Freya, the Judgement of Paris, the Gardens of the Hesperides.

Aquamarine   A gem which is related with happy marriage. It has the property of being more brilliant in artificial than natural light. Fortunate for Scorpio, for Aries in lesser degree. Curative value for disease of the throat, jaws and teeth. Preventative value for diseases of the stomach and liver.

Aquarius   Zodiacal sign. It is sanguine, aerial, hot, moist, masculine, diurnal, western and southern, humane, rational, and obeying. The House of Saturn. A fortunate sign which reigns over legs, ankles, Arabia, Russia, Denmark, Lameness, fractures, gout, cramp, rheumatism, foul blood and Hamburg. Denotes questions concerning any form of mining or ballooning.

Aquisitio   Geomantic sign meaning success, obtaining or absorbing. It is a good figure, corresponding to Jupiter, Air, Aries, and the number, 7.

Aradia   Possibly cognate with Herodias. A medieval witch goddess, supposedly the daughter of Diana, Queen of the Witches (and also the Moon), with her brother, Lucifer, the Sun. An alternative story gives Diana as being primal darkness, Lucifer as primal light, and Aradia (presumably Day or Time) as their daughter.

Ares   Greek God of War, blind courage, brutality and bloody carnage. He is also a God of Rage. His origin is probably in Thrace. He was defendant in the first Greek murder trial, being acquitted on the hill named after him, the Areopagus.

Aries   Zodiacal sign. Vernal, dry, fiery, masculine, cardinal, equinoctial, diurnal, moveable, commanding, eastern, choleric, and violent. House of Mars, Sun exalted. Hasty, violent, passionate, intemperate. A marginally fortunate sign governing small pox, measles, England, France, Switzerland, Germany, Denmark. It denotes pasture grounds, ceilings, warrens or hiding places, land recently ploughed.

Arrow   The weapon of Apollo, Diana, Artemis. Symbolic of the Sun (its rays) and also of divine light and fire. Phallic symbol.

Artemis   Greek Goddess of the Moon, chastity and the hunt. A personification of the Triple Goddess. Her arrows can kill but she is also a healer. Particularly identified with the New Moon.

Ash   Particularly identified with Odin. The World Tree, Yggdrasil, was an ash. Used for making spears and sacred to Poseidon. In Ireland, three of the Five Magic Trees which fell in A.D. 665 signifying the fall of the Old Religion to Christianity were ash trees. A symbol of rebirth and a Seat of Justice. Before Odin's ap-

215

pearance the Three Norns gave judgement beneath Yggdrasil. Highly reckoned as fireplace wood and, in older days, for oars and coracle slats.

Aspen The tree of the Autumnal Equinox, old age and shield makers. Associated with Hercules, who reportedly introduced it into Greece. Also associated with the measuring rod used in Ancient Ireland to gauge corpses for their coffins. Graves suggests that this was to remind the dead man that Hercules had conquered death, and if Hercules can do it, why can't you?

Astaroth Syrian and Palestinian Goddess, equated with Ishtar and Aphrodite. An aspect of the Triple Goddess.

Ass Associated with Saturn, death, humility, and (in alchemy) with the three material principles of matter; Mercury, Salt and Sulphur.

Assafoetida An antispasmodic herb with an extremely strong and disagreeable smell. There are associations between it and the Devil, it is used in exorcisms.

Astarte Variant of Ashtaroth, Ishtar. Another name for the Triple Goddess in her role as lover of Adonis.

Athena A Greek Goddess of War, Strategy, Law. She is a settler of disputes. In criminal trials at the Areopagus in legendary times she always voted in favour of the accused if the other judges were tied. A virgin goddess (the Maiden persona of the Triple Goddess) and is attended by an owl (wisdom) and a crow (wisdom again).

Attis Phrygian god, cognate with Adonis in some ways, who died as a result of self-castration under a pine tree. Solar connections and therefore with solar year.

Axe Symbolic of light and its power.

Baal Canaanite god whose public name was Baal, but whose 'real' or private name was sometimes Hadad. God of the atmosphere, clouds and tempests. In the legend of his death Baal was killed 'by animals as big as bulls' and, from the same account, he fell like a bull. There seems to be a similarity between the myth of his death and that of Adonis/Attis, who, in some accounts, was killed by wild boars.

Babalon Crowley's adaptation of Babylon, the city known as Mother of Harlots (in reference to temple prostitution practised there) for use as part of his sigil. It is possible that Crowley believed himself to be not only a reincarnation of The Great Beast, *To Mega Therion*, but also, in some sense, the lover of Babylon.

Bacchus A name for Dionysus (*which see*).

Basht Egyptian goddess. Either a Cat Goddess or Lioness Goddess, she represents the fertilizing warmth of the Sun, pleasure, music and dancing. Frequently depicted as having the body of a woman and the head of a cat.

Bear A lunar animal, symbolic of the lowest instincts. The She-Bear

216

was sacred in Greece to Callisto (Artemis Calliste). The bear may represent the autumn/winter months.

Bees Representatives of industry, perhaps also of social industry. Symbolic also of wealth, the soul, diligence and eloquence.

Beetle Normally a sign of things unclean or in some ways 'horrid and nasty'. Features as an ingredient in some spells, i.e. Shakespeare. Ground Cantharides Beetle is popularly known as Spanish Fly (an aphrodisiac). *For a contrasting attribution for Beetle see Kephra.*

Below As a direction a sign of mortality, flesh, human or animal intelligence as distinct from spiritual or divine intelligence.

Beryl The stone of St Thomas. Protects against hypnotism. Green Beryl was used for treating eye disease. Yellow-Green Beryl was employed in the treatment of jaundice and other liver complaints.

Black Cat Associated with misfortune, death and witchcraft. Graves mentions an oracular cave-shrine in Ireland before the coming of St Patrick where there was a 'Slender Black Cat reclining upon a chair of old silver'. She gave vituperative answers to those who tried to trick her, in keeping with her cat nature. The Black Cat may, additionally, relate to the waning moon.

Blindfold To make helpless in one sense; but additionally to give the quality of inner vision at the expense of outer, Compare, in the Waite deck, Justice (which is not but should be blindfolded) with the two, eight and nine of Swords.

Blood Life or vital power. As wine is a symbol for blood, so blood is symbolic of wine.

Boaz and Jachin Pillars which, according to tradition, stood at either end of the Temple Veil in Jerusalem before the destruction of the Temple and the Jewish captivity in Babylon. They represent, according to different sources, mercy and severity or spirit and matter.

Brahma The first person of the Hindu trinity. Father of gods and men.

Bread Life symbol, as blood, but perhaps referring more to the flesh or solid part of life. Thus, with communion, bread and water/wine could represent solid or tangible life united with intangible or spiritual life.

Broken Blade As the sword is a symbol of manhood, the broken blade must represent castration. In its other sense of bravery and freedom is the origin of the broken sword as a symbol of fear and imprisonment. Not necessarily imposed from without, the owner of the sword can refuse to use it or to keep it in good repair. In which case something more involved than simple imprisonment is involved.

Bull At various times symbolic of the Sky, Sun, Moon, and Earth. Its attributes always include masculinity if not hyper-masculinity.

Bulrush A phallic plant which features in the legend of Moses as well as in other birth stories. Used by the American Indians as a medicine for diarrhoea.

217

Burin	An engraving tool, used on copper or marble.
Butterflies	Emblematic of the living soul, rebirth, attraction towards the light, joy, and perhaps conjugal happiness and freedom.
Cactus	Symbol of keeping one's own counsel, surviving where nothing else can, and also (because of the thorns) self-protection, possibly virginity.
Caduceus	One of the immemorial complex symbols, being found in Ancient Sumeria, India and Rome. Symbolic of right conduct, moral balance, the union of the four elements, healing, Kundalini or Serpent Power on the Axis of the World, a balance of two different kinds of strength between the Wings and the Snakes. Broken up into separate parts the Wand signifies Power or Earth, the Wings are Diligence or Air, and the Snakes are Wisdom or Water and Earth.
Caliban	The savage and deformed slave of the Magus, Prospero in Shakespeare's play, *The Tempest*.
Camphor	A volatile, aromatic oil. An excitant. It is used in incenses manufactured for divination.
Cancer	Zodiacal sign of the Crab. It includes the summer solstice. An unfortunate sign ruling Scotland, Holland, Africa, asthmas, lung diseases, cancer, insanity. After all this it is also reckoned to be the most fruitful sign, House of the Moon with Jupiter exalted. Cold, watery, phlegmatic, feminine, cardinal, northern, commanding, nocturnal, moveable, weak. Denotes seas and watery places, hydraulic machines, and aquatic experiments.
Capricorn	Zodiacal sign of the Goat. Cold, earthy, arid, melancholy, nocturnal, southern, obeying, moveable, cardinal, changeable, Sign of the Winter Solstice. A barren sign which governs sprains and broken limbs, India, Macedonia, Thrace, Greece, Morocco and Oxford. Denotes barns, hot-houses, storage rooms, barren fields, tombs, mausoleums etc.
Carcer	Geomantic sign meaning prison or to be bound. It is either good or bad according to the nature of the question. It has the nature of Saturn, it is earthy, its zodiacal sign is Pisces and its number is 10.
Castor & Pollux	Greek Mythology, the Heavenly Twins. They exist in most mythologies with similar attributes: they are born of an Earth mother and a Heaven father, one represents Light (spirituality) and the other Darkness (humanity or evil). The sum of the myth seems to be the desirability of having the spiritual strangle the human for the sake of psychic evolution. (*See Merti*).
Cat's Eye	In an amulet this stone protects from witchcraft and death. It confers invisibility in battle. In some areas a man about to go on a trip gives his wife milk to drink which has been used to wash a Cat's Eye. Then, if she is unfaithful in his absence, there will be no children of the affair.
Censer	Incense was used in Ancient Egypt, Greece, Rome, India and China. Almost all religions incorporate it with the exception of the

218

Protestants and some Mohammedan sects. Its power is that of cleansing (both in the physical and spiritual sense) message carrying (i.e., 'My words fly up to heaven, my thoughts stay here below . . . ') and as an adjunct to social intercourse in ages before mass use of deodorants. The censer, then, has the function of carrying incense and therefore carrying out the purposes of incense.

Centaur   A fabulous being, half man and half horse. Symbolic of the spiritual nature unable to control the animal. Also symbolic of wisdom. Centaurs were known to have the twin gifts of prophecy and divination. Because they got fighting mad easily on liquor (in one case just by smelling it) they had a reputation for intemperance.

Cerberus   The three-headed dog who guards the Greek Tartarus or Hades. Dogs are frequently associated with death and another guardian of the Death-world, in another culture, is similar to Cerberus but with only two heads.

Ceres   The Greek Mother Goddess. The Triple Goddess in her second, fruitful phase. Equivalent to the Full Moon. A corn and grain goddess. When her daughter, Kore, was seized by Hades and dragged off to Hell, Ceres wandered the Earth looking for her, permitting no thing to grow until her grief had been satisfied. Eventually Hermes rescued Kore. She was permitted to stay with her mother six months of the year, but had to spend the other six months with Hades as a punishment for having eaten six (or seven) pomegranate seeds while with him before. The story probably forms the basis of the Eleusinian Mysteries.

Ceridwen   A Celtic goddess. Brewing up a potion to confer on her otherwise ungifted ugly son the gift of tongues, she unwisely invites a neighbour boy to stir for her. A drop of the liquid falls on his finger, he licks it and understands the speech of all things. (And also that she will now kill him if she can catch him.) So he flees, she chases, the two of them changing into a series of pairs of animals. Finally she swallows him (a grain of wheat) while she is in the form of a brown hen. She thinks she's got him; and, in the folk poem that is based on this story so far, she has. But this particular legend of Ceridwen goes on to say that nine months later the Brown Hen, by now Ceridwen again, gave birth to the Bard, Taliesin, when the seed had sprouted. And Taliesin wasn't just the son of the neighbour boy, he *was* the neighbour boy, come back to life again.

Cernunnos   The Celtic Horned God. Probably a solar divinity with other tie-ins with the annual ritual slaughter of the King of the Grove, the Mountain, etc.

Chalcedony   Protects from the Evil Eye, gives a peaceful disposition, protects against fever and gallstones.

Chalices (Cups)   Cognate with the Celtic Cauldron of Inspiration, the Cup of Life, the Grail, etc. A female symbol signifying something holy which receives or contains something equally holy.

Chalice of Blood As for chalice, but with the added implication of cruelty or pain.

Chandra The Hindu Moon God, the moon being regarded as a source of fertility and growth. A later name for him was Soma, the divine drink or drug which gave immortality or forgetfulness.

Chen The Chinese trigram ☳ which signifies Moving or exciting power, the north-east, inciting movement.

Cherub As it is now the Cherub signifies childish innocence, the head of a baby, with or without halo, with or without wings. Usually blond to further increase the innocence. Older representations of the cherub: as an adult angel . . . as the spirit of water; as a lion . . . spirit of fire; as a bull . . . spirit of earth; as an eagle . . . spirit of air. In still older times the Cherubim were the second order of angels, excelling especially in knowledge. And in Babylonia the Cherubim were guardians, half human, half animal . . . figures of terror.

Chi Chi (After Completion) An I Ching Hexagram formed from the two trigrams, Li (below) meaning the clinging fire, and K'an (above) meaning The Abysmal or Water. The significance of the figure of perfection and the pause for thinking that perfection brings, things can only get worse.

Ch'ien The trigram from the I Ching ☰. Its significance is Untiring Strength and Power, its direction is South.

Circle One of the most important and at the same time oldest of symbols. In its numerical sense it makes, as zero, the entire number system after nine. It is vital for any mathematician who wants to proceed beyond fingers. Its occult senses include: Sun, Moon, imprisonment or enclosure, protection, exclusion, division, perfection, control. Circles were used by the Essenes for meditation, and for Hercules King-sacrifice by many nations. It is symbolic of heaven (the zodiac and many other representations of the sky) and therefore symbolic of earth (as above so below). As a sign of power or of the retention of power the circle is used in ceremonial magic and telepathy.

Civet A musk derived from the anal pouch of a carnivorous mammal. The substance is used in commercial perfumes as well as in witchcraft preparations designed to arouse lust.

Clover Symbol of domestic virtue and good luck for women, of the Trinity and all trinities.

Club As a weapon it is almost always associated with giants or heroes of gigantic strength. Hence: Herne, Hercules, the Cyclops, giants from fairy stories, etc. These heroes or giants always function between Earth and the Sun, they are fertility sacrifices, they are King of the mountains; but they are never associated with either water or air. It is further interesting to note that Clubs (a late

220

development in the Tarot deck) as a name for the suit is probably closer to the actual meaning of the suit than is Wands.

Cocaine A stimulant alkaloid drug derived from the leaves of the Coca plant which is native to Bolivia and Peru. It acts on the central nervous system, producing first stimulation, then depression. It is habit forming but non-addictive.

Cock The connection between cock, sun and phallic symbol is as old as the hills. Nearly. The rooster is also the legendary father of the basilisk. The rooster lays an egg which is hatched out by a toad. The animal born of all this is frequently represented as a crowned lizard. The Basilisk was reputed to kill with a glance (connecting it with the Gorgons and the Evil Eye) and was known as either Basilisk or Cockatrice. According to legend the Basilisk would itself die if it heard the crowing of a cock (similar to Vampire legends, where, in some versions, the Vampire dies if touched by the rays of the Sun). The Cock was also a symbol of the Priests of Attis and of Corn Gods generally.

Coconut Symbol of purity and/or chastity.

Corn Adonis, Attis, Osiris, Demeter, Kore, and Tammuz are all Corn Gods. The divinity was usually dual in person: a sacrificed male and a Mother/Wife consort who mourns for the death. In the case of Osiris Corn was believed to have actually sprouted from the body of the slain god. Corn is always a symbol of plenty and of fertility, like other grains; but in the context of its mythology it is also a referrent to resurrection.

Corn Woman A Demeter figure.

Crab The sign of Cancer, sacred to Diana. In the Crab is the symbol of the fertilizing power of water.

Crane Sacred to Dorian Apollo, Theseus, Athena, and to Artemis. It was worshipped by the Etruscans and figures prominently in the fable of the invention of the Alphabet by Hermes. Cranes witnessed the murder of the sixth century Greek poet Ibycus and avenged his death by terrifying the murderers into confession. The bird is a symbol of justice, wisdom, longevity and the good and diligent soul. Dances, in the manner of its movement, were performed at Delos in honour of the Moon Goddess.

Crayfish Said to represent the unconscious mind.

Crescent Symbol of the waxing or waning Moon and therefore of the Maiden and Crone personae of the Triple (Mother) Goddess.

Cross A symbol of balance between opposites: Heaven and Earth, Fire or Air and Earth or Water, Male and Female. Similar in effect to the T'ai Chi, but lacking the T'ai Chi's implicit motion. More a symbol of resolution than of resignation or punishment. The axis of creation. Death on the Cross, or Crucifixion, is usually a sign of Solar Sacrifice and was practised long before Christ.

Crossed Swords A symbol of fighting.

221

Crown	Crown, hat, head-dress and hair dressing date from the earliest recorded times. In symbolic terms it is of cosmetic purpose; but even more important would probably be the need to indicate hierarchies: royal status, divinity, priesthood for example. Crowns and hair dressing probably also have ritual meaning.
Crux Ansata	The ankh.
Crystal	Earliest meaning is 'Frozen Ice', but it soon acquires its primary significances: for healing and protection and as a tool for seeing. Several Scottish clans had Crystal as a 'Stone of Victory'; and the water in which these stones were washed was said to have medicinal value. Crystal was also used powdered as a medicine and as a burning glass in operations. It was also employed as a tool for 'scrying' (divination with a Crystal), sometimes as a substitute for the more highly valued Scrying Tools: Diamond or polished Coal.
Cube	The square in three dimensions, carrying the same suggestion of dependability; but, in the case of the cube, this dependability has become almost sacramental. In many Tarot decks the Emperor is seated upon a cubic throne.
Cupid	Roman God of Love, son of Venus and Mercury. Equated with Eros. Too frequently he appears as a cherubic babe with soggy bow and arrows.
Cypress	Associated with sanctuaries of Aesculapius and with cemeteries. Symbolic of death and resurrection. In the Old Testament they form part of a Tree Riddle which may have been answered, Chokmah, Wisdom.
Daffodil	Also called Lent-Lily. One of the first spring flowers.
Dagger	Features in Egyptian incantation. One of the legions of Satan was formed of dagger-bearers in the first great battle against the Hosts of Heaven. A weapon of treachery.
Decagram	A ten-pointed star. Could represent return to unity, spiritual achievement, death, perfection, or totality (of the self, the Universe).
Demeter	Greek Corn Goddess. Represents the middle part of the Triple Goddess: Maiden/Mother/Crone, and was the mother of Kore. Also associated with figs and the Eleusinian Mysteries and, oddly enough, swine. The reason given for her connection with swine is that in early times of agricultural society swineherds were also magicians and seers. She is the most familiar form of the Corn Goddess, the same in most of her attributes as Isis, Ishtar, Cybele. Fertility.
Diamond	Significant both for its extraordinary hardness and for its usefulness as a Scrying Glass. Reckoned in ancient times to be one of the most powerful of stones: because of its hardness it could drive away the Devil himself, it protected against the Evil Eye, rendered all poisons neutral and cured madness. Symbolic of great power and sometimes of great wealth.

Diana	Roman Goddess of Light, groves and forests. Another personification of the Triple Goddess and equates with Rhea (wife of Chronos or Time) and with Artemis. Her attributes are jointly chastity and cruelty. She is also apparently cognate with Dione, a titaness who presided over the Planet Mars and who was a Goddess of Moisture.
Diana of Ephesus	A variant on Artemis. She is closely related to Ceres, being thought of as the Mother of her people and frequently represented as being many-breasted.
Dionysus	In later times a Greek God of wine, madness, drunkenness, terror and joy. He is associated with the vine and with grapes, with the pomegranate which sprouted out of his death, and with the pine cone which he carried at the end of his staff, the Thyrsus. Dionysus is a hermaphroditic God, having been raised as a girl to protect him from the jealousy of Hera who was trying to kill him. He is attended by troops of women, the Maenads, who tear people to pieces, if they do not believe with sufficient conviction. He also, on at least one occasion, transformed himself into a girl. His shape changing also included: lion, panther and bull. A horned god being variously horned as Stag, Ram, Bull or Goat. He was himself torn to pieces by the Titans in his first birth, which may account for this feature occurring several times in his legends. Unlike his later image of debauchery his first birth was as a horned child crowned with serpents (in this case probably signifying wisdom rather than evil). His gifts are madness, life and death.
Dog	Faithfulness, Guardian. One of the signs of the Chinese Zodiac. Dogs figure in several mythologies as Guardians of Hell. In Egypt the gall of a Black Dog was used to clean and fumigate the house. In Babylonia Dog amulets were buried underneath the doorstep to guard those within. In British and Celtic Mythology the dog features in the Hounds of Hell or the Gabriel Hounds, hunting doomed souls across the sky. This legend seems to parallel that of the Hounds of Artemis, as they hunted to death Actaeon who had seen the Goddess naked.
Dog Tree	Another name for Dogwood. I have been unable to find its significance for Crowley.
Dolphin	Associated with Dionysus and from ancient times as a friend to mankind, particularly to sailors.
Door	*See window.*
Double headed	Related to the letter, Tau, therefore to the Tau Cross. Associated with Crete and with bull sacrifice. As the Bull is, in Crete, an oceanic figure the double axe may be associated with Poseidon.
Dove	Sacred to Astarte and to Aphrodite. Additionally a sign of the Holy Ghost descending upon the Apostles.
Dragon	An enormously complex symbol, known to most civilizations in its

223

own right but also in the form of the great serpent (for instance, the Midgaard Serpent in Norse Myth). It stands for evil, wisdom, the celestial kingdom, celestial order established upon earth, the waters of the earth, the air, the guardian of esoteric wisdom or of great wealth.

Dragon's Blood Used as an ingredient of sachets and incenses governed by Mars which are to be used in magical attacks. It is a resinous material.

Eagle Cherub of Air and a sign of Scorpio regenerate. Scorpio is a double sign containing both Scorpion and Eagle. Associated with Zeus and other sky gods, particularly with the myth of Ganymede (abducted by Zeus in the form of an Eagle) and that of Europa (abducted by Zeus as Bull, but raped by Zeus as Eagle). A bird of freedom, majesty and strength.

Ear Hearing, probably the most important of the secondary senses. (Sight being the sole primary sense). Hearing and the Ear are reckoned holy as it was through them that man first learned to apprehend God.

Earth One of the four Greek elements. Almost always feminine and frequently maternal. The strength of Earth is represented in the myth of Antaeus and Hercules, which takes place during Hercules' 11th Labour. After Hercules had returned from the Garden of the Hesperides he wrestled with the Giant King Antaeus in Libya. When Hercules won the first fall he was astonished to see Antaeus regain his strength. The second fall Antaeus didn't even wait for the throw but threw himself down. Hercules took all this in and ended the fight by strangling Antaeus in mid-air.

Egg A symbol of immortality and resurrection. The cosmic egg is the world egg, containing all levels of creation. A golden egg was the birthplace of Brahma. Eggs are associated with Ra in the mythology of Egypt and with Easter in all Christian countries but particularly in Greece and Russia. The Egg with the Serpent around it, as found in one Greek Creation myth, can represent wisdom producing or nursing life. With wings the Egg can represent spiritual life or life ascending. A Gnostic symbol.

Eight The number of that force which is intermediary between terrestial order (the square) and eternal order (the circle). Eight is associated with the Serpents of the Caduceus, with infinity, with the balancing of forces or with the equilibrium of different forms of power. The number of regneration and of the company of Gods who accompanied Thoth. Signifies genius, strength, inspiration, evolution, justice. Demeter.

Elephant Symbol of tremendous power. So great was this power that natives of Malaya and India used to refer to the Elephant indirectly, as 'Father' or 'Grandfather' or even 'Tall one who turns himself about', rather than use his real name which might call down unwelcome attention from him upon themselves and their families. The Elephant is further identified with Chieftains and Wielders of

224

	Strong Magic and also with invisibility because of the Elephant's vast cunning in being able to hide its bulk.
Emerald	Emeralds were used to cure diseases of the eye, to protect against the Evil Eye and to ward off hypnotic influences. It was also a protection against epilepsy. Budge says that 'the sight of an emerald struck such terror into the viper and cobra that their eyes leaped out of their heads'. It preserved a man from accident, stimulated mental powers. Emeralds are symbolic of fidelity, unchanging love and can help the wearer to forecast events.
Ergot	A fungus of rye wheat. In the Middle Ages Ergot developed on rye in Switzerland and led to outbreaks of Ergotomania, a disease similar in some of its effects to Schizophrenia. During research into Ergot the drug LSD was discovered.
Europa	Sister of Cadmus, abducted by Zeus who had disguised himself as a Bull. After swimming with her to Crete he changed himself into an Eagle and ravished her. Graves cites the legend as one of the Moon Goddess and the Sun Bull; but it also suggests a reason why, in Crete, the Bull was associated with the ocean and Poseidon, rather than the Sun/Apollo or the Sky/Zeus.
Eye	Organ of the primary sense, sight. Particularly associated with Ra, Thoth, and the almost universal belief in 'The Evil Eye'. As the ear is a feminine, receptive organ, the Eye is bisexual, having the faculty to receive and to transmit power.
Face	Considered by many primitive peoples to be the residence of humanity, thus taboos on painting it, drawing it, photographing it lest the soul be captured. Hunting tribes often blacken the face, apparently only partially as a means of camouflage, there is also an element of disguise, the supposition being that the animal is going to be fooled by the shadow. From this concept comes that of hunting masks or ceremonial masks, intended to placate or deceive intended prey or a God.
Falcon	Specially associated with Horus in Egypt and with Circe in Greece. (Circe translates Falcon). Its qualities are swiftness, strength, wisdom and sometimes cruelty.
Fan	Related to the Moon. Used as a symbol of power or authority as well as of air, wind and the celestial kingdoms. One of the Eight Inebriated Immortals, Chung-li Ch'uan, of Chinese Mythology, carried a feather fan.
15-pointed star	Star: symbolic of Spirit, 15 associated with the Devil and (according to Cirlot) of a markedly erotic nature. Possible symbolism for the 15-pointed Star could therefore be as a reference to the Planet Venus which appropriately enough has been also named Lucifer.
Fig	Associated with Dionysus and with Juno. It was believed to fertilize women and had a phallic significance, being carried in processions of Dionysus in that context. It is tempting to wish some further connection between Caprify (to

225

ripen figs by puncturing them, either by insects or artificially) and Capricorn. Both words have the same root, 'Capri', which comes ultimately from the Latin . . . Caper, caprum, meaning Goat. And Goats were famous for their randiness.

Fire One of the four elements of the Greeks. It is associated with the Sun, with lightning, with light, with gold and with volcanoes. Some volcano myths assert that man first obtained fire from the earth, from volcanoes.

Fire Opal A hyacinthine-reddish variety of Opal from Mexico. Opals are reckoned by some to be an Evil stone, possessing the Evil Eye. But they are also said to be capable of relieving pain from eye diseases and of increasing the powers of the eyes and of the mind.

Fish A symbol to the Early Christians of Christ, but also a religious symbol to the Greeks, Egyptians and Syrians. Fish figured in processions of Dionysus, as erotic symbols, possibly of the Yoni and not, as might seem likely, of the lingam. Legend says that fish were Virgin born, which may account for Virgin Birth legends of the Christ.

Five Considered by some to be most holy or lucky, by others to be a number of uncertainty or discouragement. The Pentagram. Man. The five senses. The four cardinal points plus the centre. The five elements of Chinese philosophy or the four Alchemical elements together with that which encompasses them all. Five frequently occurs in nature and is associated with an erotic meaning. As most odd numbers it is a male number, perhaps associated with Hermes the Magician.

Fortuna Major Geomantic Sign meaning Great Fortune, Success, Interior Aid and Protection. A very good sign which equates to Sun, Earth, Aquarius, and the number 12.

Fortuna Minor Geomantic Sign meaning Lesser Fortune or External Aid and Protection. Not a very good figure. It equates to Sun, Fire, Taurus and the number 10.

Fountain Symbol of peace, rest, spiritual strength or nourishment, the Water of Life (Inner Life, Celestial Life or Eternal Life) coming forth in abundance to give strength.

Four The world, the earth, the establishment, rational thinking generally. The number of the elements, the winds. A totally 'safe' number. The square, and by implication the cube and the tesseract. It may not be a complete accident that most western architecture depends on the Square and on the number four. In addition to its obvious structural advantages the number and the form may have unexplored psychic reassurance built-in. The World, generally. A feminine number.

Four, Sign of The planetary sign for Jupiter in Astrology. It has been pointed out that the figure can be formed by taking the plantetary sign for Venus (A Circle with a Cross at the botom), rotating it 90 degrees counterclockwise and removing three quarters of the Circle.

Another likely origin would be from the Indian number 4, invented about A.D. 500. The numerological associations of 4 are such that it could then have been applied to the planet which has similar associations.

Freya Norse Goddess who is a composite form of Venus, Hera and Ceres.

Furnace Symbolic of testing, trial, purification or sacrifice by Fire. Used in some Eastern ceremonies as a symbol of renewal by Fire.

Ganymede The cup-bearer to the Greek Gods and bedfellow of Zeus. He was abducted by Zeus in the form of an Eagle from the Trojan plain.

Gate Contains the meanings of Door (*see Window*) with the additional connotation of keeping the wild and therefore unfamiliar out and the tame and known in. It is a symbol of ingress of any kind, but equally of egress, things or forces let out.

Gemini Zodiacal Sign, The Twins. Castor and Pollux in Greek Mythology, Shu and Tefnut in Egyptian. They stand for the duality of all things, the T'ai Chi.

Geomancy Literally, divining by Earth. Term used to describe a system of divination in which marks are made upon the ground or upon a piece of paper. Four lines of dots are made, keeping the mind blank so that the forces of Earth can control the hand of the Reader. The process produces a Geomantic Figure. The same process is then repeated to produce three more figures. These first four figures (the Mothers) are used to produce four more figures (the Daughters). These, in turn make four more (the Nephews) which produce two (the Witnesses) and a final figure is at last formed from the two Witnesses. This final figure is called the Judge and forms the basis for the reading with qualifications from the witnesses.

Geranium Used as an herb in Midsummer Fires in Morocco. It can also be used in magical perfumes for arousing lust.

Girdle Associated with werewolves in Germany where it was believed that a man could turn himself into a wolf by wearing a girdle made from a strip of wolf's hide. The King of Tahiti wore a feather girdle which identified him as both King and as one of the Gods. Wreaths or girdles of mugwort were worn or burned for various illnesses including backache, ghosts, magic, misfortune, sickness, headache, eye disease, dry cattle, thunder, thieves, and spells upon butter. The Girdle is associated in Greece with Aphrodite, whose girdle caused men to love her.

Gnomes Spirits of Earth.

Gnostic Sun Wheel A symbol of the Christ and probably also of Pistis Sophia, Holy or perhaps Heavenly Wisdom.

Goat Associated with Pan, with Dionysus and hence with the Devil.

Grapes Fertility and sacrifice. Associated with Dionysus and Bacchus in

227

Classic Mythology, with Noah and Satan in Hebrew legend, and with Ham and Satan in Muslim teaching.

Great Mother The Triple Goddess. She is Kore/Ceres/Hecate in Greece, representing Maiden/Woman or Mother/Crone or New/Full/Waning Moon. Graves says that the worship of the Mother Goddess or Triple Goddess was the religion of Greece before the invasion which brought with it the worship of Zeus and Apollo, the Sky/Sun Gods of the Patriarchal Pantheon which supplanted the matriarchy. For further information see *The White Goddess* and *The Greek Myths*.

Greek Cross A cross in which the upright and transverse limbs are of equal length.

Green Man A composite of at least two legends: that of the Gaulish God, Cernunnos (The Horned God), and that of Robin Hood. Robin Hood has itself elements of other traditions, that of Robin Goodfellow and Puck.

Hades The Greek God of the Underworld as well as being a name for the Greek Underworld. The afterlife, according to the Greeks, was divided into the Asphodel Meadows (a sort of waiting room where heroes and common folk could wander about), the fields of punishment (where the guilty benefitted from their crimes), and The Elysian Fields or Orchards of Elysium, where the virtuous were condemned to suffer for their virtue. Notwithstanding all this radiance, the favourite occupation of the Greek Dead was drinking blood offerings. For then they had a semblance of life.

Hanuman Hindu Monkey God, son of Vayu, the Wind God. Similar in some of his attributes, trickery particularly, to Hermes/Loki.

Harmachis The Greek version of Hor-m-akhet, meaning Horus who is upon the horizon. It is the proper name for the Sphinx and a symbol of the rising sun and of resurrection.

Hathor The Egyptian Cow-Goddess (or cow-headed goddess) who is associated with Aphrodite. Sky-goddess, the celestial cow who created the world and the sun, wielder of the Sistrum, protectress of women and presider over their cosmetic arts, goddess of joy and love and, in the last stages of Egyptian history, she becomes the presider over funerals, supplanting Osiris in that function.

Hawk The soul, Solar transfiguration, possibly it refers to either the evil mind of the sinner or to victory over sin. In Egypt the Hawk was a symbol similar in its meanings to that of the Dove as Holy Ghost at the coronation of the Pharaoh. It is associated with Isis and Osiris and worshipped by some tribes as a totemic animal.

Hazel Hazel rods are used in Water Divining and have been used for rain-making.

Heart The Egyptian priests of the dead removed all of the viscera from the body before embalming it, except the Heart, which was left inside as being necessary to the dead man at his resurrection. The association of 'love' with the Heart apparently stems from the consideration of the Heart as the Centre of the Body and the seat of Intelligence within the Body (therefore, presumably, of emotion as well). The Heart pierced with an Arrow has been said to represent conjunction. It is even more likely, however, that it is symbolic of pain.

Hecate   The eldest of the three persons of the Triple Goddess. She was a Greek underworld Goddess, being Goddess of Witches. Crossroads were sacred to her, particularly a place where three roads met. She had three heads and three bodies: lion, dog and mare.

Hellebore   In Greece it was customary to face eastward and curse while cutting Black Hellebore for medicinal use. It is also used in exorcism incense.

Heptagon   The geometrical figure which can be derived from a Heptagram or 7-pointed Star. Takes on the dual meanings of 7 (number of spirituality and mysticism or wisdom and success) and Star (also a symbol of the spirit). Crowley uses both Heptagon and Heptagram in his Tarot Deck.

Hercules   One of a great number of heroes whose exploits have been gathered under a single name. Either a Solar God (weapons bow and arrow) or an Earth God (weapon the club). Graves divides his Labours into 12, which could correspond with the 12 Houses of Heaven, the 12 Signs of the Zodiac, or the 12 Hours that form half a day.

Hermaphrodite   According to Greek legend the son of Hermes and Aphrodite. He was bisexual. In later times the Gnostics adopted the figure of Hermaphrodite as being a man created before Adam. In Alchemy both the Lion and Mercury are hermaphroditic as was Quetzalcoatl in Mexico and Ardanari Iswara in India. As a symbol the Hermaphrodite is roughly analogous to the T'ai Chi, union of opposites.

Hermes   Hermes in his capacity as conductor of the souls of the dead. Re-
Psychopomp   lated to Thoth, Anubis, Hathor.

Herne   A British Oak God, Herne the Hunter. Legendary in the Windsor Forest Area. A horned God (Cernunnos) who hunted the sky with a pack of Hell hounds. Also a historical forester of the time of Henry VIII.

Hexagon   A six-sided geometrical figure. See Hexagram.

Hexagram   A Six-pointed Star, sometimes referred to as the Star of Solomon, but more properly it is the shield of Solomon, the Star of Solomon being the Pentagram. It is a symbol of magical power and used in witchcraft. Union of the triangles of water and fire, therefore a hermaphroditic symbol and also representative of the human soul or the human soul perfected.

229

Hibiscus	Used by some primitive tribes in the making of fire drills.
Hippogriff	A composite mythological animal formed from a Gryphon (Head of an Eagle, body and hind quarters of a Lion) and a Horse. As a symbol it is a union of Fire (Lion) Earth (Horse) and Air (Eagle).
Holly	Now associated with Christ, but probably represented at one time in Britain either the Mid-winter Sun or the Mid-winter Sun King.
Horse	Associated in Greek and other mythologies with Apollo, Poseidon, Hades, the Moon Goddess, Demeter and many others. It is associated with Air (Pegasus), Water (Sea Horses and various legends), with Fire (Phoebus Apollo) and with Earth (Demeter as Corn Goddess and Great Mother). Its most likely attribution is Earth, with the added meanings of wisdom and ferocity.
Horus	One of about 20 Egyptian Gods bearing this name. Symbolized by the Falcon. A Solar Divinity who was husband of Isis. The son of that Solar Divinity and Isis, also a Solar Divinity. Continual warrior against and eventual victor over Set (the principle of Evil or Darkness). He is also sometimes the son of Osiris. A symbol of the light, Solar and masculine principle which, things being what they were, had to be victorious in Egypt.
Hourglass	A symbol of time passing, but also relates to the lemniscate, an hourglass on its side, which is a symbol of infinite time.
Hyssop	In the Near East a plant of the Winter Solstice.
I (Increase)	An I Ching Hexagram:
Ibis	The bird of Thoth. Graves points out the resemblance between the Crane and the Ibis to develop his theory concerning the invention of the Crane Alphabet.
Iceland Spar	A transparent variety of Calcite, found in Iceland. Carbonate of lime in crystalline form.
Indian Hemp	Marijuana.
Indigo	Although it may possibly be used as a scent its primary use is as a dye. Egyptian.
Indra	Indian Sky God, roughly analogous to Zeus.
Iris	The plant, but also the Greek Goddess, messenger of the Gods. The Rainbow. Her chief shrine was on Delos.
Ishtar	The Babylonian/Assyrian Goddess who corresponds to Isis/Ceres.
Isis	The Egyptian Moon-Goddess. Equates with the Triple Goddess, with Ceres, with Hera and eventually to Hathor. A Mother figure. When she tried to interfere with the vengeance of her son, Horus, against her brother, Set, who had killed and mutilated the Elder Horus, the younger Horus got so angry at his mother (and also probably at the confusion of everyone having the same name) that he cut off her head. Thoth thoughtfully replaced it with a cow's head, which is why she is sometimes represented thus. Another reason may be that by this period in Egyptian religion (a late period) everyone was so confused that they couldn't distinguish between Isis and Hathor.

Jacinth	Also known as Hyacinth. As a talisman it is a symbol of fidelity, assistance in childbirth, protection from evil spirits, protection from bad dreams or fascination or flatulence or grief and melancholy. It strengthened the members, fortified the heart, restored the appetite and produced sleep.
Jackal	The animal form of the Egyptian God, Set.
Jester	The Court Fool. Appears in the Tarot Deck as the Fool, in the playing card deck as the Joker, and in comic books, literature, paintings and music from the Middle Ages down to present times.
Juniper	Used in Northern Italy and Germany as a protector against evil spirits, in Germany as a protector against thieves, in Italy as a Christmas decoration. It was a protection against witchcraft and ghosts, the berries were worn by mourners at funerals and it forms a frequent ingredient in love potions and other magical compounds for both vengeance and attack.
Juno	The Roman equivalent to the Greek Hera. The wife of Jupiter (Zeus).
Jupiter	Roman Zeus.
K'an	A Chinese Trigram, ☵ one of the eight which together make up the I Ching hexagrams. It means Peril, Difficulty, or Danger. West.
Karma	Fate seen as a reward for good or evil acts performed in previous lives.
Ken	A Trigram, ☶ one of the eight Trigrams, meaning Resting, the act of arresting or keeping still, northwest.
Kephra	The Scarabaeus Beetle, a dung beetle which pushes a ball of dung around all day. From this it was transformed in Egyptian legend to a Beetle God, pushing the Sun. It has been imitated countless times in amulets, rings and other jewelry. Symbolizes the rising Sun and the transformations of life.
Key	That which opens, frees, allows and (conversely) closes, imprisons and forbids.
Keys	The Crossed Keys are a symbol of the Pope and of Papal Authority as being derived directly from Christ. They also relate to Janus.
Keys of St. Peter	The crossed keys.
King of the Mountain	A children's game which is a pale survival of the ancient customs in many countries of killing the Solar King at the end of a Solar Year.
Knight	Emerges as a symbol about the time of the Crusades and the concept of Chivalry. It is therefore coeval with the development of the Tarot Cards, with Alchemical research, with Arthurian tradition and with many of the Grail legends.
Kore	Persephone. The Triple Goddess as Maiden. Abducted by Pluto (Hades) and condemned to spend half of the year with him for having eaten 7 Pomegranate seeds in defiance of the warning of

231

Hermes against eating any food in Hades' domain. She signifies the New Moon and the Virgin Huntress.

Kronos In Greek myths one of the Titans who led his brothers in an attack upon their father, Uranus. Kronos, himself, castrated Uranus and threw the genitals into the sea. In falling, drops of blood which struck the Earth became the Three Fates (a disguise of the Goddess) and foam from the severed flesh which fell into the sea gave birth to Aphrodite (Foam-born) according to another story. Kronos means either Crow or Time, perhaps both.

K'un One of the eight Chinese Trigrams, ☷, meaning Capaciousness, submission, yielding quality. North.

Kundalini Tantric Yoga or Serpent Power, the Yoga of Energy rising through the chakras.

Ladder Ladders, climbing ropes, beanstalks or pine trees . . . the variants are many and the meaning usually the same: a vertical bridge between Heaven and Earth. So, in a sense, the Tao.

Laetitia A Geomantic Sign meaning Joy, Health or Laughing. A good sign attributed to Jupiter, Air, Taurus and the number 15.

Lamb A symbol of Christ particularly the risen Christ. In older times a Golden Lamb seems to have been an emblem of kingship; and, of course, there is the Golden Fleece of Colchis. The contrast between the Lamb of God and the Ram of Dionysus, one meek and the other randy, may not have escaped th e early church fathers.

Lantern Symbol of the seeker or of the lost one.

Lapis Lazuli One of the most used stones in Egypt, India, Persia, and Mesopotamia by royalty and high officials. It was used for seals, scarabs, memorial tablets and the wearer of an amulet made from lapis lazuli was said to be wearing the God. Powdered it was administered for sleeplessness, fever, gallstones and melancholy. As late as the 19th Century it was still being used in Northern Greece to ward off calamities in general and to prevent miscarriage and abortion.

Left Associated traditionally with Sinister (Latin for left) and with sneakiness in general.

Lemniscate A Figure 8 on its side, what would be in American cattle brands a 'Lazy Eight'. The symbol for Infinity in Mathematics and Eternity or Infinity in occult studies.

Leo Zodiacal Sign of the Lion. Hot, dry, burning, fiery, choleric, feral, furious, brutish, barren, strong, eastern, masculine, northern, diurnal and violent sign. It governs fevers, convulsions, pestilence, small-pox, measles, jaundice, explosions, accidents by fire, Italy, Bohemia, France, Sicily Bath, Taunton and the West of England. Associated chiefly with fire, wild beasts, wild places, ovens, etc. Generally a fortunate sign.

Leopard A composite word formed from the Greek for Lion and the Greek for Panther. The Assyrian Devil-Goddess, Lamashtu, was said to resemble a Leopard. As the panther is associated with Dionysus, the Leopard may be as well.

Li The I Ching Trigram $\equiv\equiv$, meaning brightness, elegance, light-giving. East.

Libra The Zodiacal Sign of the Scales. Includes the Autumnal Equinox. Hot, moist, airy, sanguine, western, diurnal, cardinal, equinoctial, moveable, masculine, humane and obeying sign. The House of Venus with Saturn exalted. Equilibrium. A fruitful and fortunate Sign.

Lightning The voice of God, the right manifesting itself, inspiration, just punishment.

Lingam A phallic symbol, representative of the Hindu God, Siva.

Lingam and Yoni The male and female symbols joined as a symbol of procreation and delight.

Lion One of the four Cherubic Animals. Symbolizes Fire, the Sun, and the Zodiacal Sign, Leo, as well as being the sign for the Apostle Mark and the city of Venice. The Lion is associated with royal power in particular and with heraldry in general. The wild lioness is a symbol for the Great Mother.

Llew A Celtic Solar God and also a God of Light. (In this context they appear to be different things.) His legend contains the conflict between light and darkness, with darkness initially triumphant and light winning out at the end. Llew could not be slain within a house or without it, on horseback or standing.

Lobster Symbolic of the unconscious mind.

Loki Norse Fire God. Also a God of mischief and, in some cases, outright Evil. His main object in life seems to have been stirring things up just for the fun of it. It was Loki who eventually brought about Ragnarok, the Twilight of the Norse Gods.

Lotus Symbolic of birth, evolution, the Mystic Center, the last Revelation, the intersection of Heaven and Earth, the Universe, bisexuality and the completion of a created being into a single unified whole. The totality of its meaning is also derived from the following elements: it is watergrowing (therefore connected with the unconscious); it is circular (therefore a symbol of completion . . . actual or potential); the number of its petals gives a final meaning to it. Generally speaking the simple numbers 1-10 have similar meanings to that of their numerological interpretation. More complex structures (100 petalled, 1000 petalled etc.) bear a relationship to Divinity which is increased as the number increases and which also indicates the character of the person borne by or bearing the Lotus.

Lugh A Gaelic Solar God, corresponding to Llew, and also in many respects to Apollo and to Hercules.

Maenads The followers of Dionysus. They were to be avoided, if possible, as it was their habit to tear to pieces those who had incurred their God's wrath.

233

Magi	Probably they were originally a group of Fire Priests who became, under the Sassanid Dynasty, the controlling Priesthood of the Sun in Persia. According to tradition three of their number were present at the birth of Christ.
Magpie	A trickster God, like Coyote, among the Blackfeet Indians of Northwestern America. They may have formed the basis of some form of rural divination in Europe. They are related to crows, highly social birds, regarded in some areas as devil birds. Magpies are also known in folklore as thieves easily fascinated by bright objects, especially jewellery.
Mallow	A wild plant with reddish-purple flowers, hairy stems and leaves, sticky.
Maltese Cross	Symbolic of the coming together of different forces.
Mandala	Basically a circular symbol which proves to the beholder the movement of all things toward a centre, away from a centre, or both. It is the simplest expression of complex order, as the T'ai Chi is the simplest expression of simple order in creation.
Marjolane	Archaic form for Marjoram. Used in love philters and in protective rituals.
Mars	The Roman God of War, corresponding to the Greek Aries. The Planetary Sign of the same name. Its metal is iron, its nature, in a world longing for peace, is irony.
Menstrual Blood	Used, or said to be used, in a number of witchcraft spells in Satanism. Possibly in classic times it had other connotations; but since the Middle Ages it is likely that it has been used primarily with malefic intent.
Mercury	Roman Hermes.
Mercury	A Metal. To the Alchemists. Mercury was an indispensable part of their attempt to make gold. When Alchemy became less a practical exercise and more a philosophical discipline Mercury represented the Human Soul, Conscience, or the Feminine Principle. It was described by such epithets as: Green Lion, the Serpent, the Dragon, Mercurius Animatus etc. It was believed to be either Feminine or Hermaphroditic in character.
Mercury	A Planet. The Planet of Hermes. Rules the whole of the rational and intellectual faculties, wit, ingenuity, discovery. It is considered cold, dry, earthy and melancholy. When well-dignified makes for a strong, vigorous and active mind with a retentive memory. No one can become distinguished or eminent in life, says Raphael in 1828, unless Mercury is well-placed in horoscope.
Merman	The medieval concept of the Merman probably originates in that of Triton, the son of Poseidon and his wife, Amphitrite. Triton was half man and half fish. In other forms the same figure appears as Oannes or Dagon, a Babylonian or Sumerian fish-god. And as Jonah in the Old Testament.
Merti	The Twin Cobra Goddesses of Egypt. They are known individually

as Isis and Nepthys; but their collective name is Merti and they are collectively addressed.

Minerva   Roman Goddess of wisdom, corresponding to Pallas Athena.

Minos   The King of Crete whose wife, Pasiphae, conceived a gigantic lust for a White Bull and thereby gave birth to the Minotaur, a creature half man and half bull. Minos then instructed his architect, Daedalus, to build for him the Labyrinth (variously described as a Maze or as a Palace) and retired to it in shame, there spending the remainder of his life. Upon his death Minos became one of the Three Judges of the Underworld.

Moira   Probably a variant of the collective name for the Three Fates: Clotho, Lachesis and Atropos.

Monkey   Hanuman, the Monkey God, or perhaps simple mischief. See Loki.

Moon, Full   The Triple Goddess as Mother. Fruitfulness, generosity.

Moon in Glory   Pictorial representation of the Full Moon, sometimes incorporating the New Moon and sometimes the Waning Moon as well. It depicts whatever personae of the Goddess are included, i.e.: Mother, Mother + Maiden, Mother + Maiden + Crone. Around the disc are rays, straight or wavy, symbolic of spears or shafts of light.

Moon, New   The Maiden part of the Triple Goddess. Diana the Huntress, Aradia, Artemis, Kore.

Moon   The Planet. As an Astrological sign is cold, moist, watery, phlegmatic, variable in the extreme. Enemies are Mercury and Saturn, friendly with Jupiter, Sun, Venus, and Mars. Governs aquatic animals and birds, night birds, and amphibious beasts.

Moonstone   Protects men against epilepsy. Insures good crops on fruit trees. Assists vegetation generally. Also protects against wandering of the mind and insanity.

Moon, Waning   The Triple Goddess as Crone. Hecate or Atropos.

Moon, Waxing   The Maiden Goddess, Artemis, Kore etc.

Moonwort   A type of fern, used in modern witchcraft as an ingredient of Sabat Oil.

Mother Goddess   The Triple Goddess.

Mouth   The organ of communication, therefore of consciousness expressed. The organ of eating and, to some extent, breathing. Its function is bisexual, being both receptive and generative.

Mugwort   A member of the Artemisia Family and closely related to Wormwood.

Musk   An animal secretion which is part of many magical potions, principally Sabat Oil and Perfume.

Myrrh   Used as an incense for Vengeance, Exorcism. Used also in funeral rites.

Myrtle   A tree of Death and, at the same time, sacred to Aphrodite.

235

Graves suggests that she 'purifies with Myrtle', thus possibly purifying with Death?

Narcissus   The Greek youth who fell in love with himself so passionately and hopelessly that he killed himself, being driven to this sad extreme by Artemis who was punishing him for his thoughtless cruelty. After his death he was changed to a flower which was incorporated into the rites of Demeter and Persephone. It may have further associations with Dionysus and through him with legends of a murdered God: Dionysus: Attis: Horus: Osiris: Tammuz.

Nephthys   The Egyptian equivalent of Hecate.

Nettle   A medicine, a food, and ingredient used in magic.

Nightshade   Used in hex powders and sachets.

Nine   Consciousness and psychism, efficiency, renewed energy. The triad of triads and therefore a number of great power. Frequently associated with the occult and with the triple synthesis or disposition on the corporal, intellectual and spiritual levels simultaneously. A male number. Perhaps, in a decimal system, a number representative of Chronos.

Nuit   The Sky Goddess, Egyptian equivalent of the Greek Rhea. She was the mother of Osiris, Horus the Elder, Set, Isis, and Nephthys. Like Hathor and Isis she is sometimes represented as a cow. She most often appears, however, as a woman, body elongated, touching Earth only with the tips of her fingers and her toes. She was considered to be the mother of the Sun (Osiris) and, at the same time, his daughter (Ra).

Nymphs   Greek minor divinities, goddesses who inhabited fountains, streams, rivers, lakes, oceans and trees.

Oak   The tree of Zeus, Jupiter, Hercules, Thor, and all other Thunder Gods. A royal tree, the Midsummer Fire is built with Oak.

Odin   The chief of the Norse Gods, corresponds to the German Wodin (Wotan), to Hermes and to Zeus. The Norse Gods, unlike most of their Greek counterparts, could die and did so at Ragnarok, the final battle between the Gods and the Frost Giants.

Octagon   A symbol of regeneration as it is mid-way between the square and the circle (Terrestial and celestial order). (Squaring the circle? Perhaps an expression of bringing eternal or celestial order into existence here on Earth.) As a geometric figure it is derived from the octagram. It is also symbolic of totality.

Octagram   An eight-pointed Star. Frequently employs a pair of implied Greek Crosses in its structure, therefore combines the meanings of Cross and Star. The Cross is symbolic of balance between opposites and a Fire symbol. The Star is significant of the forces of the Spirit fighting against darkness and of the Collective Unconscious. Total meaning perhaps equlibrium of opposing forces of destruction.

Ogma   A Celtic God of eloquence, healing, fertility and prophecy. A heroic figure, the inventor of Ogham (an Alphabet) and, in character, a mixture of Chronos, Hercules and Apollo.

Ogyrvran   Also given as Ogyr Vran. Guinevere's Giant (or ogre) father.

Olibanum   Frankincense. Used in many religious and occult rituals.

Olive   Associated with Zeus and Hera at Olympus as a symbol of victory, as a symbol of fruitfulness by the Jews, and as part of Hercules' funeral pyre. But its main significance is as an emblem of peace and plenty, conferred upon the Greeks by Athena.

Omega   The final letter of the Greek Alphabet. In its shape it resembles that of the Egyptian Sky-Goddess, Nuit.

One   The Prime number. The number of Genesis, of consciousness, unity, light, Ego, Creation, Being, the Active Principle. Perhaps eccentricity or egoism. God/Man. Adam or the Paradise state. The Prime Masculine number.

Onyx   Worn in India and Persia to protect against the Evil Eye. Said to reduce the pain of childbirth and to assist in delivery. Among other peoples it is thought to induce strife, cause contention between friends, bring nightmares and cause premature births.

Opal   Said to (at the same time) bring the Evil Eye and to cure diseases of the eye. It increases the powers of the eyes and of the mind.

Opium   The dried juice from a poppy, Papaver Somniferum, native to the Far East. It induces sleep, some dreams and addiction.

Orb   Common symbol having to do with royalty. It signifies the World and dominion over it; but with a Cross surmounting the Orb it has the added meaning of worldly dominion under the Lord.

Orchid   Orchid root, Satyrion, is used in some magical potions, chiefly love philtres.

Orchis   Another name for Orchid.

Ouranos   According to Graves, the first of the Patriarchal Gods. Ouranos (Uranus) was the son and lover of Gaea (Earth) and the father of the Giants, Cyclops and Titans. He was castrated and killed by his youngest son, Chronos, who was armed with a flint sickle. (*See Aphrodite*)

Oval   Horizontal it is most frequently used in the West as a halo, symbol of Godhood on Earth, almost as if it were a boundary line for Heaven: beyond this point all is God. If, however, the main axis of the Oval is vertical then it usually stands for Egg and therefore Creation.

Owl   Owls have a reputation for prophetic wisdom. Associated with Hecate (Goddess of Death or Hell), Athena and Kore.

Ox   A symbol of sacrifice, patience or cosmic forces. It is associated with the Moon. (In contrast to the Bull which is usually associated with the Sun.) It is also a symbol of great strength.

Palm   The palm tree is a symbol of victory, fruitfulness and birth. In the Babylonian version of the Garden of Eden story the Palm takes the part of the Tree of Life. It is associated with Isis, Ishtar, and Appollo. The Phoenix was believed to be born in a nest in a Palm Tree; and it was to the Palm that he returned to burn, only to be born again.

Pa   His chief characteristics are his randiness and his goatishness. Additionally he had the gift of prophecy which he taught Apollo. He made the first Pan Pipes, the design of which was later copied by Hermes.

Parsifal   The Holy Fool of the Grail Legends. A symbol of total innocence and purity.

Pasiphae   Wife and Queen of Minos (*which see*).

Peacock   Traditionally sacred to Hera and Juno. Among other associations the Peacock is symbolic of immortality, the immortal soul, twilight, the night stars and (if paired on either side of a tree) psychic duality nourished by unity.

Pear   As it is a close relative to apple (grafts between them are possible) it is likely that the Pear takes on some of the significance of the Apple. Additionally the Pear Tree was used in Russia as a protective charm for cattle, and in Switzerland as the Life Tree of a girl. If it flourished, so did she. If it died, likewise. The Pear was sacred to Hera and pruned by Priapus.

Pearl   The soul, combination of fire and water, that which is hidden, that which is deformed and becomes transformed, associated with the Moon.

Pennyroyal   A kind of Mint. Raised for herbal value and for use in Summer Sabat incense preparations.

Pentacles   The suit Pentacles in the Tarot is made up of three elements: the Circle, Pentagram, and Coin. Symbolically they total: Sun (Solar Power and Fire) + Pentagram (figure of Power, the Erotic Use of Power, the four cardinal points with Centre) + Money (Gold, physical wealth, tangible power). The total of power repeated in all three parts is manifest with the added question as to the use of that power.

Pentagon   The Geometric figure derived from the Pentagram. It shares the significance of the Star but is directly 'physical' in its effects, the binding or confining of a kind of physical power.

Pentagram   As a figure it is the prime symbol for power (frequently thought to be demonic) confined or constrained. More than any other the five-pointed Star is part of Earth and Heaven combined.

Pentagram Inverted   Power constrained for evil purposes.
Used in incense preparations designed to torment or punish.

Pepper   Used in amulets to protect against the Evil Eye. It can also free the mind from envious thoughts and temporarily relieve diseases of the liver and dropsy.

Phoenix   The Solar Bird. (See Palm Tree).

P'i   An I Ching Hexagram, ☰☷, indicating standstill or a time of confusion and disorder. A good time for the Superior Man to withdraw into seclusion and sit this one out.

Pillar   Not only a figure of support but also a phallic figure, pillars having been worshipped as phallic symbols in Greece and the Near East. The pillar represents, as it is usually stone, that which is established, firm and Earth connecting Men and everything below with Gods and all that is above.

Pine Cone   Symbol of fruitfulness, particularly associated with Dionysus and Attis.

Plum   Associated with Christmas in the Plum Pudding and, in France, with the Yule Log. And according to Chinese legend the Plum sprang from the blood of a Dragon which had been punished by having its ears cut off.

Pisces   The Zodiacal Sign of the Fish. The House of Jupiter and Exaltation of Venus. Moist, cold, watery, phlegmatic, nocturnal, bicorporeal, effeminate, sickly, southern, obeying sign. At the same time it is an exceedingly fruitful and luxuriantly productive sign. Symbolic of all places having to do with water: Seas, rivers, lakes, reservoirs, marshes, wells, etc. Unfortunate.

Pomegranates   A symbol of paradox: it is a death sign (Kore) and a sign of resurrection (Dionysus). Additionally, because of the prominence of its seeds, a symbol of fruitfulness and fecundity.

Popular   The White Poplar is the same as Aspen, as noted earlier the tree of the Autumnal Equinox, old age, shield makers, and, apparently, of resurrection. The Black Poplar was a funereal tree dedicated to Mother Earth in Early Greece. It was also used in divination, apparently a yes/no sort, together with the Silver Fir. In that usage the Silver Fir stood for 'Hope' and the Black Poplar stood for 'Hope Not' or 'Abandon Hope'.

Populus   A Geomantic figure meaning people and which is neither good nor bad. Corresponds to the Moon, Capricorn and to the number 16 as well as Water.

Poppy   A Death Flower, associated also with Sleep. Kore.

Poseidon   Brother of Zeus, ruler of the Sea. He is associated with Horses and with the Bull, is likely to have been a Sky God before Zeus. His Homeric nickname, Earthshaker, gives some idea of his titanic tempers which expressed themselves in Earthquakes and Tempests. (Perhaps also in volcanic eruptions as Poseidon is associated with Crete, therefore possibly with the eruption of Thera). He is symbolic of the unconscious generally because of the oceanic associations and more specifically symbolic of uncontrolled or unpredictable rage.

Priapus   The son of Aphrodite and Dionysus, depicted as being ugly and with enormous genitals. He is a gardener and is associated with the Pear-Tree, sacred to Hera. He is symbolic of lust in the flesh.

Puella   A Geomantic Sign meaning Girl or pretty face. A pleasant but not

239

very fortunate reading. Corresponds to Venus, Water, Libra, and the number 2.

Puer A Geomantic Sign meaning Boy, rash and inconsiderate. It is more good than bad, corresponds to Mars, Fire, Taurus and the number 3.

Pyramid Corresponds to Fire, Earth, the Mystic Centre, divine revelation and creation. It may also be said to indicate the upward striving of material which is essentially Earth-bound, a contradiction but one which provides its own dynamic.

Pyromancy The magical art of using the shapes of flame or of smoke patterns in divination.

Ra Egyptian Solar God and Creator.

Rabbit A Fertility symbol, associated with the Moon. Among some South African tribes a rabbit is burned to end a period of prolonged rainfall. Among the Cherokee, Rabbit was taboo, lest the warrior who ate it become confused like the Rabbit. Among the Sioux the Rabbit was a heroic figure, clever, similar to Falling Star in the Cheyenne legend.

Rainbow Associated with the Greek Goddess, Iris. She was the Messenger of the Gods (As Hermes in one of his functions); but she seems mainly to have worked as a private messenger for Hera.

Ram Associated with Zeus, Hermes and with Robin Goodfellow, a ram-horned and ithyphallic God of the Witches in England in 1639. It is also the Astrological Sign for Aries.

Ranunculus The commonest member of the family is the Buttercup. Ranunculus features in many spells and potions.

Raphael One of the three great angels. A guide in the Underworld but also the regent of the Sun.

Red Roses Symbol of passion, supposedly red roses were so dyed by the blood of Aphrodite.

Rhadamanthus Son of Zeus and Brother of Minos, King of Crete. He was famous as a legislator and, after his death, became one of the Three Judges of Hades with Minos.

Rhombus Elongated it forms a lozenge which was symbolic of Victory to the Chinese. It also indicates communication between inferior and superior.

Right As a direction or point of orientation 'right' has come to symbolize that which is just or good, thus differentiated from what is left or wrong. Both meanings probably arise from the fact that most people are naturally 'right'-handed.

Ring Like all circular forms it relates to the Sun, but is also an enclosure of safety or trust or terror.

Rose Associated with Venus (or Aphrodite), Eros, the Garden of Eros or Paradise, the loved one, love, death. Not unnaturally, it is also used in love philtres.

240

Rubeus	Geomantic Sign meaning passion, redhead, vice or fiery temper. It is a bad sign corresponding to Mars, Fire, Gemini and to the number 13.
Ruby	Used to protect from Witchcraft of all kinds, plague, pestilence and famine. Ruby water (in which a ruby had been washed) was given for stomach trouble. Ruby powder was an ingredient of medicines to stop bleeding.
Rue	A medicinal herb used also in Summer Sabat incense, in love sachets and in spells to bring about inertia.
Rush	Used by Cherokee Indians in homeopathic magic to enable ballplayers to spring quickly to their feet after falling. Rushes were strewn in Churches and chambers in England during the Middle Ages to make them fresh. And at one time rushes were used to make rings from. These rings were then used for the plighting of troth. Later on rush-rings were used on phony marriage ceremonies carried out to help seduce virtuous country maidens.
Saffron	Used at one time by the Persians to raise the wind. It may, additionally, be the 'Flower of Zeus' which was used to resurrect the dead hero, Tylon. It is an ingredient of some aphrodisiacs and is used in traditional recipes for Sabat Oil.
St. Andrew's Cross	A cross in the form of the Greek Letter 'X', and which signifies the union of the upper and lower worlds.
Sagittarius	The Zodiacal Sign of the Archer, or Centaur. Because he is an Archer there is a Solar Connection. Additionally: Hot, fiery, choleric, dry, masculine, diurnal, eastern, common, bicorporeal, changeable, southern and obeying sign. House and Joy of Jupiter, Cauda Draconis exalted. Fruitfulness, fireplaces, hills, high lands, military weapons etc. Fortunate.
Salamander	A fire-living lizard.
Salt	As an Eastern symbol it is, in some ways, similar to bread. Custom had it that if you took salt with someone you could not then turn around and stab him in the back. (This custom occurs in the story of Ali Baba from the Arabian Nights.) Salt plays an important part in all countries, ancient and modern, in religious ceremonies connected with birth, circumcision, initiation, marriage, death, private and public worship. It was used to ward off the Evil Eye, evil spirits and witchcraft. It is unlucky in most western cultures to spill salt. Its alchemical significance was as the primal material of which the transformation took place.
Sandalwood	Used in many occult preparations for Love, Self Defence, and for divination.
Saturn	Planetary Sign. As a God, Saturn was the equivalent of Chronos. He was a symbol of abundance and was associated with Corn. In the astrological sense he was considered to be the most powerful, evil and malignant of planets. Cold, dry, earthy, melancholic,

masculine, malignant and solitary. Friendly with the Sun, Jupiter, and Mercury. Enmity with Mars, Venus and the Moon. Rules poisons and trees of Death. Delights in deserts and ruins. Generally sly, pernicious and malignant.

Scales   The symbol for Libra. A sign of balance, consideration, thought.

Scallops   Normally associated with Aphrodite or Venus. Supposedly Aphrodisiac in effect.

Scammony   A strong purgative.

Scarabaeus Beetle   *See Kephra*

Sceptre   Related to all of the following: Cross, wand, club, thunderbolt, sword, phallus, Thor's hammer and the arrow. Straightforward Earthly power is its main implication. That power may take the form of fertility, or implied physical force.

Scorpio   Zodiacal Sign, the Scorpion or the Eagle. Mars. Cold, moist, watery, phlegmatic, feminine, nocturnal, fixed, mute, southern, extremely fruitful sign of long ascension. It is an unfortunate sign which takes much of its nature from the two animals which represent it.

Scorpion   A symbol of treachery in the Middle Ages and also representative of the Jew (in an anti-Jewish period). It has also been connected with the Hangman. Its obvious significance is that which is hidden and potentially of great danger.

Scythe   Traditionally the implement of Death. But also associated with Ceres and all Corn Goddesses or Gods (for example Saturn). The scythe is also connected with Father Time, who is, himself, probably derived from Medieval conceptions of Chronos/Saturn.

Sekhet   The Egyptian Goddess, Hathor, in her Lion-headed manifestation. Which all comes about on the occasion of a rebellion of Gods and Men against the ageing Ra. So he sends Sekhet to punish them, kill a few and bring them back to the straight and narrow. She goes too far though, and won't stop killing when he figures that it's time. So Ra wheels out a mixture of barley beer, mandrake and blood and puts her to sleep. (Another account says barley beer and pomegranate juice). When she woke up she was controllable. So the whole thing was afterwards celebrated by annual festivals.

Set   The Egyptian God of Evil, God of the Night Sky, twin of the God of the Sky by Day, Heru-ur (Horus the Elder). He was the son of Seb and Nut. He was also the brother of Isis, Osiris and Nephthys and the husband of Nephthys. And was also the father of Anubis. Set was a Jackal God, usually depicted as having a Jackal's head. The mythology of Egypt is filled with stories of the struggle between Set (darkness) and Light personified by (1) Horus the Elder (his twin), (2) Ra, (3) Osiris, and (4) Horus the Younger (his nephew). Note that 2 and 3 are both the Sun.

Seven   A specially sacred and mystic number in almost all Societies. An

242

indivisible number and therefore compared to God. Associated with the Moon (4 phases of the Moon of 7 days each making a total of 28 days or a Lunar Month). Possibly associated with Saturn and with autumn.

Ship If the Ocean and Water are both Symbols of the Unconscious and Darkness, then the ship is symbolic of the voyage across darkness, across terror, life, as expressed by the Solar Boat. As the ship of death it is the means by which the body is carried from one life to the next.

Shiva The Hindu Prince of Demons, the Dancer. God as Destroyer and as motion between birth and death, Life and Not-life. He is indifferent to pleasure and pain, spending much of his time meditating.

Sickle The implement with which Chronos castrated his father, Uranus. Related to the scythe in its significance.

Sistrum A hand-held percussion instrument, Egyptian, consisting of metal rods loosely placed in an oval frame. The noise that it made when shaken was supposed to drive away evil spirits. Associated with Hathor and with Isis.

Six Symbolic of the union between Fire and Water and therefore of the human soul. Ambivalence and effort. The number of days of Creation, therefore symbolic of the cessation of effort. A Hermaphroditic number, possibly representative of Diana or Janus.

16-pointed Star Stars tend to indicate their proximity to God or Heaven by the number of points which they have. Thus, this Star is closer to God than a four-pointed Star.

Snake In most societies a symbol of treachery, cruelty, death and evil. Additional meanings of cunning, wisdom or magical power. Associated with Thoth as Moon God. Snakes are also associated with Athena, Hermes, Hercules, Quetzalcoatl, and many other figures. Also a Greek creation symbol in connection with the Cosmic Egg which is laid by Eurynome, Goddess of all things and is hatched by Option, the Great Serpent who was fashioned out of the North Wind. The Snake is connected with the Lemniscate and with Ouroboros, the serpent which swallows its own tail.

Two-headed Snake, The symbolism of the Snake, with the added meaning of conflict between equals.

Snakestone A porous stone which was ground and used to cure snakebite.

Snowdrop An early-flowering spring bulb, therefore possibly associated with spring myths.

Solar Cross Specifically the cross within a wheel forming the Solar Wheel. Any wheel may be said to represent the Sun and the Cross does likewise, being also the usual method of Solar Sacrifice. Any method of sacrifice by Fire is also usually Solar in nature.

Sparrow According to one legend, the Sparrow was a guardian of fire for the Devil and pursued the Swallow when he stole it to bring to men

243

(Prometheus). It also may have functioned as a scapegoat in Mosaic Law in connection with the curing of Leprosy.

Spear   A Solar Weapon. The Spear of Longinus is another correlation between Solar Sacrifice and the Crucifixion.

Sphere   As the orb it is a symbol of power over the Earth. It can also represent the Sun or the Moon. Can indicate perfection.

Sphinx   Harmakhis.

Spider   Creation, aggression and convergence. Creation as in the myth of Arachne and Athena. Arachne was so skilled at weaving that Athena turned her into a spider. (Weaving being the special province of Athena and Arachne being a mere mortal, Athena was all overcome by jealousy.) Aggression in spiders toward their food, toward their enemies . . . even very large ones, and of the female of some species toward the male is well known. Convergence occurs in the spider's web, with the spider occupying the centre. The idea of the web, with all lines converging toward a central hairy horror, has been throughly exploited by thirty years of thrilling films. In Hindu myth the Spider's web represents Maya, illusion. And many legends correlate the Spider with the Moon in the sense of the thread of destiny, thus connecting it with the Three Fates, who are themselves the Triple Goddess and the Moon. The associations of the Spider (and the Snake and the Scorpion as well) with Fear/Evil seem totally out of proportion to the number of poisonous kinds and irrational if one considers the likelihood of being bitten. Nevertheless Fear and Evil must be considered in relation to Spiders when they appear as a symbol.

Square   A symbol of Earth, of Earthly order, of established strength, everything neatly sorted out and put away in little boxes.

Square surmounting a Triangle   Earthly order (or in this case the conscious mind) moving downward or inward toward the unconscious or the animal.

Stag   Associated with Dionysus, Cernunnos, and with the Moon (Artemis) in the myth of Actaeon.

Star   The forces of the spirit fighting against darkness, the Collective Unconscious, the Spirits of Heaven or the Souls of Men.

Sulphur   In the Alchemical process Sulphur stood for the Sun. In the simplest known form of Alchemy Sulphur (described in old texts as being reddish and incombustible) was combined with Mercuι (also described as red). Which seems to point to simple Solar/Lunar symbolism. Sulphur as a bi-product of volcanic activity has also come to be associated with Hell and with the Devil, which is perhaps why it is used in ceremonies of exorcism.

Sun   Fire, Life, Light, Celestial Intelligence, Creator and the Eye of God.

Sun   The Planet. His total astrological significance according to Raphael (writing in 1828) is magnificence in all things whether for good or for evil, in the animals which he rules (lion, wolf, ram, boar, bull, horse); in his jewels (among them diamonds); and the places over which he rules (palaces, splendid apartments, etc.). He is most fortunate in Taurus (The Bull) or Leo (The Lion) or Sagittarius (The Archer). Bull, Lion, and Archer are all well-established in Solar Mythology.

Sun   The Trigram, ☴ , which is one of the ten basic Trigrams of the I Ching. It stands for flexibility, penetration, harmony, unison or relatedness and decrease.

Sunflower   The Sun. Called Heliotrope, meaning Sun-turning, that is, Following the Sun.

Sun in Glory   A medieval design to represent the Sun with rays at the Cardinal and Ordinal points. Symbolic of the Majesty of the Sun and emphasizes its power.

Swallow   Connected with spring and fertility rites, a legendary fire-bringer, used medicinally in connection with diseases manifesting themselves in chattering or frenzy or incoherence. The flight of swallows served as an augury in Ancient Greece.

Swan   A Sacred Bird, in England it still is a Royal Bird. Associated with Zeus (Leda and the Swan), Brahma (probably as a Sun Bird), and the many variants of the Swan-Maiden theme in Ireland and Scotland. Its nature is probably bi-polar, having to do with the Sun, as above, and with the Moon (Triple Goddess).

Swords   The weapon of Air and of thought, for example, a cutting remark. There may be a connection between Sword and Word and Weird, all English terms arising from similar Old Norse roots. Additionally, the Sword has a phallic meaning (Life) and a fatal meaning (Death) making it yet another ambivalent symbol.

T'ai   Peace. An I Ching Hexagram, ䷊ , indicating the departure of the small and the arrival of the great. A sign of good fortune or success.

T'ai Chi   The Chinese symbol which is one of the most satisfactory representations of the motion of all things. Eternal change between polar opposites: Masculine and Feminine, Feminine and Masculine, Black and White, White and Black, lightness and dark etc. A sign containing incredible richness and simplicity.

Tau Cross   The cross in the form of the Greek Letter 'T' or Tau. It is also called the St. Anthony Cross or the Egyptian Cross and forms a part of the Crux Ansata.

Taurus   The Zodiacal Sign of the Bull. Raphael says of it: Cold, dry, melancholy, feminine, nocturnal, southern sign of short ascension, the House of Venus with the Moon exalted. Its diseases are melancholy, consumption, scrofula, croup, disorders of the throat. Fruitful sign but unfortunate. Denotes barns, remote pastures, trees, chimneys, cellars, etc., as well as Ireland, Holland, part of Poland and Russia, Persia, Asia Minor etc.

245

Ten	The number of completion but possibly also the number of over-completion, decadence. Death.
Third Eye	The Wisdom Eye of Shiva. As he spends much of his life in meditation some friction between the God and his wives naturally arises. One day one of them crept up behind him, while he was in the depths of meditation, and covered his eyes. The Third Eye then blazed forth, like the Sun, burning all the Himalayas and killing everything. When he realized what had happened Shiva restored everything: plants, animals and men: to what they had been before the opening of the Eye.
Thistle	Used in charms to ward off witches.
Thor	Norse Thunder God. His name has come down to us as Thor's Day, Thursday. He corresponds to Jupiter, Bel and Marduk (therefore having a Solar connection). He is also associated with the Oak Tree.
Thorn	Used to ward off witches, ghosts and strangers.
Three	The symbol of the Child, of birth, life and death. Beginning/Middle/End. Childhood/Manhood/Old Age, Heaven/Earth/Hell or Underworld, the Frost World/The Earth/the Fire World. Trinities, generally. The solution of the conflict posed by One (Male) and Two (Female). The World, on the seventh day.
Throat	Bears the connotation of Mouth plus the added meaning of a place in the body where blood is readily accessible. Which in turn leads to the use of the Throat in sacrifice and its meaning in legends of Vampirism. The Throat is, perhaps not coincidentally, ruled by the Zodiacal Sign, Taurus the Bull. And Bulls were sacrificed by having their throats cut to Solar Gods and to Poseidon.
Tiger Lily	Could well be used in Amatory sachets.
Topaz	Has the same virtues as Peridot, (*which see*).
Tora	Wisdom. In the Jewish religion the Law, specifically the Ten Commandments given to Moses on Sinai and written in letters of black fire on skins of white fire. It is also the personification of the Law, a Woman or Angel, who intercedes twice for mankind: once before the Creation when she pleads with Jehovah to invent Man so that there will be someone to adore Him, and second after the reading of the First Commandment from the skies over Sinai. All of Jehovah's listeners were so terrified that they dropped dead and Tora pleaded for their resurrection.
Torch	Associated with Nusku, a Babylonian Fire and Messenger God who corresponds to Agni, Loki and to Hermes. The Torch is also associated with the Sun, with Hercules (in his battle against the Hydra of Lerna), with Prometheus (who stole fire from Heaven and gave it to man), and as an allegory of truth.
Tortoise	Corresponds to the Zodiacal Sign of Cancer the Crab in the

246

Babylonian Zodiac of Marduk. It was sacred to Cybele (a Phrygian Goddess who corresponds to the Magna Mater). The Tortoise was used as a phallic amulet and also probably as protection against the Evil Eye. Pliny cites 66 uses of the Tortoise in medicine, including repelling malpractices of magic, neutralizing poisons, improving eyesight, removing cataracts, as an aphrodisiac, as an antaphrodisiac, as a remedy for scrofula etc. In Hindu legend the Tortoise is an Avatar of Vishnu. In China and Japan the World or the Islands of the Blest were believed to be supported by Tortoises. The chief western associations for Tortoise/Turtle are longevity, slowness and deliberation and in the Greek legend of the invention, by Hermes, of the invention of the lyre from a tortoise shell.

Tourmaline   A semi-precious stone from Ceylon which has the property of sometimes having separate colours associated with separate facets.

Tree of Life   A diagram of Creation showing the Divine manifesting itself downward to the lowest levels of existence and back upward again. In Kabbalistic interpretations of the Tarot each card is related to one of the 10 points on the Tree or to one of the 20 Paths which connect the points.

Triangle   Apex upward a sign of Fire, Apex downward a sign for Water, Apex downward with a line parallel to the base a sign for Earth, Apex upward with a line parallel to the base a sign for Air. A combination of the Fire and Water or the Earth and Air triangles produces the Hexagram or Shield of Solomon. The simplest geometric figure, the triangle also signifies motion in the direction of its Apex.

Triangle Surmounting a Square   The Square being significant of established order and the Triangle signifying upward motion the two together are significant of Earth establishments tending toward 'Good'.

Triple Cross   Probably significant of the Pope's vicarage over Heaven, Earth and Hell.

Triple Crown   The Papal Crown. Like the Papal Cross (The Triple Cross) it is probably representative of the Three Worlds: Heaven, Hell and Earth.

Triple Goddess   The Great Mother Goddess of Phoenicia, Egypt, Babylonia, Greece, Rome etc. She is represented under many different names by the three phases of the Moon, by the Three Fates, by the Maiden/Mother/Crone . . . she who spins she who weaves, and at the last, she who cuts. Her worship antedates that of Zeus or Odin or Jupiter and refers to earlier Matriarchal civilizations.

Tripod   A pot or cauldron associated with the worship of Apollo at Delphi.

Tristitia   A Geomantic Sign meaning Sorrow, grief, perversion or condemnation. It is a bad sign, corresponding to Saturn, Earth, Aquarius and the number 14.

247

Tui The Trigram, ☱, meaning Pleasure, complacent satisfaction, the joyful.

Tulip Associated with Magyar marriage customs.

Turquoise Associated by the Hindus with Buddha who employed Turquoise as a weapon to vanquish a monster. Carried by many peoples as an amulet to ward off the Evil Eye. In Arabia it is believed to change colour to warn the owner of his impending death. It is said to protect from poisons, reptiles and eye disease. It also figures in ritual jewelry of New Mexico, Arizona and Northern Mexico.

Turtle See *Tortoise*.

Two The Prime Feminine Number. The sign of duality and of change. The number One is fulfilled only through the number Two, producing Three. All pairs, oppositions, conflicts, supplements, complements, partners. The number of the T'ai Chi. Also indicative of man's awareness of his existence and therefore the number of the beginning of intellect as distinct from ego. The number of perception. Man conscious of some: thing/one/where/time condition other than himself. Woman in every sense.

Typhon The Egyptian God of Evil, Set (*which see*). Some confusion exists about Typhon, many writers think of him as a sort of Egyptian version of the Midgaard Serpent; but it would appear that Typhon is just an alter ego of Set and that he has no separate identity. In Greece Typhon was the monster son of Hera, brought forth parthenogenetically. He was nursed by the monster snake or dragon, Python, whom Apollo later slew. Typhon was the father of Cerberus, Hydra, Chimaera, and Orthrus (a two-headed hound) and the grandfather of the Sphinx and the Nemean Lion. He was eventually brought down by Zeus after a running battle that wound up at Mount Aetna in Sicily. The volcano, it is said, owes its fire to Typhon, still alive, below.

Undines Water Nymphs.

Uraeus The Royal Snake of Egypt, forming part of the Double Crown. It signifies the Lower or Northern Kingdom. It may represent an Asp (Cleopatra) or a striking Cobra.

Urim & Thumim According to modern Tarot tradition the Breastplates or Shoulderplates of the Jewish High Priest. According to Jewish tradition they were stones, carried by the High Priest, perhaps of different colours or perhaps marked, used in some kind of simple 'Yes or No' oracular divination.

Urizen Name for the God of this world invented by Blake from the Greek or from the pun (you reason). He stands for reason and for the limitation of Energy. Blake uses the term in a pejorative sense indicating constraint and possible tyranny.

Vampire A symbol for a stealer of life, the usual form of that life being fresh blood; but psychic or spiritual vampires also exist. It is,

248

especially in present day horror films, a blatant sexual symbol, the act of vampirism being used as a euphemism for rape.

Venus Roman Goddess of Love and Beauty, equivalent to Aphrodite. Astrologically the Planet Venus is probably the third oldest in Astrological Systems (after the Sun and the Moon). She is feminine, nocturnal, benevolent, friendly to every Planet except Saturn. She rules fragrant spices, fruitful plants and her general attributes are those which one would expect of Aphrodite or the Goddess as Mother.

Vervain Used in Winter Sabat Incense, purifying baths before conjuration or witchcraft, and in Love Sachets, philtres and incense.

Vesta The Roman Goddess of the domestic fire. The equivalent of the Greek Goddess, Hestia.

Via Geomantic Sign meaning Street or Way. It is neither good nor bad. Its attributes are the Moon, Water, Leo, and the number 7.

Vine Always a symbol of life and abundance or (or drunkenss and debauchery). Frequently associated with Dionysus.

Virgin A reference to chastity, to the New Moon (The Triple Goddess as Chaste Maide, Artemis), to the Virgin Mary.

Virgo Zodiacal Sign, The Virgin. According to Raphael, Virgo is dry, cold, earthy, feminine, nocturnal, melancholy, barren, humane and commanding. It denotes studies or libraries, cabinets, concealed or private drawers, hot houses etc. Generally reckoned unfortunate.

Vishnu Originally a Solar Deity; but later, in the Hindu religion, attracts many other attributes and personalities. Legend has it that every cycle of Creation is represented by an Avatar of Vishnu, thus making ten in all; but popular myth has added to these making many. The Avatars of Vishnu include incarnations as a Fish, Turtle, Wild Boar, Lion, Dwarf, as Krishna, and as Rama, the Hero of the epic, Ramayana. In all of his many incarnations Vishnu is an extremely popular God.

Volcano Associated with Fire worship. As is logical the main areas in which volcanoes are worshipped are West Coast U.S.A., Mexico (Popacateptl), the Hawaiian Islands, Sicily, Italy, Greece and Japan. All of these areas are those in which vulcanism occurs. In Greek Mythology volcanoes are associated with Hephaestus, the Blacksmith of the Gods, who was also the jailer of Typhon underneath Mount Aetna. His Roman counterpart was Vulcan, from whose name comes Volcano.

Vulcan See *Volcano*.

Vulture In Egypt the Vulture was the symbol of the Goddess Nekhebet. She was the Goddess of the South or Upper Egypt, the Mother of the Sun (and therefore Pharaoh), she was the primeval abyss which brought forth the light and the twin sister of Uatchet, Goddess of the North or Lower Egypt. Together their symbols form the

249

	Double Crown, which was a symbol of the sovereignty of the Pharaohs over the Two Kingdoms, Upper and Lower Egypt.
Wands	Symbolic of magical power. The Wand is used in divination, prophecy, necromancy and magical ritual. A full description of the Wand and of its construction occurs in Paul Huson's book, *Mastering Witchcraft*.
Water	Symbolically represents the source of the First Creation, the home of the Dragon in Chinese Myth, that which preserves life, the Alpha and Omega, the potential and the actual, the unconscious or intuition, cleansing rebirth and baptism, the origin of wisdom, the female and moving part of creation as opposed to/joined with/complementing the masculine and fixed part of creation.
Watercress	Used medicinally at one time as a toothache remedy. Its cruciferous structure would lend itself to some works of magic.
Wheat	A symbol of fruitfulness. As it is one of the oldest of symbols from the Natural World it is nearly always associated with the Triple Goddess in her second and maternal aspect. Her priesthood was most cases female and the secrets of agriculture were for the most part kept by women.
Wheel	A symbol of motion, but basically it is representative of the Sun and its motion and power.
White Rose	Purity, but in alchemical terms inferior to the red rose as red is the ultimate colour on the alchemical colour scale together with gold.
Wildcat	Associated with the Moon Goddess.
Window	The significance of the window and that of the door are parallel. The Door is a symbol of physical going out and coming in. The window indicates the same two-way motion; but in the case of the window that motion is of the mind, the soul, or the spirit or, in some cases, to the mind/soul/spirit. Both shapes, being square, are symbolic of established order. And both are affected by the number of panes or divisions of the total shape. (See also *Gate*).
Wine	Relative to Dionysus, Bacchus, life, blood, and of course Christ and the Devil. Further symbolic of any alcoholic drink or the effects therefrom.
Witches' Sabbath	According to Huson, *Mastering Witchcraft*, a witches' meeting at quarterly and cross-quarterly intervals.
Wodin	The Germanic equivalent of the Norse Odin.
Wolf	Sacred to the Moon, symbolic of the wild, the dangerous in nature, the beast in man.
Wormwood	A vital ingredient in Absinthe, a drug, and a common constituent in the Materia Medica of witchcraft.
Yama	One of two Hindu Kings of the Dead, judge of men and king of the spiritual world. He was the first of all created beings to die. Corresponds to Hades, to Hermes Psychopomp and, in a sense, to Adam Cadmon.

Yew   As Graves says, a Death tree everywhere in Europe. He also attributes it to the Winter Solstice. A favourite tree for the makers of bows. An ingredient in Saturnian Hex Powders for the purpose of bringing restriction, inertia or lethargy.

Yod   A Hebrew letter which has come to symbolize the Voice of or the Power of Jehovah descending to Earth. In the Old Testament it may mean roughly the same as the Dove does in the New. Its origin as a symbol may arise from the fact that it is the first letter of Tetragrammaton, the Unutterable Name of God. That Name, in English, is Yod-Heh-Vau-Heh or Jehovah.

Yod-Heh-Vau-Heh   Tetragrammaton or Four Letters. See *Yod*.

Yoni   The female symbol of the Hindus.

Zeus   The Greek Sky God, a patriarchal figure who took over according to legend from his father, Chronos. In reality it is more likely that the male-oriented worship of Zeus supplanted that of the Triple Goddess of the Moon and of Agriculture.

Bibliography of Primary Works Used

BARING-GOULD, Sabine *Curious Myths of the Middle Ages* Rivingtons, London, 1873
BENHAM, W. Gurney *Playing Cards* Spring Books, London, no date
BUDGE, E.A. Wallis *Amulets and Talismans* Collier Macmillan, New York, 1970
BUDGE, E.A. Wallis (trans.) *The Book of the Dead* Routledge & Kegan Paul, London, 1953
BUDGE, E.A. Wallis *The Gods of the Egyptians* Dover Books, New York, 1969
CABLE, James *The Death of King Arthur* Penguin Books, London, 1971
CAMPBELL, Joseph *The Masks of God* Viking/Compass, New York, 1970
CASE, Paul Foster *The Tarot* Macoy, Richmond, 1947
CHRISTIAN, Paul *The History and Practice of Magic* Citadel, New York, 1969
CIRLOT, J.E. *A Dictionary of Symbols* Routledge & Kegan Paul, London, 1971
CROWLEY, Aleister *The Book of Thoth* Weiser, New York, 1971
CROWLEY, Aleister *777* Weiser, New York, 1970
DAVIDSON, Gustav *A Dictionary of Angels* Free Press, New York, 1971
DORESSE, Jean *The Secret Books of the Egyptian Gnostics* Hollis & Carter, London, 1960
DOUGLAS, Alfred *The Tarot* Gollancz, London, 1972
ELWORTHY, Frederick *The Evil Eye* Collier Macmillan, New York, 1970
FRAZER, Sir James George *The Golden Bough* Macmillan, London, 1932
GRAVES, Robert *The Greek Myths* Penguin Books, London, 1955
GRAVES, Robert *The White Goddess* Faber, London, 1972
GRAY, Eden *A Complete Guide to the Tarot* Bantam, New York, 1972
GUERBER, SPENCE, ROLLESTON, NIVEDITA, COOMARASWAMY, PETROVITCH, EBBUTT and DAVIS *Myths and Legends Series* Harrap, London, various dates
GUIRAND, Felix (editor) ALDINGTON, Richard and AMES, Delano (translators) *Larousse Encyclopaedia of Mythology* Paul Hamlyn, London, 1961
HALEVI, Z'EV ben SHIMON *Tree of Life* Rider, London, 1972
HARGRAVE, Catherine Perry *A History of Playing Cards* Dover, New York, 1960
HARTMANN, Franz *The Principals of Astrological Geomancy* Rider, London, 1913
The Holy Bible Collins, London. n.d.
HUSON, Paul *The Devil's Picture Book* Abacus, London, 1972
HUSON, Paul *Mastering Witchcraft* Hart Davis, London, 1970
JONAS, Hans *The Gnostic Religion* Beacon Press, Boston, 1970
JUNG, C.G. HULL, R.F.C. trans. *Collected Works* Routledge & Kegan Paul, London, various dates
KAPLAN, S.R. *Tarot Cards for Fun and Fortune Telling* U.S. Games Systems, New York, 1970

253

KHAN, Yitzhac *Tarot and The Game of Fate* Sebaac, San Francisco, 1971

KNIGHT, Gareth *A Practical Guide to Qabalistic Symbolism* Helios, Toddington, 1969

KOCH, Rudolf HOLLAND, Vyvyan (trans.) *The Book of Signs* Dover Publications, New York, n.d.

LEHNER, Ernst *Symbols, Signs & Signets* Dover Publications, New York, 1969

LELAND, Charles Godfrey *Aradia, The Gospel of the Witches* Buckland Museum, New York, 1968

LEVI, Eliphas WESTCOTT, W. Wynn (trans.) *The Magical Ritual of the Sanctum Regnum* Crispin Press, London, 1970

LIND, Frank *How to Understand the Tarot* Aquarian, London, 1971

MASTERS, Anthony *The Natural History of the Vampire* Hart-Davis, London, 1972

MATHERS, S.L. MacGregor *The Tarot* Redway, London, 1888

MAYANANDA *The Tarot for Today* Zeus Press, London, 1963

MAC CANA, Proinsias *Celtic Mythology* Hamlyn, London, 1970

MACKENZIE, D.A.; RAPPOPORT, Angelo S.; MONCRIEFF, A.R. Hope; and SQUIRE, Charles *Myth and Legend in Literature and Art* Gresham, London, n.d.

MOAKLEY, Gertrude *The Tarot Cards Painted by Bembo* New York Public Library, New York, 1966

PAPUS *The Tarot of the Bohemians* Wilshire, Los Angeles, 1971

RADIN, Paul *The Trickster* Routledge & Kegan Paul, London, 1956

RAPHAEL (SMITH, R.C.) *A Manual of Astrology* Arnold, London, 1828

REGARDIE, Israel *The Golden Dawn* Hazel Hills Corp., River Falls, Wisconsin, 1970

SADHU, Mouni *The Tarot* Allen & Unwin, London, 1970

SCOTT, George Ryley *Phallic Worship* Panther Books, London, 1970

SHAH, Idries *The Secret Lore of Magic* Muller, London, 1969

SHUMAKER, Wayne *The Occult Sciences in the Renaissance* University of California Press, Berkeley, 1972

SILBERER, Herbert JELLIFFE, Smith Ely (trans.) *Hidden Symbolism of Alchemy and the Occult Arts* Dover, New York, 1971

SPENCE, Lewis *The History and Origins of Druidism* Aquarian Press, London, 1971

SPENCE, Lewis *Magic Arts in Celtic Britain* Aquarian, London, 1970

SPENCE, Lewis *The Mysteries of Britain* Aquarian Press, London, 1970

THOMPSON, C.J.S. *The Hand of Destiny* Rider, London, 1932

THIERENS, A.E. *The General Book of the Tarot* Rider, London, no date

TILLEY, Roger *Playing Cards* Weidenfeld & Nicholson, London, 1967

USSHER, Arland *The XXII Keys of the Tarot* Dolmen, Dublin, 1969

WAITE, A.E. *The Pictorial Key to the Tarot* Rider Books, London, republished 1971

WELSFORD, Enid *The Fool* Faber, London, n.d.

WERNER, E.T.C. *A Dictionary of Chinese Mythology* Julian Press, New York, 1961

WILHELM, RICHARD BAYNES, Cary F. (trans.) *I Ching* Routledge & Kegan Paul, London 1968